Teaching Strategic Management

ELGAR GUIDES TO TEACHING

The Elgar Guides to Teaching series provides a variety of resources for instructors looking for new ways to engage students. Each volume provides a unique set of materials and insights that will help both new and seasoned teachers expand their toolbox in order to teach more effectively. Titles include selections of methods, exercises, games and teaching philosophies suitable for the particular subject featured. Each volume is authored or edited by a seasoned professor. Edited volumes comprise contributions from both established instructors and newer faculty who offer fresh takes on their fields of study.

Titles in the series include:

Classroom Exercises for Entrepreneurship
A Cross-Disciplinary Approach
James D. Hart

Teaching the History of Economic Thought
Integrating Historical Perspectives Into Modern Economics
Edited by Daniela Tavasci and Luigi Ventimiglia

Teaching Benefit–Cost Analysis
Tools of the Trade
Edited by Scott Farrow

Teaching Human Resource Management
An Experiential Approach
Edited by Suzanne C. de Janasz and Joanna Crossman

Preparing for High Impact Organizational Change
Experiential Learning and Practice
Edited by Gavin M. Schwarz, Anthony F. Buono and Susan M. Adams

Teaching Cultural Economics
Edited by Trine Bille, Anna Mignosa and Ruth Towse

Teaching Nonprofit Management
Edited by Karabi C. Bezboruah and Heather Carpenter

Teaching the Essentials of Law and Economics
Antony W. Dnes

Teaching Strategic Management
A Hands-on Guide to Teaching Success
Edited by Sabine Baumann

Teaching Strategic Management

A Hands-on Guide to Teaching Success

Edited by

Sabine Baumann

Professor, Jade University of Applied Sciences, Germany

ELGAR GUIDES TO TEACHING

Cheltenham, UK • Northampton, MA, USA

Published by
Edward Elgar Publishing Limited
The Lypiatts
15 Lansdown Road
Cheltenham
Glos GL50 2JA
UK

Edward Elgar Publishing, Inc.
William Pratt House
9 Dewey Court
Northampton
Massachusetts 01060
USA

Paperback edition 2021

A catalogue record for this book
is available from the British Library

Library of Congress Control Number: 2020938001

This book is available electronically in the **Elgar**online
Business subject collection
http://dx.doi.org/10.4337/9781788978361

ISBN 978 1 78897 835 4 (cased)
ISBN 978 1 78897 836 1 (eBook)
ISBN 978 1 80220 167 3 (paperback)

Typeset by Servis Filmsetting Ltd, Stockport, Cheshire
Printed and bound by CPI Group (UK) Ltd, Croydon, CR0 4YY

Contents

PART I   TEACHING STRATEGIC MANAGEMENT HISTORY AND NEWLY EVOLVING FIELDS

PART II   METHODS FOR TEACHING STRATEGIC MANAGEMENT

Figures

Tables

Contributors

Sabine Baumann is Professor of Business Administration in the College of Management, Information, Technology at Jade University, Germany. Before rejoining academia, Dr. Baumann worked in senior management positions for Bertelsmann, Germany's largest media conglomerate. Her interdisciplinary research addresses digital business model transformations and strategic exploitations of network structures. Her work has been published in journals such as *Journal of Media Business Studies*, *International Business and Economics Review*, and *Journal of Business Economics*. An award-winning teacher, she has initiated the panel series "Turning Teaching Failures into Teaching Successes" at Strategic Management Society.

John Bourke is the President of The Business Excellence Institute, the only global membership body for business excellence professionals. With 30 years experience in a wide range of industries and countries, he has worked in both large multinationals and small companies, founded three businesses, and consulted for governments and companies such as Google. John holds a BSc in Applied Physics (NUI Galway), an MBA (UCD Smurfit Graduate Business School) and an MSc in Business & Management Research (Henley Business School).

Britta Boyd is an Associate Professor of Business Administration at the University of Southern Denmark and Adjunct Professor at Beijing Institute of Technology. She has published articles in international journals and books within her research interests of family business, entrepreneurship strategy, international marketing and sustainable management. At the University of Southern Denmark she mainly teaches in International Marketing, Business Marketing, Corporate Social Responsibility and Entrepreneurship.

Geoffrey Graybeal, Ph.D. is a Clinical Assistant Professor in the J. Mack Robinson College of Business at Georgia State University. Dr. Graybeal is a media management scholar and entrepreneur who uses management theory to explore issues of media sustainability. He has published research in journals such as the *International Journal on Media Management* and *Journal of Media Business Studies*. He co-founded Lede, LLC, a social media and business model innovation consultancy, while earning his doctorate.

Sven-Ove Horst is Senior Assistant Professor of Media and Creative Industries at Erasmus University Rotterdam. He is interested in exploring emergent phenomena, such as strategy, identity work and digital media entrepreneurship. His research has been published in e.g. the *International Journal on Media Management*, the *Journal of Media Business Studies*, and the *Journal of Media Management and Entrepreneurship*, for which he serves as associate editor. He enjoys speaking at conferences and connecting theory with practice through leadership development workshops, networking activities, and systemic consulting.

Rita Järventie-Thesleff is Professor of Practice and CEMS Academic Director at Aalto University, Finland. Prior to joining academia, Dr. Järventie-Thesleff worked as a business executive in the forest industry. Over the years she has taught Global Strategy, Leadership and Self-development and Global Responsible Leadership. Her current research interests center on identities and practice-based approaches to management and organization. Her work has been published in journals such as *Organization Studies*, *Scandinavian Journal of Management*, *Journal of Organizational Ethnography* and *Journal of Media Business Studies*.

David R. King earned his Ph.D. in strategy and entrepreneurship from Indiana University's Kelley School of Business. After retiring from the U.S. Air Force, he joined academia and he is currently an Associate Professor in the Florida State University where he teaches undergraduate business strategy. Dave's research focuses on complementary resources, merger and acquisition (M&A) integration and performance, technology innovation, and defense procurement. An award-winning researcher, his research appears in leading management journals.

Päivi Maijanen, D.Sc. (Econ. & Bus. Admin.), is Associate Professor at the School of Business and Management at the LUT University, Lappeenranta, Finland. Her research interests and teaching are focused on strategic management, and in particular, on the resource-based view, dynamic capabilities, managerial cognition, and ambidexterity. She has applied these concepts in case studies on digital transformation in the media industry. Before starting in academia, she had a long career as a journalist and manager at the Finnish Broadcasting Company.

Sabine Reisinger is a strategist with parallel academic and business consultancy backgrounds. She is a Senior Lecturer in Strategic Management at the Johannes Kepler University Linz. Her research, teaching and consultancy interests include strategy processes, change processes, competitive strategy, and the human factor of strategy. In her most recent research, she addresses competitiveness issues in a globalized and digital world.

Norman T. Sheehan, MBA, Ph.D, FCPA, FCMA, CGA, ICD.D is a Professor and CPA Scholar at the Edwards School of Business, University of Saskatchewan. Norman has published a number of award-winning cases and interactive educational activities that he enjoys using in his strategy classes and sharing with others. He also publishes articles in the areas of strategy, governance, risk management and performance measurement. Norman was recognized as a Master Teacher at the University of Saskatchewan in 2013.

Aiden E. Sizemore earned his degree in English Literature from Florida State University. Upon graduation, Aiden joined the Florida State University Office of Distance Learning as an operations assistant in Testing & Assessment and transitioned to the online programs manager for the Dedman School of Hospitality. He joined the College of Business in 2013 and is currently the Director of Academic Technology. Outside the office, Aiden enjoys the many outdoor activities that north Florida offers with his wife and four dogs.

Richard R. Smith is a Professor of Strategic Management at Singapore Management University. His research on strategy execution centers on human capital as a strategic resource of the firm in building effective organizations. Prior to joining SMU, he spent 30 years in global consulting firms as a partner, managing director, and CEO. Rick serves on the Board of Directors for the Singapore Civil Service College, the advisory board of AACSB Asia, and several non-profit boards.

Uwe Stratmann is a Professor of Strategic International Marketing and Sales Management in the faculty of business and management at the University of Applied Sciences Kempten (Germany). Besides that, he is responsible for an MBA course "Strategic Sales Management" at the Professional School of Business and Technology in Kempten. Uwe Stratmann has a strong focus on the international automotive industry, for example, he worked for AUDI AG (in the area of dealer performance management) before he took over the professorship.

Patrick Tan is a Senior Lecturer of Strategic Management at Singapore Management University (SMU). He has taught undergraduate, postgraduate and executive development courses in design of business, strategy, business model innovation, and entrepreneurship, using the experiential and case method approaches. Prior to joining SMU, Patrick had more than 30 years of management experience in global financial services corporations, such as ANZ Bank, AXA, and Cigna International.

Candace M. TenBrink, Ph.D., is an Assistant Professor of Management at the University of Houston-Downtown. Her research interests include the strategic aspects of turnarounds and life cycle issues. She was recently awarded a Fulbright Scholar grant to study turnarounds, corporate rejuvenation, and innovation in Poland. She enjoys strategy-related consulting projects. Prior to entering academia, she was the managing partner of a film production firm and an award-winning analyst in investment banking. Dr. TenBrink received an MBA from the Ross School of Business, and a B.A. from Michigan State University.

Janne Tienari is Professor of Management and Organization at Hanken School of Economics in Helsinki, Finland. Dr. Tienari's research and teaching interests include strategy work, managing multinational corporations, mergers and acquisitions, gender and diversity, and branding and media. His latest passion is to understand management, new generations, and the future. His work has been published in leading journals such as *Organization Studies, Human Relations, Organization, Journal of Management Studies, Organization Science*, and *Academy of Management Review*.

Krysti Turnquest is the Director of the Accelerated Transfer Academy at the University of Houston-Downtown (UHD). She is the former Assistant Director for UHD's Center for Community Engagement and Service Learning. Krysti is pursuing her doctorate in Measurement, Quantitative Methods and Learning Sciences at the University of Houston. She holds a bachelor's degree in sociology from the University of Texas at Austin and a joint master's degree in urban and environmental policy and planning, and human development from Tufts University.

Dianne Tyers is the President of Advance Consulting for Education and the Dean of Dalhousie University's College of Continuing Education. Over her almost 30 years of experience in adult education across multiple sectors, Dianne has addressed the learning needs of varied stakeholders in for-profit and non-profit organizations through appropriate teaching methodologies and education technologies. Dianne has a Ph.D. (University of Toronto), an MBA (Western University), and an MA (University of Queensland). Dianne is a Fellow of the Business Excellence Institute.

Robert P. Wright is an Associate Professor of Strategy at The Hong Kong Polytechnic University. He is a multi-award-winning teacher and researcher. Outside of academia he is a Fellow of the Hong Kong Institute of Human Resource Management, Fellow of the Australian Institute of Management and Fellow of the Hong Kong Institute of Directors. Dr. Wright is a graduate of executive development programs in IMD in Switzerland, and the Harvard Business School.

Introduction: learning from teaching failures, achieving teaching successes

Sabine Baumann

To have failed is to have striven, to have striven is to have grown.
(Maltbie Davenport Babcock)

Failure is disguised success.
(Matshona Dhliwayo)

Teaching is personal. Teaching is challenging. Teaching is diverse. Teaching can be messy. Teaching – even the same module – is always different. Teaching is about people.

The idea for *Teaching Strategic Management: A Hands-on Guide to Teaching* came from a curiosity about why we as faculty and instructors rarely share our personal stories of failure in the classroom, but instead place so much emphasis on celebrating streamlined and frequently impracticable "best" practices. We all know these moments when well-planned teaching concepts fall apart in the classroom, when students become disengaged or when we realize during grading that the flaw was in the concept or our teaching rather than students' being unprepared for the assessment. However, experienced faculty also know that what may have started out as a failure often turns out to be the root of wonderful teaching successes. Therefore it is so important to share what it takes to turn failures in the classroom into those marvelous moments when our hard work and meticulous preparation culminate in students' finally mastering difficult concepts and when a sense of enlightenment and deep satisfaction fills the classroom.

Teaching is diverse. Teaching is truly challenging. There is an extensive array of diverse challenges ranging from dealing with heterogeneous student groups to teaching specific methods such as design thinking, grading, teaching strategic management to particular student groups such as non-business students or executives, how to bring practice into the classroom, teaching online, and so on. Especially junior faculty find the first steps as a teacher a tough contest. Nevertheless, experienced faculty know that you never stop growing as a teacher and that the next challenge is just around the corner. Regardless of their experience, what they all need are teaching resources with true applicability: What works and what doesn't work, and why?; How to . . .?; and lessons learned and feasible practices. In other words: hands-on advice!

Teaching is personal. Teaching is about people. Therefore this guide for teaching strategic management grounds in a deeply personal approach and provides a teaching resource with a high degree of applicability for the classroom. In all chapters, experienced contributors share individual accounts of classroom experiences and offer insightful advice on how to address the teaching strategic management challenge they cover in their chapter. Each chapter also provides specific examples such as syllabi, teaching plans, reading lists, case studies, assignments, and exercises that can be directly used in teaching. We wanted to not only make this an interesting read, but to also make this volume truly relevant for teachers of strategic management.

The first part of this volume covers "Teaching Strategic Management History and Newly Evolving Fields." In her chapter on "Teaching the History of Strategic Management" Päivi Maijanen provides a historical perspective to strategic management and its core question of why some firms outperform others. This question is used to elucidate the evolution of strategic management as a field where theory and practice are tightly connected. Consequently, teaching about the history of strategic management combines teaching changes in the business environment and the related theoretical developments. Maijanen presents course material covering the core theories and concepts of strategic management and suggestions for course assignments.

Chapter 2 covers "Teaching Strategy as an Ethical Practice." Sven-Ove Horst describes strategy as a reflective practice that entails ethical responsibilities and explains how strategy can be taught with a strong ethical sensibility. After reviewing some relevant discussions around strategy teaching, Horst develops a frame for seeing the ethical side of strategy as part of a strategy-as-practice approach. He connects this frame with his experience of teaching a course on strategic management at the University of Navarra in Spain to discuss value-based strategy teaching in this context. He shows how the university's core values provide the basis for learning how to act with care and responsibility as a strategist. Provided course assignments demonstrate potential student learning outcomes.

In the third chapter "Teaching Sustainability in Strategic Management," Britta Boyd addresses sustainability as an increasingly prominent part of corporate social responsibility within strategic management. The objective is to provide students with an understanding and comprehensive knowledge of the development of sustainability, legal responsibilities of different actors and corporate social responsibility (CSR) activities in strategic management. The chapter attaches special importance to the conceptual evolutionary path of theories and practices in sustainability development and provides assignments for student reflection on its implications.

Part II of this volume covers "Methods for Teaching Strategic Management." Candace M. TenBrink and Krysti Turnquest in their chapter on "Service Learning in Strategic Management: Opportunities, Challenges, and Examples" explain how the experiential teaching method of service learning can help students of strategy overcome a lack of strategy knowledge and experience and help them grasp the breadth and depth of strategy. After a brief description of the history of service learning the authors discuss why this pedagogy may be a positive learning tool in strategic management and offer benefits and obstacles in deploying it. The chapter provides several cases to assist with planning a service learning course and questions to invoke an insightful discussion.

In a similar vein, Richard R. Smith and Patrick Tan in Chapter 5 further explore the "Experiential Approach to Strategy Formulation." They argue that the methods for teaching strategy formulation are often left to conceptual frameworks and generic toolsets in the business school classroom while, ultimately, strategy formulation is about taking action. Therefore, one of the best ways to teach it is through physical application via the experiential approach. Their chapter introduces the background associated with teaching strategy and experiential approaches, provides an overview of the concepts used to making teaching in an experiential format most effective, demonstrates a proven process for teaching in this method, and considers several discussion questions. The authors share their experiences, challenges and insights as they experimented with and taught business practicum courses.

In Chapter 6, Uwe Stratmann shows how "Writing and Using Your Own Case Study for Strategy Teaching" is a very effective instrument to combine theory with practice and to involve students in a very active way. Different to the use of existing, secondary teaching cases, his chapter focuses on the production and use of a teacher's own case study. Writing and integrating one's own teaching case is very beneficial in terms of the alignment between teaching content and the case as well as the overall involvement of both sides, the lecturer and the students. The chapter describes an effective case study writing process as well as methods to integrate the case into the teaching concept. The writing process and didactical methods are exemplified by a case study on Nespresso, in order to provide pragmatic advice and to show outcomes in terms of learning and teaching success.

Sabine Reisinger in Chapter 7 evaluates "Interactive Exercises, Peer

Coaching, and Videos in Strategic Management Education" to help students develop the strategic competences needed to run a business in today's digitized, highly connected, globalized world. By integrating interactive methods into strategic management courses, students of Generation Y and Z can build conceptual and analytical knowledge as well as develop strategic, personal and interpersonal competencies. Her toolbox for strategic management courses provides interactive methods to discuss different beliefs, views and perspectives and to facilitate the understanding of complex topics and theories. Most of the described methods can be used in class and/or online. Two comprehensive teaching designs show in detail how interactive methods can be integrated into a strategic management course. The first is suitable for teaching complex theories and concepts of strategy and/or new subjects like platform industries, value networks or business ecosystems. The second enables students to develop an understanding of the complexity of strategy by applying strategy tools in peer groups.

In Chapter 8, Norman T. Sheehan introduces "Tailored Methods of Strategizing in Undergraduate Education: From SWOT to the 6Ps of Business Strategy." His experience is that while students are typically able to leverage their SWOT analysis to formulate potentially profitable strategies, their proposed strategies are often incomplete or the elements of strategy are not aligned with each other. His chapter provides a strategy formulation tool, the 6Ps of Business Strategy, which instructors can use to help students formulate business strategies that are comprehensive and coherent as well as profitable. The framework can also be used to compare and contrast business strategies as well as diagnose why some strategies have failed. The 6Ps reinforce that effective strategies fully integrate all functional areas and they have been successfully applied by undergraduate and masters' students, managers and company directors.

Chapter 9, "Teaching Strategy by Not Teaching Strategy," completes the second part on methods. Robert P. Wright shares his discovery that when teachers teach less, students end up learning more. The author demonstrates the benefits of going back to the basics of children's learning – enthusiastically and with a lot of fun. He outlines his strategies for better preparing, cultivating and nurturing the next generation of thought-leaders in the teaching of strategic management. In this process of continuous renewal he presents a pedagogical innovation – the FOCUSED framework – that has enriched and enabled students to learn beyond the domain of strategy, strategizing and strategic management. What started off as a simple fun teaching tool is now being used by senior executives to help them better deal with their unsolved problems, issues and challenges.

Part III of this volume addresses "Teaching Strategic Management for

Particular Groups of Learners and Teaching Settings." David R. King and Aiden E. Sizemore, Chapter 10, start off with "Strategic Management in Online and Hybrid Courses." They explain that after developing techniques to teach in traditional classrooms, a move to teach online can be daunting. In their chapter, the authors provide the background on online classes and important considerations specific to online instruction. They discuss common challenges and their solutions prior to specific sections that outline how to develop a syllabus, grade online, adapt exercises and case assignments online for different size course enrollments, and how to design and manage discussion boards. They also identify tools and resources available for making the transition to online teaching easier.

In Chapter 11, Geoffrey Graybeal provides insights on "Teaching Strategic Management for Media Students." Being an educator who has taught both majors, he discusses differences between teaching business students and teaching media students. His chapter outlines three primary challenges and solutions to teaching strategic management to media students. It explores syllabus development for strategic management courses for media students and presents a list of suggested textbooks and resources for developing courses while providing an overview of some of the top scholarly journals and organizations dedicated to the academic subdiscipline of media management, economics and entrepreneurship. Methods of delivery for course material and themes for course discussion questions are also offered in the chapter, as are sample assignments that could be incorporated or adapted into undergraduate or graduate level courses on strategic management for media students.

"Teaching Strategy Work to Business Students" is explored by Rita Järventie-Thesleff and Janne Tienari in Chapter 12. They start out with a brief introduction to the "relevance debate," whether business schools offer students the knowledge and skills needed for success in an increasingly complex and volatile world including the necessary ethical grounding of their business education. Moreover, the uncertainties of the operating environment set new requirements for teaching strategic management – or strategy work, as the authors prefer to call it – to digital-native business students. In their chapter, they argue for an approach based on strategy-as-practice as an alternative to teaching traditional positivistic techniques of strategic inquiry. The authors offer concrete suggestions regarding teaching methods and learning outcomes based on their teaching experiences. They propose inclusion of a set of themes in course curricula and discuss pedagogical methods that will facilitate a synthesis of research and business practice.

Dianne Tyers and John Bourke complete Part III and also this volume with their contribution on "Teaching Strategic Management for

Executives." Chapter 13 discusses the unique characteristics executives have as learners that need to be addressed when considering how best to enable them to learn about strategic management. The authors outline the challenges educators face and how to overcome them, covering everything from course design to delivery. Central to their approach is the content that goes into the course syllabus and the approach to delivering it. The authors hold that educators need to achieve more than merely succeed in having executives learn about strategic management – they need to be able to apply their learning. This requires executives to learn how to manage strategically, something that starts with understanding strategy, and how to craft and implement it, and continues with embracing leadership for organizational adaptability. The authors explore a repertoire of approaches from which teachers of strategic management can select to meet the needs of executive learners.

Teaching Strategic Management: A Hands-on Guide to Teaching Success aims to provide instructors, faculty, and program directors of strategic management courses at undergraduate, graduate, and executive levels with an enlightening and instructive guide for teaching and for creating course syllabi and teaching plans. The editor of this volume and the contributors hope that the wealth of material provided in this guide benefits faculty and instructors of strategic management, be they experienced and seeking inspiration for new methods, or needing guidance for developing a new course. We hope this guide sparks an ongoing sharing of teaching experiences and advice, and paves the way to those "marvelous moments" when the classroom is full of inspiration, insight, and fun.

PART I

Teaching strategic management history and newly evolving fields

1. Teaching the history of strategic management

Päivi Maijanen

INTRODUCTION

When learning about strategic management, it is not only important to study the main concepts and theories but also their historical evolution. The historical perspective provides us with an in-depth understanding of what strategic management is all about. Importantly, learning about the history is not only learning about the theoretical developments and trajectories but also about changes in the business environment. Addressing these changes and new phenomena has forced and inspired scholars to refine the old concepts and theories or create new ones. We can say that the evolution has taken place in two ways: through accumulation of scientific knowledge and through empirical inputs from the changing business environment. Learning a history of a discipline of any kind may sound boring and irrelevant, but in fact it can be seen as an exciting journey to study how the theory and practice have coevolved and intertwined; how new phenomena and questions arise and how this evolutionary process deepens our knowledge and understanding.

It is worth noting that the history of the actual independent discipline of strategic management is fairly young. The early history goes back to the 1970s. Its main professional forum, the Strategic Management Society (SMS), was not established until the year 1981. Naturally, the field has long roots in the earlier developments of military and later business strategy that finally led to the situation where the scholars of strategic management saw the need for creating a more solid foundation for the field. From the very beginning, the core question of strategic management has been why some firms are more successful than others and how firms can sustain their competitive advantage. What can be more relevant questions for business! Learning about strategic management and its history provides us with a profound understanding of these highly important questions of every single entrepreneur.

Through its core question, strategic management research expresses its practical relevance and a close link with the changes taking place in the global business environment. The question has not become less relevant during the past decades. Quite the opposite. Since the establishment of the SMS in 1981, the business environment has gone through enormous changes, such as the rise of networks instead of conglomerates, keen competition based on globalization, and the digitalization-based rise of the platform ecosystems, to name a few. These all have disrupted and challenged established industries and companies' competitive advantage and made them ask the question how to sustain it.

From the practical perspective, the importance of strategic management is to be motivated by its ability to answer everyday problems faced by companies. In a way, strategic management offers us a checklist to look at when trying to understand, for instance, why some companies in an industry outperform the others and why some formerly strong companies rapidly lose their leading position (e.g. Nokia vs. Apple). The answers given by strategy research help also understand more "local" problems. If you have to give answers why some of your neighborhood restaurants or corner shops succeed or fail, just start to look at their competitive position following the guidelines of Porter. Or, if you would like to start a company of your own and you are asking which kind of resources you should have to be successful, have a look at the so-called VRIN (valuable, rare, inimitable, non-substitutable) attributes offered to you by the resource-based view. If your company or the company you are consulting is losing its competitive advantage due to rapid changes in the business environment then it is advisable to look at the checklist given by the dynamic capability view. Briefly, knowing the basic ideas of strategic management and its evolution helps you understand the business world much more than just analyzing it from the more specific perspectives of, let us say, economics, finance, accounting or marketing. Strategic management puts those complicated things together by asking how to achieve and sustain competitive advantage.

This chapter is organized as follows. After the introduction, the course design for teaching the history of strategic management is briefly presented followed by the main theoretical outlines of strategic management. The overview of the history is followed by suggestions for course assignments.

COURSE DESIGN

As general advice for teaching the history of strategic management – or any discipline – I would emphasize the importance of "keeping it simple." It is important to focus on the main trajectories and core concepts and theories. Going into details may confuse and distract and even hamper learning, especially for beginners. In the later and more advanced stages, it is possible to go into more refined and profound issues.

The course that I am suggesting would consist of lectures (12–15 hours) with some discussions and short team assignments in the class and larger individual or team work conducted independently after the lectures. The bigger team (or individual) work could be, for example, an analysis of a case company or industry based on quantitative or qualitative analysis methods and using theories of strategic management. The course can be supported by online course material of lectures and articles. This would be the structure for a full module. When the history of strategic management forms only a part of a module I would suggest having some smaller-scale assignments (see suggestions at the end of the chapter) instead of a larger assignment conducted individually or in teams.

This chapter provides the basic lecture material to cover the core developments, theories and concepts of strategic management. The course design is targeted especially to bachelor students but also master's and doctoral students with no previous knowledge of the discipline. The chapter includes some concepts that I would recommend only for students at a more advanced level (master's and Ph.D. students), such as the discussion on transaction cost economics (Coase, Williamson) and the Chandlerian analysis on the structure and strategy. The teaching can be supported with some readings. This would be particularly recommended for students at a more advanced level. The chapter provides a rich reference list of articles for both teachers and students. For example, the students could be required to read 1–2 articles before class in order to be able to discuss and reflect on them during class.

EARLY HISTORY OF THE STRATEGY CONCEPT

This chapter will briefly present the main trajectories, concepts and definitions of strategic management research. The word "strategy" has its origin in the Greek word "strategos," meaning "the art of a general" and referring to the "army" and "the art of leading." The Greek verb "stratego" means to "plan the destruction of one's enemies through effective use of resources" (Bracker, 1980, p. 219). Later many leading war strategy theoreticians, for example the Prussian general Clausewitz, used the concept of strategy when referring to the long-term goals of a nation and its ability to win wars instead of winning single battles. However, it was only after the Second World War when the idea of a business strategy (or business policy as it first used to be called) and a bit later also the idea of strategic management were introduced. The goal of the business strategy was to achieve competitive advantage, that is, to outperform the rivals. According to Ansoff (1965), the rise of business strategy research was triggered by rapid changes in the business environments. Especially the increasing role of science and innovations contributed to rapid technological changes. In the more competitive environment, the firms were forced to react or, in fact, to pro-act to the maneuvers of the rivals (see Bracker, 1980).

THE RISE OF MODERN STRATEGIC MANAGEMENT

The rise of modern strategic management can be traced back to the late 1950s when a sociologist, Philip Selznick (1957), and economist Edith Penrose (1959) published their insightful books. Selznick launched the concept of "distinctive competence" and emphasized the role of leadership thus focusing on firms' internal strengths as a source of competitive advantage over the rivals (Hoskisson et al., 1999, p. 421). In a similar way but from the perspective of economics, Penrose emphasized the importance of a firm's internal resources. She focused on leadership and management as the most important production factors and engines of growth. According to Penrose, firm-specific and path dependent resources and the ability to manage them make it possible to explain the success (and failure) of organizations. As will be shown in the chapter, the later developments of strategic management, such as the resource- and knowledge-based view and the dynamic capability view, are based on these path-breaking ideas from the 1950s.

In the 1960s, strategy scholars focused on firms' internal success factors by conducting extensive case studies in order to demonstrate their impacts. These studies were titled as business policy studies, even if they, in fact, dealt with long-term strategy issues from the managerial perspective. A Harvard economic historian, Chandler, published in 1962 an important book called *Strategy and Structure* in which he managed to show how large multi-divisional companies developed their strategies to be successful. Chandler's main thesis was that "strategy creates structure." According to him, main administrative changes within an organization are reactions to new opportunities or threats created by competitive environments, very often by innovations. Chandler (1962, p. 13) also launched a compact definition of a strategy:

> The determination of the basic long-term goals and objectives of an enterprise, and the adoption of courses of action and the allocation of resources necessary for carrying out these goals.

The focus was on large companies, for example, in chemical, automobile, energy, and steel industries and Chandler managed to explain the rise of the multi-divisional organizational structure as a rational response to the changes in business environments. He also highlighted the important role of top managers as catalysts of organizational changes. In a way, Chandler also managed to validate the importance of transaction costs introduced by the Nobel laureate Coase already in 1937 in his influential article "The Nature of the Firm."

Coase's (1937) basic idea was that in addition to traditional production costs, there are also costs of using markets – that is, costs relating to information searching, negotiating, contracting, and so on – that he called transaction costs. When the market-based transaction costs happened to be higher than the costs of using the firm's own organization it was advisable to internalize the activity (transaction). According to Coase, this was the main reason for the rise of giant multi-divisional conglomerates since the 1920s. Chandler's (1962) influential historical case studies produced strong empirical evidence that supported Coase's theoretical idea.

About ten years after the publication of Chandler's book, another Nobel laureate, Williamson, further developed theoretical ideas of Coase and created an important branch in economics called transaction cost economics. It also had a strong impact on strategic management when trying to understand where the boundaries of a firm are. Williamson (1975, 1981, 1985) specified the determinants of transaction costs (e.g. bounded rationality, uncertainty, opportunism, small number of alternatives, and asset specificity) and claimed that the stronger these determinants are the better it is to internalize transactions instead of using the markets and vice versa. These ideas were largely utilized by strategy scholars when trying to explain diversification decisions of the firms. Later, in the 1980s and 1990s, strategy scholars applied Williamsonian ideas when explaining the rapid rise of networks (or "hybrids" as Williamson (1991) called them) and the "flattening" of organizational hierarchies within the companies (Williamson, 1991; Teece, 1998). Briefly, networks, such as joint ventures and strategic alliances, are outcomes from the situations where there exist both pro-market and pro-hierarchy-determinants.

Another influential early strategy scholar was Ansoff (1965) who also used case studies as a method. He defined strategy (see Bracker 1980, p. 220)

> as a rule for making decisions determined by product/market scope, growth vector, competitive advantage, and synergy.

In their historical case studies, Ansoff and Chandler were looking for managerial best practices that could be generalized. The roles of top managers were highlighted, since their strategic decisions determined the organizational structures of companies. This perspective also indirectly resulted in the idea of sustainable competitive advantage, that is, the ability of a firm to outperform its rivals for a long period. Interestingly, however, the pursuit of achieving sustainable competitive advantage shifted the focal point of strategy research from firm internal strengths and weaknesses toward the externally determined opportunities and threats of competitive environments of the firm. At the end of the 1970s, strategic management research took the pendulum-like shift, as Hoskisson et al. (1999) aptly call it, from internal factors analyzed by business policy case studies toward more economics-based strategic analyses that emphasized the connections between the competitive situation of the firm, especially its ability to utilize monopoly power and its economic performance (Hoskisson et al., 1999, pp. 424–425). At the same time, the research methodology took a shift from large qualitative case studies toward quantitative surveys and increasing use of econometric methods when trying to identify factors behind successful performance of the companies.

SUSTAINABLE COMPETITIVE ADVANTAGE AND PORTER'S FIVE FORCES MODEL

As Nag et al. (2007, p. 936) state, perhaps the first scholars who renamed the field of business policy as strategic management were Schendel and Hofer (1979) in their influential textbook called *Strategic Management*. According to their definition (Schendel and Hofer, 1979, p. 516):

> Strategy provides directional cues to the organization that permit it to achieve its objectives, while responding to the opportunities and threats in its environment.

At the same time, the first attempts to use economics-based concepts in the context of strategic management took place. The Harvard economist Michael Porter (1980, 1981, 1985) started to analyze the relationship between the firm's competitive environment and its performance. Porter used the traditional monopoly model and especially the anti-trust ideas developed in the context of the industrial organization (IO) tradition launched by Mason (1939) and Bain (1956) in the early 1950s. The IO school launched the so-called "Structure–Conduct–Performance"-model to fight against the monopoly power of large companies (cf. Scherer, 1980). The idea was simple. IO scholars looked at the industrial structure, especially its concentration ratios that were interpreted as a measure of the monopoly power in the industry, and the way in which the firms conducted their pricing strategies. If high concentration rates and monopolistic behavior were associated with high rates of profit, the anti-trust authorities used their anti-trust policy instruments to weaken the monopoly power of large companies concerned. The idea was, of course, to minimize the social cost of monopoly power and to promote more competition in order to increase the social welfare. Interestingly, Porter's idea was to turn this model upside down: What was bad for the customers was good for the companies. Porter concluded that the more monopoly power the firm can gain and the less dependent it is on the bargaining power of the rivals, the more competitive advantage it could achieve.

In order to concretize this basic view, Porter launched the so-called *five forces model*, in which the main idea was to position the firm so that it could maximize its monopoly power at the same time as the bargaining power of other players was minimized. In the five forces model, the players were *competitors*, *suppliers*, and *customers* on the horizontal level and the threat of *new entries* and the threat of *new substitutes* on the vertical level. The idea was to look at all of these five factors and to evaluate the threats related to them from the perspective of monopoly or bargaining power. For instance, the fewer potential suppliers or customers there are, the more dependent the firm is on them, and the more bargaining power the suppliers and/or customers have. Porter called the use of the five forces model as a competitive analysis. The model provided a tool for a firm to create its competitive strategy in order to achieve and sustain its competitive advantage. According to Porter, the main strategies for a firm are (i) the *cost leadership strategy* based on the economies of scale and scope, (ii) the *differentiation strategy* based on the ability to differentiate its products/ services, that is, to make its demand curve more inelastic, and (iii) the *focus-based* or *niche strategy* based on the ability to find a small market segment or niche that is not too attractive for larger companies.

The *cost leadership strategy* can be applied by large companies, which already have a dominant position in the market based on economies of scale and scope and nowadays even more on network externalities as, for example, Facebook, Google, and Amazon manifest. By means of its monopoly power, a dominant firm can achieve lower unit costs than its rivals or control the whole supply chain. The idea of the *differentiation strategy* is to create brands that offer unique value to some buyers/ customers who are not price-sensitive and who have unsatisfied needs, that is, they are willing to pay extra for the products/services. The *niche strategy* focuses on small market segments where the threat of substitutes is small and the competition is not too keen.

Porter's strategy view, based on the idea of analyzing firm-external factors arising from the competitive environment, was very successful in the 1980s, both on the practical as well as theoretical level. Nowadays, almost every company makes its competitive analysis along the lines of Porter and looks at their external threats from this perspective. Theoretically, Porter's main contribution was to put strategic management on a higher scientific level based on microeconomics. His approach made it possible to utilize advanced econometric methods and extensive databases in order to identify the determinants of competitive advantage. He focused on the industry level, thus following the anti-trust tradition of Bain and Mason. Later, Porter and his followers analyzed the so-called strategic groups within one industry and tried to find out the determinants behind their success.

Unfortunately, however, Porter's theoretical success was overshadowed by new empirical results that showed that the role of firm-external competitive advantage determinants were minor when compared to the firm-internal determinants, such as resources, competencies, and capabilities (Rumelt, 1991). These findings caused a new swing of a pendulum in the strategic management research (Hoskisson et al., 1999), this time from firm-external to firm-internal determinants of competitive advantage. Interestingly, now the shift was based on strong empirical evidence gained by sophisticated econometric methods. The theoretical challenger this time came from the group of microeconomics-oriented strategy scholars who were also looking for the market imperfections and monopoly profits associated with them. Interestingly, now the focal point was on the resource markets instead of Porterian product/service markets. The founding fathers of the challenging theoretical school, called *the resource-based view*, had their eye on factor market imperfections and hence mainly on firm-internal resources, routines, capabilities and on different ways to utilize them to achieve sustainable competitive advantage.

RESOURCE-BASED VIEW

Following the old Ricardian (1817) land rent idea that the ownership of a scarce, value-creating resource can be very profitable for its owner, the resource-based view theoreticians Wernerfelt (1984), Barney (1986, 1991) and Rumelt (1984) managed to show that especially the scarce firm-internal resources can create market imperfections and result in sustainable competitive advantage.

A Danish economist, Birger Wernerfelt (1984), elegantly launched a simple mathematical model that showed how resource markets really could create monopoly profits for the owners of scarce resources in imperfect markets. Jay Barney (1986) wrote the same Ricardian story in a more pragmatic way, emphasizing the strategic factors that the firm can use in order to create sustainable competitive advantage. In his very influential article, Barney (1991) finally revealed the core of the resource-based view by explicating the so-called VRIN attributes that a successful resource should have. The resource should be (i) valuable (V), that is, able to create new value for the customer, (ii) rare (R), (iii) inimitable (I), and (iv) non-substitutable (N). Because resources and their use are based on cumulative firm-specific learning processes, firms are necessarily heterogeneous in terms of their resources. The firm's main strategic function is to organize its business model so that it can profit from resource market imperfections by means of VRIN resources.

Richard Rumelt (1984) contributed to the theory building by launching an idea of *isolation mechanisms* that are needed to make the resources inimitable and non-substitutable. The isolation mechanisms can be based, for example, on causal ambiguity or tacit knowledge. The first one means that it is impossible for an outsider to see what the relationship between the resource bundle used and its ability to create new value is. Walmart has often been mentioned as a good example of this. All the rivals know that the secret of the success lies in Walmart's ability to utilize its extensive logistic databases efficiently but no one seems to know how they exactly do it. Deployment of tacit knowledge assets that are deeply embedded in a firm's internal organization can also efficiently hinder imitation. Together with legal means to protect knowledge assets, such as patents, trademarks, copyrights, and so on, tacit knowledge creates the so-called *appropriability regime*. As Teece (1986, 1998) has shown, the tighter the appropriability regime is, the harder it is to copy the value creating strategies and the more sustainable the competitive assets are.

During the last thirty years, the resource-based view has no doubt become the dominant strategy school that has been utilized by both strategy consultants and strategy scholars when explaining the sustainability of competitive advantage (see Peteraf, 1993). Together with the Porterian competitive analysis that analyzes the threats and opportunities arising from the external competitive environment, the resource-based view focusing on the firm's internal resources and their ability to create sustainable value are nowadays the building blocks of a useful strategy.

However, there are some drawbacks in the resource-based view. The main problem when using it in the real world is its static or at least retrospective nature. The strategy view offered by the resource-based view is like a snapshot picture. It tells where we are and perhaps also why we are there but it does not tell us that much about the future. A good example can be found from the recent mobile smartphone market. In the beginning of the year 2007, the Finnish company Nokia was a dominant market leader with a market share of about 40 percent, and there existed many good resource-based explanations why they were so dominant. Especially their capability to orchestrate a global supply chain and their excellent technological resources were highlighted. Everything seemed to be fine with Nokia. However, at the end of the same year, Nokia had lost its leading position and after some more years they stopped manufacturing smartphones. What happened? Apple's iPhone came to the market with quite different superior VRIN-attributes and stopped the rise of Nokia. Similar stories can be told, for example, about Kodak and Polaroid, which did not manage to overcome the disruption realized by digitalization.

Nokia, Kodak, Polaroid, and many other companies exemplify the main problem of the resource-based view. Because of its static nature it is unable to deeply analyze change processes and to take into account the pressures arising from rapid changes in the competitive environment. These changes can be traced back into the changes in technologies, consumers' preferences, regulations or power structures. Even if the resource-based view is very useful when trying to have a bird's-eye view of the threats and potentials of a company in terms of a resource gap analysis, it is not that useful when trying to analyze the future prospects of a company. In brief, it is too retrospective. Something more is needed and this time the swing of the pendulum does not go from internal factors to external factors but from the static analysis (typical also of the Porterian strategy view) to the more dynamic and evolutionarily inspired analysis. This leads us to the domain of the dynamic capability view.

The *knowledge-based view* (Kogut and Zander, 1992; Grant, 1996) can be interpreted as a special case of the resource-based view emphasizing the role of intangible knowledge assets. A piece of knowledge has peculiar properties that deserve some extra comments. Knowledge can be either *codified*, that is, information that is easy to transfer but hard to protect, or it can be *tacit*, that is, hard to transfer and copy but easy to protect and appropriate. From the strategic management perspective, tacit knowledge is perhaps more relevant, since it enables the knowledge creator/holder to profit from knowledge assets. Following the famous quotations of Polanyi (1967), tacitness means that one knows more than one can tell. Therefore, tacit knowledge is easy to protect and hard to transfer. Based on the Teecean idea of the appropriability regime, one can conclude that the more tacit the piece of knowledge is, the tighter the appropriability regime is and the easier it is for the firm to sustain its knowledge-based competitive advantage. As the role of science-based innovations becomes more important all the time, it is clear that also knowledge becomes a more powerful resource as a special source for market imperfections.

DYNAMIC CAPABILITY VIEW

The dynamic capability view was launched in the 1990s by Teece et al. (1997) who took an important step toward dynamizing the static perspective of strategic management. Following Selznick's (1957) idea about distinctive competence and especially the evolutionarily inspired ideas of Nelson and Winter (1982), Teece et al. focused on the fundamental question of how an organization can cope with a rapidly changing environment so that it manages to sustain its competitive advantage.

Nelson and Winter (1982) used analogies borrowed from the evolutionary theory in which evolution takes place through the three mechanisms called variation, retention and selection. In the business context, Schumpeterian (1934) entrepreneurs who are able to produce new combinations (products, processes, services, business models, etc.) create the variation. The retention is established by routines that make it possible to replicate organizational structure, whereas the selection takes place through market competition. The key concept is a routine that is a cumulatively learned pattern that helps solve decision problems in a satisficing (not optimizing) way. Since the decision-makers are only boundedly rational and they are facing uncertainty, they cannot normally optimize. Instead, they use heuristic rules of thumb that result in satisficing solutions (Simon, 1962; Cyert and March, 1963). According to Nelson and Winter, there are first order routines (capable of pure replication of the existing structure) and higher-order routines (capable of changing first order routines).

Teece et al. (1997) combined the dynamic evolutionary view of Nelson and Winter (1982) and the basic ideas of the resource-based view in a way that resulted in the dynamic capability view. Based on this view, dynamic capabilities are needed to enhance a change of resource-base, that is, assets and capabilities, to address the changing business environment. According to the seminal definition launched by Teece et al. (1997, p. 519), "a dynamic capability is the firm's ability to integrate, build, and reconfigure internal and external competences to address rapidly changing environments."

There are many different definitions of dynamic capabilities. For instance, Eisenhardt and Martin (2000, p. 1117) define dynamic capabilities simply as

> the firm's processes that use resources—specifically the processes to integrate, reconfigure, gain and release resources—to match and even create market

change. Dynamic capabilities thus are the organizational and strategic routines by which firms achieve new resource configurations as markets emerge, collide, split, evolve, and die.

As for the definition of Eisenhardt and Martin, dynamic capabilities are interpreted as best practices. Hence, competitive advantage obtained by them can be only temporary. This characterization of dynamic capabilities does not highlight entrepreneurial evolutionary elements emphasized in the Teecean view.

One of the most cited definitions that summarizes the main idea of dynamic capabilities is from Helfat et al. (2007, p. 4): "A dynamic capability is the capacity of an organization to purposefully create, extend, or modify its resource base." It demonstrates the purposeful use of dynamic capabilities and links them to Schumpeterian entrepreneurial thinking where innovations ("new combinations") are of great importance. Teece (2007, 2012, 2014) has also stressed the role of entrepreneurial thinking when looking for micro foundations of the dynamic capability view.

One can conclude that the dynamic capability view sees a firm consisting of routines and bundles of routines called capabilities. As Sidney Winter (2003) aptly shows, there are both *operational capabilities*, whose main function is to replicate the existing resource base and learning-based capabilities, and there are *dynamic capabilities*, whose main function is to change the existing resource base and capabilities in order to better cope with changes of competitive environments (due to changing preferences of customers and technological or regulatory changes). When the competitive environment is not changing drastically, the firms using mainly operational or "simple" dynamic capabilities interpreted as best practices (see Eisenhardt and Martin, 2000) can do their job in a satisficing manner. However, the more rapidly the competitive environments change, and the higher the uncertainty faced by the firms, the more demanding dynamic capabilities are needed and the more important the role of entrepreneurial attitude of top managers is (Teece, 2012, 2014).

In his much-cited and celebrated article, David Teece (2007) launched the idea of the micro foundations of the dynamic capability view. Teece focused on three capacities, *sensing*, *seizing* and *reconfiguring (transforming)*, that are necessary conditions for the effective use of dynamic capabilities. Sensing deals with the ability to sense weak signals and to recognize strategic options that may prove to be successful. The more turbulent the business environment is, the more important it is to have this entrepreneurial instinct.

Seizing deals with the ability to efficiently invest in new strategic options and capabilities necessary for building up them. In many cases, the firm has also to be able to disinvest in already existing path-dependent capabilities that may have been the engines of earlier success. This kind of situation often results in difficult internal conflicts within the organization because of the change resistance due to organizational rigidities.

Reconfiguring or transforming follows sensing and seizing. It simply means the ability to change the existing resource base and operational/ dynamic capabilities in a way that promotes necessary organizational renewal.

Teece (2012) gives a good example of the smartphone business. Until the year 2007 Nokia was the leading company in this field with very good VRIN resources but within a few years it lost its market share for its rivals iPhone and Samsung. According to Teece, one of the main problems of Nokia was the lack of important dynamic capabilities that would have made it possible to generate the efficient operating system and to manage consumer-friendly very complicated copyright issues relating to different applications. Apple had already done this job when creating its successful iPod. In addition, Apple's ability to sense the preferences of customers played an important role.

COGNITION AND STRATEGY

During past decades starting in the 1990s, there has been an increasing interest in the research of managerial and organizational cognition (Kaplan, 2011). The focus has been especially on the managerial cognition with the question of how managers' knowledge structures affect a company's strategic actions, performance and renewal capacity. Organizations can be regarded as interpretation systems (Daft and Weick, 1984) where knowledge structures are created and applied to make sense of the complex reality and facilitate information processing and decision-making. Following Walsh's definition (1995, p. 281):

> A knowledge structure is a mental template that individuals impose on an information environment to give it form and meaning.

In strategic management studies, knowledge structures are called, for example, mental models, dominant logics, strategic frames or schemas, to name a few. Dominant logic is one of the concepts used in studies of managerial cognition. It specifically relates the managerial cognition to the company's business context. The concept of dominant logic was launched by Prahalad and Bettis (1986, p. 490) who define it as the way in which managers conceptualize the business and make critical resource allocation decisions – be it in technologies, product development, distribution, advertising, or in human resource management.

Dominant logic is the managerial worldview defining the key imperatives of the business. At the same time as dominant logic acts as an information filter (Bettis and Prahalad, 1995) it also provides the common strategic understanding and interpretation schema to facilitate managerial decision-making. The idea is that the key elements of dominant logic become embedded in the organizational behavior – mindsets, routines, capabilities, and processes (Bettis et al., 2011). This embeddedness may cause severe challenges in times of disruptive changes. In times of discontinuities, managers should transform their dominant logic in order to address the new demands of the changing business environment. Because of its per-sistent nature, the established dominant logic embedded in organizational behavior does not change easily and may act as a blinder (Prahalad, 2004), preventing the managers – especially those of incumbent firms – from sensing the weak signals and the rising opportunities (Vecchiato, 2017).

There is a large body of research showing how managerial cognition affects the strategic renewal and ability to adopt and address disruptive changes (Kaplan, 2011). One of the focal articles is the Porac et al. (1989) study on how managerial cognitive categorization of the competitive groups in the business led to the decline of the Scottish knitwear industry in the 1980s. Another classic in this field is Tripsas and Gavetti's (2000) study on how managers' cognitive rigidity hampered Polaroid's ability to adapt from print to digital technology. Furthermore, the story of Blockbuster and Netflix is illustrative. Blockbuster failed to reframe and transform itself from brick-and-mortar video rental to an online streaming service provider (Raffaelli et al., 2019), whereas Netflix adopted the new business design. The story of Nokia is another good example of how managerial cognitive inertia hinders necessary strategic renewal (Vuori and Huy, 2016).

In strategic management research, the research on cognition and strat-egy has diffused in various research areas, such as capabilities (Laamanen and Wallin, 2008; Eggers and Kaplan, 2009) and incentives (Kaplan and Henderson, 2005). Cognition has been used as an underlying element in some conceptual developments. Cognition has also been part of the trend toward research on a more micro foundational level. For example, Helfat and Peteraf (2015) link cognition with the concept of dynamic capabilities to provide a frame to analyze managerial cognitive capabilities. Using Teece's (2007) model (of sensing, seizing and reconfiguring) they define what cognitive competences constitute managerial sensing, seizing and reconfiguring capabilities. Likewise, managerial cognition is one of the three underpinnings – in addition to managerial human and social capital – of the concept of *dynamic managerial capabilities* launched by Adner and Helfat (2003). In line with the general definition of dynamic capabilities (Teece et al., 1997), they define dynamic managerial capabilities as "the capabilities with which managers build, integrate, and reconfigure organizational resources and competences" (Adner and Helfat, 2003, p. 1012). The idea of the new concept is to analyze how individual managers differ in terms of their decision-making and change management.

AMBIDEXTERITY AND CHANGE MANAGEMENT

In the past few decades, ambidexterity has become a widely used concept of strategic management to analyze companies' ability to manage change. It is originally based on March's (1991) study on organizational learning and the concepts of exploration and exploitation. Later, especially O'Reilly and Tushman (Tushman and O'Reilly, 1996; O'Reilly and Tushman, 2004) refined the concepts of exploration and exploitation in their research on ambidexterity (ambidextrous organization). According to the basic idea of ambidexterity, managing change requires the ability to simultaneously exploit the current businesses and explore new businesses. This is especially relevant during disruptive changes, during which companies need to radically renew themselves to adapt to the new business logics. During the transformation, the current business provides the required stability and necessary resources to run the old business, whereas exploration is needed to constantly search and create new business opportunities (March, 1991). In terms of the concepts presented in this chapter – resources, capabilities and cognition – exploitation can be said to be based on current and learned resources, capabilities and cognition, whereas exploration requires new and often very different resources, capabilities and cognition.

The challenge for managers is how to balance exploration and exploitation. The more radically the business is changing the more exploration is needed. However, as March (1991) emphasizes, too much exploration on the expense of exploitation may destroy valuable resources and routines that are needed to run the current business. On the other hand, too much exploitation may lead to stagnation and inability to maintain competitive advantage in the changing business environment. Especially incumbent firms with strong learned work cultures have a bias toward exploitation (March, 1991). The balance between exploration and exploitation creates challenges for managers to find ways to overcome the organizational rigidities and manage the tensions that arise between the often opposite activities of exploration and exploitation (Smith and Tushman, 2005; Raisch et al., 2009; O'Reilly and Tushman, 2011). As O'Reilly and Tushman (2016) emphasize, ambidexterity requires good leadership skills from managers to cope with the many challenges and commit the organization to work toward the same strategic goal.

The ambidexterity literature provides solutions and tools for managers to manage and organize the two often opposite activities of exploitation and exploration (O'Reilly and Tushman, 2016). The literature identifies three solutions to implement ambidexterity: structural, contextual and temporal ambidexterity (O'Reilly and Tushman, 2013; Birkinshaw et al., 2016). Structural ambidexterity is based on establishing separate development units for exploration activities. In contextual ambidexterity, exploitation and exploration are pursued within the same unit. Contextual ambidexterity emphasizes individuals and their possibility to make choices between exploration and exploitation on an everyday basis (Gibson and Birkinshaw, 2004). Temporal ambidexterity means sequential alteration between exploitation and exploration. In practice, they all have their pros and cons (O'Reilly and Tushman, 2013) and therefore companies may end up applying a mixture of different solutions.

During the current times of technological discontinuity, it is clear that there is an urgent need for ambidexterity in practically all industries. It could be claimed that ambidexterity is needed now more than maybe ever before. No matter what industry – banking, travelling services, automobile, media, and so on – digital technologies are disrupting the dominant business logics at all levels and dimensions.

THE EVOLUTION OF STRATEGIC MANAGEMENT IN A NUTSHELL

The above section launched a brief and compact history of the rise and development of the "strategic management" concept. After a very short historical review, the rise of the so-called "business policy" was discussed and its focus on firm internal, historically motivated case studies was stressed. These analyses were mostly practical and meant to help managers when facing uncertainties arising from the changes in the business environment. During the 1970s, the analysis took a more scientific stance, trying to use statistical data and trying to derive more generalizable conclusions relating to strategic managerial problems. Following and extending the "swings of a pendulum" idea introduced in the insightful article of Hoskisson et al. (1999) we then looked at the rise of the microeconomics-based Porterian view that highlighted the strategic importance of the competitive environment. Now the focus was clearly on the firm external side and the methods were based on large databases and econometrics following the lead of economics.

In the mid-1980s, however, we noticed the swing of a pendulum toward the firm internal factors. Based on empirical criticism of the Porterian five forces model, some strategy researchers (Wernerfelt, Rumelt, Barney and Peteraf) challenged the Porterian view according to which the competitive advantage was based on the ability to exploit market imperfections in the product/service markets. Instead, the followers of this new resource-based view gave a look at firm internal factors, such as resources, routines and capabilities and the resource market imperfections as main sources of competitive advantage.

In the late 1990s, the next swing of a pendulum took place. This time the static nature of both the Porterian and resource-based view was challenged by dynamization of the resource-based view. The new approach, called the dynamic capability view, analyzed the firm's ability to transform its resource and knowledge base in order to better cope with drastic changes of the competitive environment. Especially the apt operationalization of the dynamic capability view launched by David Teece (2007) opened up a new and more detailed way to look at the challenges faced by modern companies. Teecean concepts of "sensing," "seizing," and "reconfiguring" enabled researchers to analyze different strategic actions taken by entrepreneurially oriented business managers. Figure 1.1 illustrates the idea of the swing of a pendulum utilized in this chapter.

Figure 1.1 shows first the swing from the historically oriented and case-

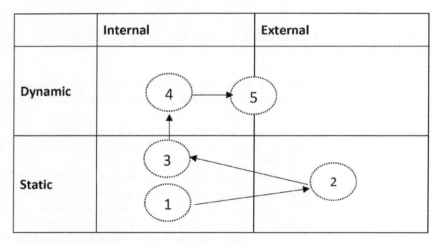

Figure 1.1   The development of the basic ideas of strategic management

based business policy models (1) toward the economics-based Porterian view (2) that stressed the product/service market imperfections. The next swing went toward the resource-based view (3) stressing the role of firm internal factors and market imperfections related to them. The last swing went from the static toward dynamic approach and resulted in the rise of the dynamic capability view (4). My guess is that the next swing will be the step toward what I would call "the modern synthesis" (5) that simultaneously includes both resource and product/service market imperfections and analyzes them in the dynamic context. Some recent advances in the field of the dynamic capability view already hint to this direction (see Teece, 2018; Helfat and Raubitschek, 2018). These insightful analyses look at the dynamic capability view in the context of digital platform-based ecosystems, in which strong network externalities create new sources for competitive advantage.

CONCLUSIONS

The target of the course that I am suggesting in this chapter is to provide a clear understanding of the main concepts and theories and the main trajectories of strategic management since the 1970s when it became an independent discipline. In addition, the students should understand the relevance of the concepts and theories for managers. Students should be able to apply these concepts in real-life business cases to better understand their relevance as managerial tools in decision-making and managing change.

The application of theoretical concepts in real life cases is significant but naturally also challenging. Therefore, the teacher's role and support are of great importance in helping and guiding the students to understand the theories' practical relevance and impact. Furthermore, it is important that students dedicate time to assignments and discussions during the course. Below I suggest some assignments that help and guide students to reflect theories of strategic management through real life examples.

ASSIGNMENT 1

The assignment can be carried out as a group discussion in the classroom or as a written assignment carried out as group work or individually.

Read the following article:
Barney, J.B. (1991). Firm resources and sustained competitive advantage. *Journal of Management*, 17(1), 99–120.

1. Discuss/review the main ideas of the article focusing on the following questions:
   - What are the resources defined by RBV? What are the so-called VRIN resources?
   - What are they like and why are they relevant for firms?
   - What are the mechanisms that help sustain the competitive advantage?
   - How can firms use and benefit from applying the RBV frame?
2. Think of a firm, organization, sports team etc. which is a market leader having a competitive advantage over others. Make reflections of the case by analyzing, for example, the following questions:
   - Why is this case interesting?
   - How would you explain the success of your case company (team) in terms of the resource-based view (which resources might be behind the success etc.)?
   - How would you study this case by using the RBV (research target/s, methods)?

ASSIGNMENT 2

The assignment can be carried out as a group discussion in the classroom or as a written assignment carried out as group work or individually.

Read the following article:
Tripsas, M. and Gavetti, G. (2000). Capabilities, cognition, and inertia: Evidence from digital imaging. *Strategic Management Journal*, 21(10–11), 1147–1161.

1. Discuss/review the main ideas of the article focusing on the following questions:
   - Based on the case study, what is managerial cognition and why is it relevant for firms' strategy?
   - Make reflections on the Polaroid story: how did managerial cognition affect Polaroid's business? (What was Polaroid's dominant logic in the beginning? How did the technology challenge the business? etc.)
2. Think of a firm, which has succeeded or failed in renewing its business.
   - Describe the case and its business context.
   - What do you think about the role of managerial cognition in the success or failure?

3. Think of a firm or industry that is currently facing a disruptive change. Make reflections of the case in terms of managerial cognition and ambidexterity, for example:
   - Describe the case. What generates the disruption?
   - How do you see that the changing business environment is challenging existing and path-dependent managerial cognition?
   - How would you see the renewal process in terms of ambidexterity?

ASSIGNMENT 3

The assignment can be carried out as a group discussion in the classroom or as a written assignment carried out as a group or individually.

Think of a firm (or sports club etc) that is more successful than others in its business area. Describe the case and industry and analyze the firm's superior performance in terms of:

a) Porter's five forces model
b) Resource-based view
c) Dynamic capability view.

REFERENCES

Adner, R. & Helfat, C.E. (2003). Corporate effects and dynamic managerial capabilities. *Strategic Management Journal*, 24(10), 1011–1025.

Ansoff, H.I. (1965). *Corporate Strategy*. New York: McGraw-Hill.

Bain, J.S. (1956). *Barriers to New Competition*. Cambridge, MA: Harvard University Press.

Barney, J.B. (1986). Organizational culture: Can it be a source of sustained competitive advantage? *Academy of Management Review*, 11(3), 656–665.

Barney, J.B. (1991). Firm resources and sustained competitive advantage. *Journal of Management*, 17(1), 99–120.

Bettis, R.A. & Prahalad, C.K (1995). The dominant logic: Retrospective and extension. *Strategic Management Journal*, 16(1), 5–14.

Bettis, R.A., Wong, S., & Blettner, D. (2011). Dominant logic, knowledge creation, and managerial choice. In Easterby-Smith, M. & Lyles, M.A. (Eds.) *Handbook of Organizational Learning and Knowledge Management*. Chichester: John Wiley & Son, 367–381.

Birkinshaw, J., Zimmermann, A., & Raisch, S. (2016). How do firms adapt to discontinuous change? Bridging the dynamic capabilities and ambidexterity approach. *California of Management Review*, 58(4), 36–58.

Bracker, J. (1980). The historical development of the strategic management concept. *Academy of Management Review*, 5, 219–224.

Chandler, A. (1962). *Strategy and Structure: Chapters in the History of the American Industrial Enterprise*. Cambridge, MA: The MIT Press.

Coase, R.H. (1937). The nature of the firm. *Economica*, 4(16), 386–405.

Cyert, R.M. & March, J.G. (1963). *A Behavioral Theory of the Firm*. Englewood Cliffs, NJ: Prentice Hall.

Daft, R.L. & Weick, K.E. (1984). Toward a model of organizations as interpretation systems. *Academy of Management Review*, 9(2), 284–295.

Eggers, J.P. & Kaplan, S. (2009). Cognition and renewal: Comparing CEO and organizational effects on incumbent adaptation to technical change. *Organization Science*, 20(2), 461–477.

Eisenhardt, K.M. & Martin, J.A. (2000). Dynamic capabilities: What are they? *Strategic Management Journal*, 21(10–11), 1105–1121.

Gibson, C.B. & Birkinshaw, J. (2004). The antecedents, consequences, and mediating role of organizational ambidexterity. *Academy of Management Journal*, 47(2), 209–226.

Grant, R.M. (1996). Toward a knowledge-based theory of the firm. *Strategic Management Journal*, 17(S2), 109–122.

Helfat, C.E., Finkelstein, S., Mitchell, W., Peteraf, M.A., Singh H., Teece, D.J., & Winter, S.G. (2007). *Dynamic Capabilities: Understanding Strategic Change in Organizations*. Malden, MA: Blackwell Publishing.

Helfat, C.E. & Peteraf, M.A. (2015). Managerial cognitive capabilities and the microfoundations of dynamic capabilities. *Strategic Management Journal*, 36(6), 831–850.

Helfat, C.E. & Raubitschek, R.S. (2018). Dynamic and integrative capabilities for profiting from innovation in digital platform-based ecosystems. *Research Policy*, 47(8), 1391–1399.

Hoskisson, R.E., Hitt, M.A., Wan, W.P., & Yiu, D. (1999). Theory and research in strategic management: Swings of a pendulum. *Journal of Management*, 25(3), 417–456.

Kaplan, S. (2011). Research in cognition and strategy: Reflections on two decades of progress and a look to the future. *Journal of Management Studies*, 48(3), 665–695.

Kaplan, S. & Henderson, R. (2005). Inertia and incentives: Bridging organizational economics and organizational theory. *Organization Science*, 16(5), 509–521.

Kogut, B. & Zander, U. (1992). Knowledge of the firm, combinative capabilities, and the replication of technology. *Organization Science*, 3(3), 383–397.

Laamanen, T. & Wallin, J. (2009). Cognitive dynamics and capability development paths. *Journal of Management Studies*, 46(6), 950–981.

March, J.G. (1991). Exploration and exploitation in organizational learning. *Organization Science*, 2(1), 71–87.

Mason, E. (1939). Price and production policies of a large-scale enterprise. *American Economic Review*, 29(1), 61–74.

Nag, R., Hambrick, D.C., & Chen, M.-R. (2007). What is strategic management, really? Inductive derivation of a consensus definition of the field. *Strategic Management Journal*, 28(9), 935–955.

Nelson, R.R. & Winter, S. (1982). *An Evolutionary Theory of Economic Change*. Cambridge, MA: Harvard University Press.

O'Reilly, C.A. & Tushman, M.L. (2004). The ambidextrous organization. *Harvard Business Review*, 82(4), 74–81.

O'Reilly, C.A. & Tushman, M.L. (2011). Organizational ambidexterity in action: How managers explore and exploit. *California Management Review*, 53(4), 5–22.

O'Reilly, C.A. & Tushman, M. L. (2013). Organizational ambidexterity: Past, present, and future. *The Academy of Management Perspectives*, 27(4), 423–338.

O'Reilly, C.A. & Tushman, M.L. (2016). *Lead and disrupt. How to solve the innovator's dilemma*. Stanford, CA: Stanford University Press.

Penrose, E.T. (1959). *The Theory of the Growth of the Firm*. Oxford: Basil Blackwell, (2nd edition 1980).

Peteraf, M.A. (1993). The cornerstones of competitive advantage: A resource-based view. *Strategic Management Journal*, 14(3), 179–191.

Polanyi, M. (1967). *The Tacit Dimension*. London: Routledge and Kegan Paul.

Porac, J., Thomas, H., & Baden-Fuller, C. (1989). Competitive groups as cognitive communities: The case of Scottish knitwear manufacturers. *Journal of Management Studies*, 26(4), 397–416.

Porter, M.E. (1980). *Competitive Strategy: Techniques for Analyzing Industries and Competitors*. New York: Free Press.

Porter, M.E. (1981). The contributions of industrial organization to strategic management. *Academy of Management Review*, 6(4), 609–620.

Porter, M.E. (1985). *Competitive Advantage*. New York: Free Press.

Prahalad, C.K. (2004). The blinders of dominant logic. *Long Range Planning*, 37(2), 171–179.

Prahalad, C.K. & Bettis, R.A. (1986). The dominant logic: A new linkage between diversity and performance. *Strategic Management Journal*, 7(6), 485–501.

Raffaelli, R., Glynn, M.A., & Tushman, M. (2019). Frame flexibility: The role of cognitive and emotional framing in innovation adoption by incumbent firms. *Strategic Management Journal*, 40(7), 1013–1039.

Raisch, S., Birkinshaw, J., Probst, G., & Tushman, M.L. (2009). Organizational ambidexterity: Balancing exploitation and exploration for sustained performance. *Organization Science*, 20(4), 685–695.

Ricardo, D. (1817). *The Principles of Political Economy and Taxation*. London: John Murray.

Rumelt, R.P. (1984). Towards a strategic theory of the firm. In Lamb, R.B. (ed.) *Competitive Strategic Management*. Englewood Cliffs, NJ: Prentice Hall, 556–570.

Rumelt, R.P. (1991). How much does industry matter? *Strategic Management Journal*, 12, 167–185.

Schendel, D.E. & Hofer, C.W. (1979). *Strategic Management: A New View of Business Policy and Planning*. Boston: Little, Brown and Co.

Scherer, F.M. (1980). *Industrial Market Structure & Economic Performance*. Chicago, IL: Rand McNally.

Schumpeter, J.A. (1934). *The Theory of Economic Development*. Cambridge, MA: Harvard University Press (original edition 1912).

Selznick, P. (1957). *Leadership in Administration*. New York: Harper & Row.

Simon, H.A. (1962). The architecture of complexity. *Proceedings of the American Philosophical Society*, 106(6), 467–482.

Smith, W.K. & Tushman, M.L. (2005). Managing strategic contradictions: A top management model for managing innovation streams. *Organization Science*, 16(5), 522–536.

Teece, D.J. (1986). Profiting from technological innovation: Implications for integration, collaboration, licensing and public policy. *Research Policy*, 15(6), 285–305.

Teece, D.J. (1998). Capturing value from knowledge assets: The new economy, markets for know-how, and intangible assets. *California Management Review*, 40(3), 55–79.

Teece, D.J. (2007). Explicating dynamic capabilities: The nature and microfoundations of (sustainable) enterprise performance. *Strategic Management Journal*, 28(13), 1319–1350.

Teece, D.J. (2012). Dynamic capabilities: Routines versus entrepreneurial action. *Journal of Management Studies*, 49(8), 1395–1401.

Teece, D.J. (2014). The foundations of enterprise performance: Dynamic and ordinary capabilities in an (economic) theory of firms. *Academy of Management Perspectives*, 28, 328–352.

Teece, D.J. (2018). Profiting from innovation in the digital economy: Enabling technologies, standards, and licensing models in the wireless world. *Research Policy*, 47, 1367–1387.

Teece, D.J., Pisano, G., & Shuen, A. (1997). Dynamic capabilities and strategic management. *Strategic Management Journal*, 18, 509–533.

Tripsas, M. & Gavetti, G. (2000). Capabilities, cognition, and inertia: Evidence from digital imaging. *Strategic Management Journal*, 21(10–11), 1147–1161.

Tushman, M.L. & O'Reilly, C.A. (1996). The ambidextrous organizations: Managing evolutionary and revolutionary change. *California Management Review*, 38(4), 8–30.

Vecchiato, R. (2017). Disruptive innovation, managerial cognition, and technology. *Technological Forecasting and Social Change*, 116, 116–128.

Vuori, T.O. & Huy, Q.N. (2016). Distributed attention and shared emotions in the innovation process: How Nokia lost the smartphone battle. *Administrative Science Quarterly*, 61, 9–51.

Walsh, J.P. (1995). Managerial and organizational cognition: Notes from a trip down Memory Lane. *Organization Science*, 6(3), 280–321.

Wernerfelt, B. (1984). A resource-based view of the firm. *Strategic Management Journal*, 5(2), 171–180.

Williamson, O.E. (1975). *Markets and Hierarchies: Analysis and Antitrust Implications*. New York: Free Press.

Williamson, O.E. (1981). The modern corporation: Origins, evolution, attributes. *Journal of Economic Literature*, 19(4), 1537–1568.

Williamson, O.E. (1985). *The Economic Institutions of Capitalism*. New York: Free Press.

Williamson, O.E. (1991). Strategizing, economizing, and economic organization. *Strategic Management Journal*, 1(52), 75–94.

Winter, S.G. (2003). Understanding dynamic capabilities. *Strategic Management Journal*, 24(10), 991–996.

2. Teaching strategy as an ethical practice

Sven-Ove Horst

INTRODUCTION

Strategy not only involves the implementation of plans, tools, decisions and actions that have large consequences for creating a successful organizational future, but it is also a practice that carries inherent ethical responsibilities toward people, organizations and society, which have to be appreciated, reflected upon and enacted in local contexts. This understanding resonates with the strategy-as-practice approach (see e.g. Burgelman et al., 2018; Golsorkhi et al., 2015a; Vaara & Whittington, 2012), which allows studying "issues that are directly relevant to those who are dealing with strategy, either as strategists engaged in strategic planning or other activities linked with strategy, or as those who have to cope with the strategies and their implications" (Golsorkhi et al., 2015b, p. 1). Therefore, strategists need a sensibility toward acting with people, which enables them to act in a responsible yet strategic manner to situations and circumstances they face. However, this understanding of strategy and ethics as an inseparable part of the same practice is not (yet) strongly developed (Behnam & Rasche, 2009; Clegg et al., 2013; Elms et al., 2010; Statler et al., 2007; Tsoukas, 2018).

This "underdevelopment" of scholarship around strategy-and-ethics as practice may be based in the current focus of strategy research and teaching. In recent years, academic discussions often addressed questions of rigor and relevance (Grant, 2008; Kelemen & Bansal, 2002; Paton et al., 2013; Thomas & Wilson, 2011; Thorpe et al., 2011). Strategy was seen as a field in which teaching should be either "theory-based" (e.g. Grant, 2008) or which should be "practice-based" (Ghoshal, 2005). While no agreement was reached, it reminded us as scholars that *how* and *what* we teach and *how* we conduct research has significant implications and effects on how managers act. Therefore, Ghoshal (2005, p. 87) proclaimed, "if we really wish to reinstitute ethical or moral concerns in the practice of management, we have to first reinstitute them in our mainstream theory" that we teach. However, current strategic moral dilemmas within which managers navigate, for example, Brexit, #Dieselgate, Cum-Ex, trade-wars, populist tendencies, and fake-news show that this has not been done in predominant manner (Bachmann et al., 2017; Elms et al., 2010).

This may not be very surprising, because the critical scholarship around the strategy-and-ethics connection shows us that management discourses sustain distinct values and practices (Vaara & Faÿ, 2012). Moreover, while strategists have a degree of freedom and flexibility for drawing on particular discourses and enacting them in practice (Suominen & Mantere, 2010), the ideas, theories and discourses which they currently sustain, have created undesired practices which "we all now so loudly condemn" (Ghoshal, 2005, p. 75), instead of enhancing and supporting good strategic management decisions and actions (cf. Bachmann et al., 2017; Clegg et al., 2013; Tsoukas, 2018). Some say this is because of the way in which problematic beliefs, values and practices are reproduced in and through current management education (Vaara & Faÿ, 2012), and call for a more reflective approach to strategy teaching and pedagogy, which includes "action-oriented pragmatic knowledge that concerns things that are deemed good or bad" as well as discussions around this practical ethical knowledge for grounding personal experience (Clegg et al., 2013, p. 1252). Therefore, to expand our understanding and explore what teaching strategy as an ethical practice might look like, I will sketch one perspective that can help install a sensitivity for acting ethically in the context of strategy (Clegg et al., 2013; Statler et al., 2007; Tsoukas, 2018).

STRATEGY AS AN ETHICAL PRACTICE

The perspective of strategy as an ethical practice is grounded in our understanding of strategy as a practice (Vaara & Whittington, 2012; Whittington, 2007). Here, strategy is seen as something that people do, instead of something that an organization has (Whittington, 2006). As an alternative to the mainstream strategy research it shifts attention away from performance outcomes of strategy alone, to a more comprehensive and fine-grained analysis of the "thinking and doing of strategy," which includes all situational, behavioral aspects of strategy formulation, planning and implementation (Golsorkhi et al., 2015b, p. 1). It looks at how and why strategy practitioners employ different frameworks, tools and ideas and enact the corresponding practices to achieve organizational success in practice. Therefore, the three concepts "practitioners," "practices," and "praxis" are core elements of understanding strategy (Whittington, 2006).

Strategy research addresses questions of responsibility and "effects of strategy", while discussing, for example, the way in which strategy practitioners function as carriers of current practices (Vaara & Faÿ, 2012), including influential ideas like, for example, benchmarking, strategic planning and value creation, but also of more debatable ideas such as, for example, financialization, downsizing or offshoring and outsourcing. We learn that strategy as a professional field "employs, develops, licenses, and spreads particular practices and particular kinds of practitioners, with aggregate effects that can resonate through whole societies" (Whittington, 2007, p. 1580). Therefore, taking this notion of "practioners as carriers of practices" seriously (Whittington, 2006, p. 626), preparing them for practice will have to include a consideration of ethics.

This strong notion of an inseparable strategy–ethics is visible in foundational strategy textbooks. They describe that management will have to make decisions which are not only based on market opportunities or corporate competencies and resources, but also on personal values and aspirations, while acknowledging their obligations to segments of society other than stockholders (Andrews, 1971, p. 38). They underline that "coming to terms with the morality of choice may be the most strenuous undertaking in strategic decisions" (Christensen et al., 1987, p. 460). This shows the understanding of making strategic decisions in an ethical manner or under ethical premises was seen as the hallmark of strategy. "Ethics and strategy go together" and to achieve that "we need to tell a radically different story about organizational life to connect these concepts" (Freeman & Gilbert, 1988, p. xi). In that sense, they argue, strategy should be built "on a foundation of ethical reasoning" (Freeman & Gilbert, 1988, p. xiii).

Newer studies on strategy–ethics describe this connection in greater detail. Normally the "traditional strategy process models encourage managers to pursue knowledge about the environment and the organization, to make decisions and formulate strategies based on this knowledge and to implement structures and processes that serve effectively to produce competitive advantage and, in turn, financial success" (Statler et al., 2007, p. 153). But "coping with complexity" and "distinguishing those [influences] which are critical from those which are merely important, and reaching a balanced judgment, typically under conditions of uncertainty and imperfect information" is what strategy is about (cf. Grant, 2008, p. 278). This means, for example, balancing and working through contradictory tensions that arise from organizational change (Horst & Moisander, 2015), facilitating and questioning current developments, envisioning future possibilities and then co-creating organizational strategies (Bange et al., 2019; Horst & Järventie-Thesleff, 2016).

Today in fact, top-down strategic planning with pre-conceived ideas often needs to give way to more situational approaches where strategy emerges from local adaptations and responses (Horst et al., 2019a). This means "the strategist will have to recognize the limitations of predictive knowledge in the face of emergent change" (Statler et al., 2007, p. 153), and take it as an opportunity to develop and apply "practical wisdom" (Statler et al., 2007, p. 152). In this situation, ethics and strategy are perhaps most closely and visibly intertwined (Elms et al., 2010, p. 409). This is why and how a practice–theoretical lens toward strategy-and-ethics can help us shed light on this relationship and describe how and what we should look toward in our teaching.

The frame of strategy as an ethical practice further draws on our understanding of business ethics as practice. Understanding ethics as a form of practice shifts our emphasis toward the context and interpretation of ethics, the discourse in which it is enacted and its relation to organizational subjects (Clegg et al., 2007, p. 107), because "ethical issues arise in different contexts and situations, and cannot be 'solved' by a single formula" (Carter et al., 2007, p. 8). Moreover, "ethics as practice constitutes, and is constituted by, the interactions and tensions between different rationalities and values" (Carter et al., 2007, p. 8), which may clash in the moment of strategic uncertainty. This could be seen as a strategic problem, while it might in fact be an opportunity for strategy-and-ethics. As Zygmunt Bauman claims, "uncertainty is the home ground for the moral person and the only soil in which morality can sprout and flourish" (Bauman, 2009a, p. 63). Therefore, ethical practices are enacted in situations of "ethical pluralism," where moral choices are carved out from unclear situations and against potentially conflicting standards (Clegg et al., 2007, p. 108). This entails knowledge about and a sensitivity toward complex problems with insufficient solutions and engaging them in reflective manner under conditions of uncertainty (cf. Bauman, 2009b, p. 365). This reflective strategy–ethics as practice "will be enacted in situations of ambiguity where dilemmas and problems will be dealt with without the comfort of consensus or certitude" (Clegg et al., 2007, p. 109). Following Clegg et al. (2007, pp. 111–112), this means the ethical conduct of strategy will always be embedded in local practices that operate in an active and contextualized manner. For them, strategic "choice" implies a moral choice and reflection about different possibilities; choice is about interpreting and adapting rules and ideas according to local circumstances, which implies active "sense-making" (Maitlis & Christianson, 2014). At the same time, it includes a 'humbleness' toward not knowing everything, and an 'openness' toward discussing, sharing and constructing together the possibilities of action. This is related to strategic actions in the context of emergent strategy, in which the attentiveness to local circumstances and surroundings allows the creation of sensible solutions and actions (Chia, 2014).

In their context, practitioners skillfully draw on their practices as a result of habituation and enact their practices with a particular moral contour (Tsoukas, 2018, p. 333). This way, strategy as an ethical practice concerns processes of self-formation and identity-development amongst people at work (Clegg et al., 2007, p. 115). Ideally, these processes are reflective because people take the time to think about who they want to be, what they want to achieve, and how, and take these reflections as a chance for learning about themselves and their processes and possibilities of becoming. On this basis, the ethical practice of strategy is enacted through "vigorous and persistent self-critique, practiced through open dialogue and the creation of ethical spaces in which such issues can be discussed" (Clegg et al., 2007, p. 117). This is important because

> practice is an inherently value-laden array of activities, whose internal goods define a certain conception of what constitutes that 'good life' in pursuing the ends of the practice and whose members develop, through habituation, a particular character – that is, moral virtues and a capacity for the exercise of practical wisdom. (Tsoukas, 2018, p. 332)

In other words, practices are inherently "moral accomplishments" in which people uphold a set of shared standards of excellence which include applied normative values (Tsoukas, 2018, p. 333).

The literature suggests that strategists who are interested in acting in an ethical manner in the face of ambiguity should focus on the dialogical processes through which they make meaning and take creative action (Clegg et al., 2007, p. 117; Statler et al., 2007, p. 158). In developing their sense of selves, strategists are advised to balance scientific knowledge with an adaptive responsibility and focus on learning that integrates both cognitive and moral reasoning (Statler et al., 2007, p. 157). In addition, the attention to dialogue needs to go beyond a superficial inclusion of stakeholders, and ensure through a process-oriented character that the good for the stakeholder community is continuously sustained in tandem with a sensitivity for firm performance (and hence successful strategy) (Statler et al., 2007, p. 159).

Overall, strategy as an ethical practice describes strategists as moral actors which have an impact on others – locally, in organizations, in their communities and industries (Clegg et al., 2013, p. 1255). They enact values and ideals through their practices, for example, through combining practical wisdom and strategy (Bachmann et al., 2017). For strategy teaching, therefore, the ambition is to cultivate a reflective "problem orientation" to concepts, frameworks and theories and fostering attention toward the role and place of ethical judgment in strategy (cf. Clegg et al., 2013, p. 1256). Ultimately, teaching strategy-and-ethics can enable people, organizations and systems to reshape knowledge and practices to render the teaching of ethics resourceful and more than just a placebo (Clegg et al., 2013, p. 1257).

UNIVERSITY OF NAVARRA AS A CONTEXT OF STRATEGY TEACHING

The University of Navarra is a strong value-laden context, in which students and professors carry a sensitivity for values and ethical practice. It is a unique place which can serve as an example for integrating core human values into the conduct of education, research and practice. Sánchez-Tabernero and Torralba (2018, p. 3) describe the university as an intellectual community which is based on a "reflective institutional culture." This culture is driven by Christian core-principles related to education. These are "service, truth, freedom and faithfulness" (Sánchez-Tabernero & Torralba, 2018, p. 5). These principles support a holistic and "liberal" approach to education (Sánchez-Tabernero & Torralba, 2018, p. 12), which enables personal growth through continuous reflection and learning of scientific disciplines as well as through gaining an understanding for "good personal conduct." This fusion of learning about personal conduct and discipline knowledge comes to life in several "practices," which are described in the university's Statement of Core Values: "Service to Society, The Search for the Truth, Freedom and Pluralism, and Desire for Faithfulness to the Church" (Sánchez-Tabernero & Torralba, 2018). I will now briefly describe the guiding values and reflect on how they support developing reflective judgment in the context of strategy as an ethical practice.

WORK

Work is the manifestation of the dignity of each person, a factor in personality development, a bond between human beings and a driving force of progress. Among other consequences, this concept of work involves aspiring to excellence when carrying out tasks and keeping an eye on the details. (Navarra, 2010)

The quote above shows that work is understood as an expression of how one conducts oneself. Through working, people not only produce external output for an organization, but also transform and enrich themselves on a personal level (Guitián, 2015, p. 64). Furthermore, work enables connecting with other people and acting as a force of change. In this sense, "work is for making life more human, not less human" (Guitián, 2015, p. 64). Therefore, being and doing good, as part of the excellence a person strives toward in their practice and through their practices is at the heart of this guiding value.

The holistic approach is further demonstrated in that freedom is seen as an essential feature of education, alongside service and the search for truth (Sánchez-Tabernero & Torralba, 2018, p. 8).

FREEDOM

The University is a place for harmony, study and friendship, open to people of all conditions, without discrimination based on religion, race, ideology, nationality, sex, etc. The University feels called to contribute to solving the problems facing society and, without moving directly into political action or tasks inherent to other institutions, develops students' capacity to be critical, which enables each person to freely form his or her own opinions and convictions, in an environment of pluralism. Love of freedom and responsibility is the basic principle of academic and professional life, research work, medical and healthcare activity. The management tasks at the University are carried out following principles of joint responsibility and participation. (Navarra, 2010)

Freedom is seen not only as a possibility, but as a primal condition for reflective conduct. Accepting differences, yet working together constructively, and enacting freedom and responsibility through joint responsibility and participation seem to connect well with the intention of strategy as an ethical practice. As Sánchez-Tabernero and Torralba (2018, p. 8) explain, "the ideals of service and the search for truth represent the best course for developing the full potential of freedom. Put simply, the university aims to form people to become good professionals with good hearts, i.e. people with full lives and the capacity to serve others." This is closely connected with respect.

RESPECT

The university helps students acquire knowledge and develop certain attitudes, such as respect for others, the ability to listen, appropriate behavior, a civic spirit and respect for nature. All these habits help students prepare for professional life and encourage the members of the academic community to take on social responsibility. Respect for privacy is part of the commitment undertaken by those who work in the university community. (Navarra, 2010)

Developing an ability to listen and a reflexivity of one's own conduct are at the center of the university's values. Preparing for being a reflective practitioner who carries a "civic spirit and respect for nature" seems to encourage taking responsible actions. This relates to the centrality of dialogue at the university as a place to foster knowledge. It also creates the opportunity for "debate, discussion and plurivocal exchange" (Clegg et al., 2007, p. 117), which is exemplified in the idea of interdisciplinarity.

INTERDISCIPLINARITY

The University's mission statement – to seek and present the truth – is a collective enterprise that requires dialogue between specialists from different academic areas. With this approach, the diversity of the sciences is mutually enriching, students acquire an overall vision and knowledge is not overly compartmentalized. (Navarra, 2010)

Interdisciplinarity is integral to the search for truth. As Sánchez-Tabernero and Torralba (2018, p. 8) explain, "[s]pecialization in research is inevitable and necessary but must be accompanied by efforts to achieve [an] overview of the various knowledge areas." Therefore the curriculum is built to allow the specialized knowledge of disciplines to be integrated into a "comprehensive vision of humans and the world" (Sánchez-Tabernero & Torralba, 2018, p. 7). In this sense, reflective appreciation of knowledge sharing as well as enriching and constructively creating new knowledge become possible.

At the same time, any "betterment of society goes hand in hand with the question about what society needs and how to achieve it best" (Sánchez-Tabernero & Torralba, 2018, p. 7). But "betterment" also needs a sense of responsibility. Therefore, the university tries to develop "students' awareness of social responsibility so they understand their professional activity [. . .] as a way of bettering the world" (Sánchez-Tabernero & Torralba, 2018, p. 6).

RESPONSIBILITY

The work of professionals at the University of Navarra should be characterized by a sense of responsibility, and they seek to communicate this attitude to students as part of the University's educational mission. This attitude is reflected in judicious use of resources and taking care of the facilities. (Navarra, 2010)

Responsibility is seen and taught as an integral part of being human and conducting yourself as a person in the world of work today. The ideal is that students are learning to become practitioners with a strong value-ethics and a reflexive approach to seeing themselves. Developing "professional competencies and personal habits" is key (Sánchez-Tabernero & Torralba, 2018, p. 6). Being primed with these values as part of the institutional context, as well as through learning assignments and teaching with taking the role of individual responsibility into account, students may be able to connect these values with how they act in the context of strategic management.

The focus on "service" more broadly and in particular "Service to Society" underscores that work has the capacity to bring about social transformation, and that people can ensure a concern for others also in their profession (Sánchez-Tabernero & Torralba, 2018, p. 6).

SERVICE

As its founder wished, the University of Navarra has had an explicitly stated aim of service and it aspires to contribute to the material and moral betterment of society. This characteristic leads it to learn about and respond to the problems and needs of society in fields related to its teaching and research activity: medical care and healthcare, studies on current issues, university cooperation and many other social promotion activities. Solidarity is a fundamental aspect of the university spirit. The University encourages members of the academic community to participate in specific initiatives to serve those most in need. (Navarra, 2010)

Their conduct should lead toward the betterment of society. This cultivates a responsive nature in thinking and acting and is strongly aligned with the "acceptance and discussion of ethical dilemmas [. . .] as one step towards a more ethically informed management" (Clegg et al., 2007, p. 117), and as such creates the possibility for strategy as an ethical practice.

EXPERIENCES FROM TEACHING STRATEGY WITH AN ETHICAL SENSIBILITY

Course Context

The study program is the four-year bilingual BA in Advertising and Communication of the Department of Communication. Thirty-three students from the fourth year, mostly Spanish-speaking students and several visiting students from marketing and journalism programs participated in the course. They were about 19–23 years old.

The course was developed as an intense workshop-type seminar for BA students in the last year of their study. It included lectures, discussions and student presentations over the course of five weeks. The course was targeted at teaching strategic management to students in a communication and advertising program. This meant I linked a general understanding of strategy with specific circumstances and aspects of the media industry (Küng, 2017). Furthermore, I wanted to teach the practice of strategy with a high degree of reflexivity and situational awareness (Biggs, 2012), and developed my course structure and learning activities accordingly.

What Did My Course Syllabus Look Like?

My syllabus introduced strategy in a broad way, covering core aspects and theories about strategic management, but also sensitizing the students to emergent developments which create complex problems in practice:

Strategic media management involves "major intended and emergent initiatives taken by general managers on behalf of owners involving utilization of resources to enhance the performance of firms in their external environments" (Nag et al., 2007, pp. 942–943). But strategic media management isn't always that simple: How about start-ups creating a new venture that have no large resources or owners in their support? How about fast changing environments that make long-term strategic planning obsolete? How about the digitization of media products that makes previously learned practices for print and analogue environments worth-less? All these define and change strategic media management drastically.

Digital media technologies are influencing the processes and practices of product development, branding, innovation and strategy as they transform the ways in which people and companies communicate and organize themselves: we see more direct communication to audiences and new modes of work internally. They have become tools, channels, platforms and strategies for obtaining, produc-ing, and sharing knowledge about the world around us, through communication and interaction (Lindgren, 2017, p. 5). Therefore, the course will take a broad perspective toward media management, seeing it as both the management of media organizations and the management of various forms of media, through which organizational actions are achieved as a form of practical engagement.

Consequently, our focus will be on reviewing traditional approaches to strategy and how they apply to the media context, as well as discussing new developments that shift our understanding of strategy toward new digital, networked, and complex realities. The course is intended to provide the students with a reflective approach to managing that will guide the articulation and implementation of organizational strategies.

I structured the learning outcomes in a way to capture a large diversity of strategy topics, as well as highlight that the students would have to situate and make sense of these models, ideas and frameworks for their local contexts. The intended learning outcomes read as follows:

With successful completion of the course, students will be able to:

- Assess theories, concepts and tools of strategic media management
- Understand the role of industry, competitive forces and strategic positioning
- Distinguish the origins and assumptions of the resource-based view (RBV) of the firm
- Appreciate the role of dynamic capabilities (DCs) in building sustainable competitive advantage
- Understand strategy as a process and social practice
- Understand the processes and practices through which change is implemented and sustained
- Critically evaluate step-based and contingency models of change
- Evaluate the way in which communication and leadership impact strategy
- Evaluate the importance of intra-organizational politics and exercise of power for strategy
- Discuss and evaluate concepts and approaches to business ethics and ethical decision-making.

In connection to these learning outcomes, the academic program was structured as follows:

Week 1

- Day 1 (Tuesday): Introduction to Strategic Media Management. What makes media management special?
- Day 2 (Wednesday): Industrial organization. Competitive forces in the industry. Strategic positioning.

Week 2

- Day 3 (Tuesday): Creating value and the value chain. The resource-based-view.
- Day 4 (Wednesday): Strategic management as a process. Strategy emergence. Strategic learning.

Week 3

- Day 5 (Tuesday): Strategy as practice. New theoretical sophistication of strategy. Plus: Group Presentation 1 (GP1).
- Day 6 (Wednesday): Strategy, power and political decision-making. Plus: GP2.

Week 4

- Day 7 (Tuesday): Strategy, responsibility, and ethics. Corporate codes of conduct, rule following, decision-making, ethics as practice. Plus: GP3.
- Day 8 (Wednesday): Strategic change. Forces, ideals and processes. How do you manage change? Plus: GP4 and GP5.

Week 5

- Day 9 (Tuesday): Strategy, communication and leadership. Strategy discourse, storytelling. Leading through communication. Plus: GP6 and GP7.
- Day 10 (Wednesday): Strategy and entrepreneurship. Creativity and innovation. Plus: GP8.

Reading assignments covered a variety of academic journal articles and suggested a core-reading for addressing strategy as a practice: Clegg et al. (2017). This book gives an overview of core topics, which I extended through contextualizing specific questions and cases with industry-specific readings.

The learning activities focused on "what the student does" (Biggs, 2012). I wanted the students to be active and reflect with me in class on particular topics and issues. Similarly, I incorporated a big group activity to support active learning about a specific topic and share their experiences and interpretations.

I used the following evaluation scheme: Class participation 15 percent, group presentation 30 percent, individual interview assignment 55 percent. The presentation and the interview assignment are now described in greater detail:

Group Presentation: 30 percent of grade.

The idea of this assignment is that students work together to comprehend, synthesize and evaluate knowledge from one journal article and conduct additional research to underline their argumentation. This allows preparing and reflecting together on the state of knowledge on strategic media management and approaching the phenomena we face from different angles.

The presentation of the students is intended to present knowledge, insights and developments of the topic and stimulate further engagement. Furthermore, the idea is that students reflect on the meaning and relevance of the included concepts and theories for understanding and managing strategy. Therefore, the purpose of the presentations is NOT just to summarize the content or retell chosen articles, but rather to push the class discussion to consider the meaning and relevance of the theories and concepts and critically evaluate current developments around media entrepreneurship that stood out during the reading of your literature. Please incorporate other sources, own experiences and current examples into your presentation. Creative forms of class engagement are encouraged.

What I liked about the individual interview assignment, it pushed the students to connect with a strategist of their choice, gain sensitivity for the conduct of strategy in this context, and reflect on these experiences for the written report.

Individual Interview Assignment: 55 percent of grade.

The purpose of the interview assignment is to connect with and learn from a practitioner that is active in the field of strategic media management through conducting a semi-structured qualitative interview (and some fieldwork). You will search for an adequate interview partner, schedule a meeting, conduct the interview (preferably face-to-face, but Skype is possible as well), and later transcribe, analyze and reflect upon the interview.

The second half of the assignment is to use the interview material and your experiences from doing the fieldwork (searching for a practitioner, reading about strategic management in this context, conducting the interview, etc.) for reflecting on your own learning experiences and development within the field of strategic media management. Please focus explicitly on answering the following questions:

- What did you learn from the interview?
- What kinds of skills are needed to become a good strategist?
- How do digital technologies shape strategic media management?
- How does that connect to the theories and debates we have worked with in class?
- What are currently important topics for strategic management in the media context?

Overall, the assignment focuses on various levels of learning from Bloom's Taxonomy, namely comprehension, application, analysis, synthesis and evaluation.

For the interview questions I tried to include different aspects of strategy-making to enable the students to connect the issues they would hear in practice with the concepts and ideas we have discussed in class:

Entry and focus on communication:

- How has your job changed in the past 10 years? What things have become important today?
- ...

Internal developments:

- How do you manage your team (or organization) to create and share new ideas?
- What is the role of decision-making for developing new ideas?

- How would describe in your own words what strategy means?
- What is important when acting strategically today?
- How do you manage spontaneous changes or new developments?

Responsibility in communication and strategy:

- What is the role of digital communication for your job? Can you describe that?
- How would you describe the role of responsibility in communication?
- What are you responsible for when you manage your projects, ideas, your organization?
- How would you describe the role of ethics in management today?
- What does it mean to manage ethically to you?
- Can you combine managing strategically and ethically? How would you combine it?
- What can organizations do to manage well for the future?

Overall, using the idea of constructive alignment, I purposefully aligned student activities with my intended learning outcomes. I ensured an explicit focus on how ethics and responsibility are connected with the conduct of strategy in practice. Through asking "How is responsibility seen today?", "What is the role of ethics?", "What do people see as acting ethically?", and "How can strategy and ethics be connected?" I steered the students to talking with the practitioners about strategy-and-ethics in a manner that would allow elaborations and appreciation about how these are connected in practice. To prepare them in class, I envisioned how their interviews might go and primed them for how they could respond fluently to dive deeper into this topic. This way, I sensitized them to become "active listeners" and "co-construct" their interviews in a constructivist manner (Holstein & Gubrium, 1997). Later they connected these experiences back to our in-class discussions through their assignment. For completing the assignment, they had to write a reflection in which they connected: (1) theories, concepts and discussions from class with (2) their own experiences and (3) the descriptions of the strategy practitioner. I hoped this would enable them to connect different frames and develop a reflexive appreciation of the ideas and tools of strategy.

WHAT DID MY STUDENTS LEARN?

The institutional frame which guides teaching, research and personal conduct at the University of Navarra in Pamplona is respect for and adherence to a set of underlying values, which are *work, freedom, respect, interdisciplinarity, responsibility, service and international dimension.* The university embedded these values in the curriculum of all programs and disciplines to create a strong sensitivity for acting ethically. It describes these values to "guide and characterize the daily actions of those who make up the University and shape its environment and culture" (Navarra, 2010). This means the students were primed for understanding strategy as an ethical practice and connected this conception with the values they had been encountering across their studies.

Inspiring learning, pushing the students to grow beyond themselves, and making them strive toward becoming "reflective practitioners" (Schön, 1991), more reflective people, more reflective strategists was my intention. Now, as students have different interpretations of what strategy is to them, what values they draw on, and how they should act on this basis, the individual learning outcomes varied, but they all showed a strong sensitivity for making the connections between strategy theory, ethical conduct and their own development. One student who always participated in class, but who struggled with the final project wrote that:

> I've learned about strategy since my first year in college, but sincerely, it hasn't been until your class that something has made click in my mind and woke me up to the interest of strategy in some way. Because I personally am the most not-strategic person at all. (Student 24, 2019)

One student writes in his interview reflection that he now better understands what acting strategically in today's turbulent times means. He foregrounds that the values of "patience, compassion, civility and empathy [are important] as managerial practices" (Student 10, 2019). He aspires to become a successful manager and strategist through connecting the underlying values he has learned with the contexts and circumstances he finds. He has understood that in practice, he needs to act reflectively and enact the values in his daily practices. He summarizes that:

> If I am to pursue the path of managing an international marketing team, then my practices are to match those values that will effectively develop myself and my teams. (Student 10, 2019)

This shows that the core idea about strategy as an ethical practice had sunk in. In fact, other students showed similar learning experiences and connected the theories and concepts we talked about in class with the experiences of doing the strategy interview. In particular, some students explicitly highlighted the way in which they felt ethics and ethical actions are a hallmark of being a manager today, and that ethics needs to be included in today's business education:

> I really loved the way Salla descripted today's world with ethics as 'Ethics is the basis for everything in today's transparent business world'. [. . .] Ethics in business life is something that I feel strongly about and that it should be a bigger topic in schools too. (Student 32, 2019, p. 8)

The core learning outcome I wanted to create with the interview was that students developed a reflexivity about what they learn and how they act (Hibbert, 2013), and preserve this understanding for entering the business world. I wanted to push them to reflect on themselves and their actions, thereby making the connection between theory and practice. A student remarked on the learning outcome that:

> Going more deeply into the topic has helped me see what kind of colleague, manager or boss I want to be in the future. I hope I didn't slide too much off the topic, because I know that it can happen to me quite often. Also, I am much more a practical person and therefore I think that my research part might have been bit too concise, but I rather used my own experiences, thoughts and what new I have learned. (Student 32, 2019, p. 8)

This shows that the connection of strategy–ethics–practice came out strongly in the individual reflections. Students learned to make choices, reflect on their actions, and evaluate how they act and in regards to what outcomes. Even though they may not be managers yet, this learning – from my point of view – creates the conditions from which ethical strategizing can arise. Take the following example of a student:

> First of all I'll say that sincerely, I'm on a plane right now writing this essay, so again, I procrastinated up to this point. I failed again to the task of organizing; I failed to strategizing myself. I knew about this work for 2 months and didn't do much until the last possible minute. Why do we do that? Well, why do I do that? It's like if I would refuse to follow the different steps before the time is running out. And this is the most unprofessional thing to do. And it's one of the lessons I've learned, again. But lessons are there to learn from them and not stepping into the same rock again you would think, then why again? I guess because the punishment is not as big. In university you might have a lower grade and the rush in your veins, which is not pleasant at all but is tolerable. But in the professional strategic world . . . .. That's something different for sure that I'll have to learn falling again, because it is not something you change from day to night. So, for now, I'll try to do my best (knowing I could have done better with more time) in this final assignment and also knowing that strategy can be treated as something that people do (or should do) rather than what an organization has. (Student 24, 2019)

The students have understood that strategy as an ethical practice aims to connect our theoretical frames and the values they aspire to with the situation they face, be it a university assignment or a work project, and reflecting on what kind of person they become through the actions they conduct. This is exactly what the strategy as an ethical practice approach aims to accomplish, namely to "enable more reflective, nuanced approaches to strategy and organization practice" (Clegg et al., 2013, pp. 1247–1248). In particular, the role is to cultivate a problem orientation to research and strategy and a sensibility for the role and place of ethical judgment in strategy (Clegg et al., 2013; Statler et al., 2007; Tsoukas, 2018). Strategically speaking, their learning was successful.

WHAT DID I LEARN?

To conclude this chapter, I would like to highlight three take-aways for teaching strategy as an ethical practice.

First, teaching strategy as an ethical practice, in my view, is actually just "teaching strategy," but with a reflective appreciation of values which enter decision-making, actions and practices. Ethics and responsibility should never be just an add-on to what is taught, but need to be ingrained in the everyday understanding of the subject. This relates to the current and ongoing discussion that we need good practices of strategy-making which can support creating sustainable, reflective and effective solutions to complex societal and social problems (Vaara & Durand, 2012). Achieving this on a broad scale may help ensure that strategy matters for the better.

Second, strategy teaching is always context-dependent. The ethics-sensitive teaching of strategy in *this* context was supported by an institutional setting that cherishes this approach. If you plan to teach a course on strategy as an ethical practice in *your* context, be it at a university, college or even through coaching in an industry setting, you have to ask yourself: How free are you in what you teach? What are the values that your context envisions? What are current practices that can serve as an example of things working well? What needs to be improved and work better? You might even involve the course participants to create innovative ideas and envision constructive changes for your context. Overall, all these aspects should guide you toward answering one core question: What is the most meaningful pedagogical approach to ensure that strategy is seen and later practiced in an ethical manner?

Third, strategy teaching, as with all teaching, relates to who you are as a teacher and who you strive to be as a person. In particular, seeing strategy as an ethical practice highlights the enormous importance of individual responsibility as part of a reflective practice. Becoming attentive to how you are developing as a teacher, student, manager, employee or as an entrepreneur is essential for "value-based judgment" (Bachmann et al.,

2017; Statler et al., 2007; Tsoukas, 2018). This attentiveness can help build your "identity as a strategist" in reflective manner (Oliver, 2015). As an entrepreneur, for example, your personal identity and your strategy are closely aligned; you become what you do (Horst et al., 2019b). This underscores that it is good to make reflective judgments about *what* you want, *how* you want to reach that, and *who* you want to be. Furthermore, when it is hard to create a vision for the organization's future, paying attention to how you interact with others and what you want to achieve with them for the organization may create an openness to emergent strategy-making that can facilitate successful organizational development (Horst et al., 2019a).

Based on these experiences I am optimistic about the growing importance of seeing strategic management as an ethical practice and fruitful discussions around the teaching and pedagogy around these issues.

REFERENCES

Andrews, K.R. (1971). *The Concept of Corporate Strategy*. Homewood, IL: Dow Jones-Irwin.

Bachmann, C., Habisch, A., & Dierksmeier, C. (2017). Practical wisdom: Management's no longer forgotten virtue. *Journal of Business Ethics*, 1–19. doi: 10.1007/s10551-016-3417-y.

Bange, S., Moisander, J., & Järventie-Thesleff, R. (2019). Brand co-creation in multichannel media environments: A narrative approach. *Journal of Media Business Studies*, 1–18. doi: 10.1080/16522354.2019.1596722.

Bauman, Z. (2009a). *Does Ethics Have a Chance in a World of Consumers?*. Cambridge, MA: Harvard University Press.

Bauman, Z. (2009b). *Postmoderne Ethik* [Postmodern Ethics] (U. Bielefeld & E. Boxberger, Trans.). Hamburg: Hamburger Edition.

Behnam, M., & Rasche, A. (2009). 'Are strategists from Mars and ethicists from Venus?' – strategizing as ethical reflection. *Journal of Business Ethics*, 84(1), 79–88. doi: 10.1007/s10551-008-9674-7.

Biggs, J. (2012). What the student does: teaching for enhanced learning. *Higher Education Research & Development*, 31(1), 39–55. doi: 10.1080/07294360.2012.642839.

Burgelman, R.A., Floyd, S.W., Laamanen, T., Mantere, S., Vaara, E., & Whittington, R. (2018). Strategy processes and practices: Dialogues and intersections. *Strategic Management Journal*, 1–28. doi: 10.1002/smj.2741.

Carter, C., Clegg, S., Kornberger, M., Laske, S., & Messner, M. (2007). *Business Ethics as Practice: Representation, Reflexivity and Performance*. Cheltenham, UK and Northampton, MA, USA: Edward Elgar Publishing.

Chia, R. (2014). Reflections: In praise of silent transformation – allowing change through 'letting happen'. *Journal of Change Management*, 14(1), 8–27. doi: 10.1080/14697017.2013.841006.

Christensen, C.R., Andrews, K.R., Bower, J.L., Hamermesh, R.G., & Porter, M.E. (1987). *Business Policy: Texts and Cases* (6th ed.). Homewood, IL: Irwin.

Clegg, S.R., Jarvis, W.P., & Pitsis, T.S. (2013). Making strategy matter: Social theory, knowledge interests and business education. *Business History*, 55(7), 1247–1264. doi: 10.1080/00076791.2013.838033.

Clegg, S.R., Kornberger, M., & Rhodes, C. (2007). Business ethics as practice. *British Journal of Management*, 18(2), 107–122. doi: 10.1111/j.1467-8551.2006.00493.x.

Clegg, S.R., Schweitzer, J., Whittle, A., & Pitelis, C. (2017). *Strategy: Theory and Practice*. London: Sage.

Elms, H., Brammer, S., Harris, J.D., & Phillips, R.A. (2010). New directions in strategic management and business ethics. *Business Ethics Quarterly*, 20(3), 401–425. doi: 10.5840/beq201020328.

Freeman, R.E., & Gilbert, D.R. (1988). *Corporate Strategy and the Search for Ethics*. Englewood Cliffs, NJ: Prentice Hall.

Ghoshal, S. (2005). Bad management theories are destroying good management practices. *Academy of Management Learning & Education*, 4(1), 75–91. doi: 10.5465/amle.2005.16132558.

Golsorkhi, D., Rouleau, L., Seidl, D., & Vaara, E. (2015a). *Cambridge Handbook of Strategy as Practice* (2nd ed.). Cambridge: Cambridge University Press.

Golsorkhi, D., Rouleau, L., Seidl, D., & Vaara, E. (2015b). Introduction: What is strategy as practice? In D. Golsorkhi, L. Rouleau, D. Seidl, & E. Vaara (Eds.), *Cambridge Handbook of Strategy as Practice* (pp. 1–20). Cambridge: Cambridge University Press.

Grant, R.M. (2008). Why strategy teaching should be theory based. *Journal of Management Inquiry*, 17(4), 276–281. doi: 10.1177/1056492608318791.

Guitián, G. (2015). Service as a bridge between ethical principles and business practice: A Catholic social teaching perspective. *Journal of Business Ethics*, 128(1), 59–72. doi: 10.1007/s10551-014-2077-z.

Hibbert, P. (2013). Approaching reflexivity through reflection: Issues for critical management education. *Journal of Management Education*, 37(6), 803–827. doi: 10.1177/1052562912467757.

Holstein, J.A., & Gubrium, J.F. (1997). Active interviewing. In D. Silverman (Ed.), *Qualitative Research: Theory, Method and Practice* (pp. 113–129). London: Sage.

Horst, S.-O., & Järventie-Thesleff, R. (2016). Finding an emergent way through transformational change: A narrative approach to strategy. *Journal of Media Business Studies*, 13(1), 3–21. doi: 10.1080/16522354.2015.1123854.

Horst, S.-O., Järventie-Thesleff, R., & Baumann, S. (2019a). The practice of shared inquiry: How actors manage for strategy emergence. *Journal of Media Business Studies*, 16(3), 202–229. doi: 10.1080/16522354.2019.1641672.

Horst, S.-O., Järventie-Thesleff, R., & Perez-Latre, F.J. (2019b). Entrepreneurial identity development through digital media. *Journal of Media Business Studies*, 1–26. doi: 10.1080/16522354.2019.1689767.

Horst, S.-O., & Moisander, J. (2015). Paradoxes of strategic renewal in traditional print-oriented media firms. *International Journal on Media Management*, 17(3), 157–174. doi: 10.1080/14241277.2015.1084306.

Kelemen, M., & Bansal, P. (2002). The conventions of management research and their relevance to management practice. *British Journal of Management*, 13(2), 97–108. doi: 10.1111/1467-8551.00225.

Küng, L. (2017). *Strategic Management in the Media: Theory to Practice* (2nd ed.). London: Sage.

Lindgren, S. (2017). *Digital Media and Society*. London: Sage.

Maitlis, S., & Christianson, M. (2014). Sensemaking in organizations: Taking stock and moving forward. *The Academy of Management Annals*, 8(1), 57–125. doi: 10.1080/19416520.2014.873177.

Nag, R., Hambrick, D.C., & Chen, M.-J. (2007). What is strategic management, really? Inductive derivation of a consensus definition of the field. *Strategic Management Journal*, 28(9), 935–955. doi: 10.1002/smj.615.

Navarra, University of (2010). University statement of core values (pp. 1–3). Pamplona: University of Navarra.

Oliver, D. (2015). Identity work as a strategic practice. In D. Golsorkhi, L. Rouleau, D. Seidl & E. Vaara (Eds.), *Cambridge Handbook of Strategy as Practice* (pp. 331–344). Cambridge: Cambridge University Press.

Paton, S., Chia, R., & Burt, G. (2013). Relevance or 'relevate'? How university business schools can add value through reflexively learning from strategic partnerships with business. *Management Learning*, 45(3). doi: 10.1177/1350507613479541.

Sánchez-Tabernero, A., & Torralba, J.M. (2018). The University of Navarra's Catholic-inspired education. *International Studies in Catholic Education*, 10(1), 1–15. doi: 10.1080/19422539.2018.1418943.

Schön, D.A. (1991). *The Reflective Practitioner: How Professionals Think in Action.* Aldershot, UK: Ashgate Publishing.

Statler, M., Roos, J., & Victor, B. (2007). Dear Prudence: An essay on practical wisdom in strategy making. *Social Epistemology*, 21(2), 151–167. doi: 10.1080/02691720701393475.

Suominen, K., & Mantere, S. (2010). Consuming strategy: The art and practice of managers' everyday strategy usage. *Advances in Strategic Management*, 27, 211–245. doi: 10.1108/S0742-3322(2010)0000027011.

Thomas, H., & Wilson, A.D. (2011). 'Physics envy', cognitive legitimacy or practical relevance: Dilemmas in the evolution of management research in the UK. *British Journal of Management*, 22(3), 443–456. doi: 10.1111/j.1467-8551.2011.00766.x.

Thorpe, R., Eden, C., Bessant, J., & Ellwood, P. (2011). Rigour, relevance and reward: Introducing the knowledge translation value-chain. *British Journal of Management*, 22(3), 420–431. doi: 10.1111/j.1467-8551.2011.00760.x.

Tsoukas, H. (2018). Strategy and virtue: Developing strategy-as-practice through virtue ethics. *Strategic Organization*, 16(3), 323–351. doi: 10.1177/1476127017733142.

Vaara, E., & Durand, R. (2012). How to connect strategy research with broader issues that matter? *Strategic Organization*, 10(3), 248–255. doi: 10.1177/1476127012452827.

Vaara, E., & Faÿ, E. (2012). Reproduction and Change on the global scale: A Bourdieusian perspective on management education. *Journal of Management Studies*, 49(6), 1023–1051. doi: 10.1111/j.1467-6486.2012.01049.x.

Vaara, E., & Whittington, R. (2012). Strategy-as-practice: Taking social practices seriously. *The Academy of Management Annals*, 6(1), 285–336. doi: 10.1080/19416520.2012.672039.

Whittington, R. (2006). Completing the practice turn in strategy research. *Organization Studies*, 27(5), 613–634. doi: 10.1177/0170840606064101.

Whittington, R. (2007). Strategy practice and strategy process: Family differences and the sociological eye. *Organization Studies*, 28(10), 1575–1586. doi: 10.1177/0170840607081557.

3. Teaching sustainability in strategic management

Britta Boyd

As business students become more and more aware of environmental problems, they choose topics around social responsibility of companies and their interest in learning about sustainability issues increases. The objective of teaching sustainability in strategic management is to provide students with an overall understanding and knowledge of the development of sustainability, legal responsibilities of different actors and corporate social responsibility (CSR) activities in businesses. Special importance is attached to the conceptual evolutionary path of theories and practices in sustainability development and the reflection on its implications.

When designing a course in sustainable management it is not only important to include interesting cases dealing with companies solving CSR issues. A theoretical foundation should also be provided to introduce students into the subject and demonstrate how sustainable management has developed over time. Based on the latest and most central models and concepts within the area of sustainability students on Bachelor and Master level should be able to:

- Define and identify relevant and theoretical problems and discuss them in class.
- Perform in-depth analyses of practical issues and theoretical articles.
- Conclude managerial and theoretical implications of findings to argue in a scientifically appropriated way.

Students should then be able to evaluate critically and apply central concepts in connection with real business cases. Theoretical and practical solutions of certain problems should be solved based on this knowledge. The material presented here is suitable for undergraduate and graduate students in all business-related studies. On undergraduate level sustainable management is usually offered as an elective course and on graduate level it can be included as a compulsory module depending on the focus of the Master study.

The rest of this chapter is organized as follows: The next section introduces the concepts of sustainability, legal responsibilities and CSR and how to teach them. It describes the relevant models used for teaching sustainability in strategic management from a historical perspective to show developments in the area of sustainability. The following section provides a collection of scientific articles on sustainability and CSR as a basis for intense reading. A student exercise is presented in which each student selects one or more articles, summarizes and discusses them in class. The selection of relevant journal articles and a guideline how to summarize and analyze should then be specified. The chapter concludes with discussion questions and suggested solutions.

INTRODUCING THE FUNDAMENTAL CONCEPTS – SUSTAINABILITY, LEGAL RESPONSIBILITIES AND CSR

Teachers need to be familiar with the three concepts of *sustainability, legal responsibilities and CSR* which will be presented in this section. The concepts are best taught to students by first presenting and then discussing them in class. Following the theoretical introduction exercises, case studies and discussion questions related to the concepts are to be presented.

Sustainability

The term sustainability has its origin in forestry, where only so many trees were allowed to be cut as can grow back naturally. The former president of Norway, Gro Harlem Brundtland defined sustainable development as to "meet the needs of the present without compromising the ability of future generations to meet their own needs" (Brundtland, 1987). After setting up a commission for sustainable development, the meaning of sustainability according to the Rio Conference in 1992 became much more complex. The Conference of the Parties (COP) 21 in Paris tried to develop Climate Action and the United Nations Environment Programme (United Nations Climate Change, 2019).

Sustainable development has attracted many scholars to contribute with new concepts. The phrase "triple bottom line" was articulated by Elkington in 1994 emphasizing people, planet and profit goals of companies. Referring to the 1987 report "Our Common Future" of the World Commission on Environment and Development and the UNCED (United Nations Conference on Environment and Development) held in Rio de Janeiro in 1992, Elkington suggests business strategies for sustainable development. Companies facing challenges in this rapidly emerging area will then achieve competitive advantages (Elkington, 2013; 1994). In his book named *Cannibals with Forks: The Triple Bottom Line of 21st Century Business*, Elkington (1997) provides practical guidelines to companies on how to build partnerships with different stakeholders in a sustainable manner.

In the 1980s, companies began to become involved in the discussion on sustainability. Societal expectations and pressures from stakeholders increased in a globalized economy. Companies started self-regulation by formulating codes of conducts. Corporate citizenship as charitable donations and other forms of community action identified the role of corporations in administering citizenship rights for individuals (Matten & Crane, 2005).

The Brundtland Commission (World Commission on Environment and Development, 1987) defines sustainable management as "A way to satisfy today's economic, ecologic and social needs that also enables future generation to satisfy their needs." This assumption is regarded as a basis for sustainable management by Löbel et al. (2005) and can be divided into four dimensions of sustainability:

- Economic indicators: patents, cooperation, turnover, equity ratio, use of profits, investments, number of employees.
- Ecologic indicators: waste disposal, rental machines, renewable energy use, ecologic performance of products and company, product origin.
- Social indicators: regional ties, employee structure, working conditions, qualification, customer and employee relationships, family meetings.
- Long-term indicators: companies' vision and philosophy, strategic goals, succession plans.

The relevance of sustainable management and the increasing prevalence of new concepts is illustrated by the fact that the volume of national and international research is increasing. Furthermore, companies are presenting sustainability reports to a large extent now because of internal or external responsibilities (Loew et al., 2005; Boyd, 2010).

Legal Responsibilities

Companies have legal responsibilities toward external stakeholders such as suppliers, consumers, shareholders, governments and non-governmental organizations (NGOs). The roles, activities and responsibilities of these external stakeholders are described in the following four subsections.

Suppliers
Globalization and corporate scandals cause companies to set social and environmental standards for suppliers, monitored internally and by external auditors. Codes of Conduct (CoC) are used as a common way of managing corporate responsibilities in the supply chain and can be defined as "a set of standards, guidelines or rules for ethical behavior which firms impose on their suppliers as a prerequisite for entering into contract with them" (Gilbert & Huber, 2017, p. 463). According to a study from Accenture and UNGC (United Nations Global Compact) only 34 percent of CEOs think their company integrates more sustainability issues into their core business strategy than five years ago but 93 percent of the CEOs think sustainability issues will be critical to the future success of their business (Accenture, 2011). Different companies, organizations and NGOs have thus noticed the importance of integrating sustainable actions and becoming involved in developing standards and CoC for suppliers.

A CoC is seen as an important step in establishing an inclusive culture, but it is not a comprehensive solution on its own. When implementing a CoC the following steps are recommended (Mamic, 2005):

● Create a shared vision.
● Develop understanding and ability.
● Implement code of conduct in organization.
● Feedback, improvement and remediation.

The main problems associated with CoC are that they are often vague, not taken seriously and are difficult to monitor. On the one hand, a much-debated problem around the supplier CoC is suppliers cheating by employing children or subcontractors. On the other hand, buyers put pressure on their suppliers with limits for overtime and child labor but at the same time require short delivery times.

Companies who want to ensure compliance with their supplier CoC can also safeguard this with threats of direct sanctions, for example, corrective action or termination of the supplier contract. Another means to reach goal congruence can be to implement compensation schemes or rewards for suppliers with high compliance with their CoC. In some cases, a third-party intervention can be necessary via the legal system or NGOs. A trustful relationship between suppliers and buyers should aim to reduce the need for assessment or legal regulations. Moreover, reputation effects can spread information to other customers and lead to an increase of compliance with the supplier CoC (Pedersen, 2015).

Managing legal responsibilities via CoC in the supply chain of course depends on a number of other factors such as company size, geographical dispersion, industry and management competences. A multinational company, for example, with worldwide production and sales sites, needs a well-functioning management system to ensure that all suppliers behave in accordance with the CoC.

Consumers
Consumer rights are understood as the entitlement to be treated fairly and with respect when they enter an exchange with a seller (Crane & Matten, 2016). An ethical framework for treating consumer issues was formulated by the United Nations (UN) in 1985 to protect customers. The UN guidelines point out that the consumer often faces imbalances in bargaining power toward the seller and is therefore vulnerable in certain aspects (Harland, 1987).

Consumer vulnerability toward persuasion attempts of sellers depends on a number of factors (Pedersen, 2015):

- Individual characteristics, for example, psychological resilience and self-esteem, cognitive ability.
- Individual states, for example, mood as a long-lasting emotional state, motivation to resist temptations.
- External conditions, for example, social pressure by others, physical elements in a store layout.
- Marketer characteristics, for example, cognitive ability to code information, resources such as financial, technological or organizational.

Consumers are increasingly concerned about ethics when making purchases and are seeking to enhance sustainability for future generations. Ethical, conscious, sustainable or green consumerism describes an expanding social movement of consumers that cares about ethics and corporate citizenship in their purchasing decision. This decision could be to simply buy free-range eggs or avoid products from child labor (Smith, 2008).

Besides ethical motivations, the consumer's decision to act in a sustainable manner can be a result of political, environmental, social or religious considerations. An increase in ethical consumerism movement has been recognized in Western culture. As an example, the UK ethical food and drink market has risen by 16.3 percent from 2015 to 2016 including free-range eggs, vegetarian products, sustainable fish, Rainforest Alliance and Fairtrade products (Ethical Consumer Research Association, 2019). These figures show the rising demand of ethical consumption but at the same time the need for transparency in the entire supply chain.

Another issue that needs to be considered when discussing legal responsibilities and ethical consumption is that marketers face a marketing and consumer ethics dilemma. A paradox in the intention and actual behavior of ethically minded consumers could be observed. According to Futerra (2005) 30 percent of consumers in the UK intend to buy, but only 3 percent actually purchase ethical products. This so-called ethical intention–behavior gap can be explained by the following reasons (Newholm & Shaw, 2007):

- The social desirability bias: Only socially acceptable answers are given in surveys.
- Cognitive and environmental drivers: Unethical purchases are rationalized by denial, dependency or cost–benefit arguments.
- Symbolic or identity-based factors: An individual identity such as a sportsperson or student can clash with the notion of ethical consumption.

Shareholders

Milton Friedman (1970, p. 32) explained sustainability and responsibility of shareholders from the perspective that "the social responsibility of business is to increase its profits . . . while conforming to the basic rules of society, both those embodied in the law and those embodied in ethical custom." As discussed in Carroll (1979, 1991) it seems clear that Friedman is not opposing the social responsibility of companies, but embraces the economic, legal and ethical responsibility of companies. In his Pyramid of Corporate Social Responsibility Carroll (1991) adds a philanthropic responsibility as a response to society's expectation that companies should be good corporate citizens. This includes activities and donations to promote human welfare in areas such as sports, arts, education and community.

An increasing interest of shareholders to take an active role rather than simply applying the "Wall Street rule" has been observed. Shareholders have the ability and capacity to change toward sustainability and promote CSR in various ways. As capital providers and financial product innovators, shareholders can select the most socially responsible companies or projects. Moreover, shareholders can act as information providers in the investment process and evaluate the social and environmental performance of the company. Finally, shareholders can act as influencers in personal meetings or through public voicing and norm entrepreneur by shaping the norms of sustainable strategic management (Pedersen, 2015).

Responsible investment (RI), where environmental, societal and governance issues are integrated into investment decisions, is an important task of shareholders. The concept of RI concentrates on long-term stakeholder perspectives based on stimulating debates between society and corporations. The development of RI started in the 1970s when individual shareholders from the US introduced societal and environmental concerns into the world of finance. They were motivated by political and protest movements such as civil rights, women's liberation and environmental concerns. Later on, the idea of RI expanded to Europe and other parts of the world designated this idea also to green funding and sustainable investments. Beyond 2006, not only individual and institutional shareholders but also the mainstream investment community became interested in RI (Louche & Lydenberg, 2017).

In 2006 the UN launched the Principles for Responsible Investment (PRI) as a leading corporate responsibility instrument developed by the financial sector. The PRI Initiative is an international network of investors working together with the goal to understand the implications of sustainability for investors and support participants to incorporate these issues into their investment decision making and ownership practices. The PRI's six core principles require institutional investors to (OECD, 2006):

1. Incorporate ESG (environmental, social, and governance) issues into investment analysis and decision-making processes.
2. Be active owners and incorporate ESG issues into ownership policies and practices.
3. Seek appropriate disclosure on ESG issues by the entities in which they invest.
4. Promote acceptance and implementation of the Principles within the investment industry.
5. Work together to enhance their effectiveness in implementing the Principles.
6. Report on their activities and progress toward implementing the Principles.

Despite these activities to support RI, the scope, size and spread of these practices remain limited. Most investments were short-term oriented and risky in their approach. Therefore, the aim of RI becoming a mainstream practice still has a long way to go (Pedersen, 2015).

Governments
Even though CSR is seen as voluntary contribution to sustainable development that goes beyond legal requirements, governments can promote sustainable management with a variety of public policies and instruments (Pedersen, 2015):

- Legal or constitutional acts, for example laws on socially RI in government funds.
- Economic policies, for example subsidies and tax incentives for sustainable activities.
- Informational and educational activities, for example guidelines on CSR reporting or socially RI.
- Networks and partnerships, for example multi-stakeholder forums such as the Global Reporting Initiative (GRI: an international independent organization helping businesses to report on their sustainability issues while creating a framework for value creation and comparison).
- Hybrid instruments, for example involvement in labels, awards and action plans on socially RI.

These policy instruments represent a limited number of governance tools which can be employed by a government. To advance sustainable development, governments can lead by example in various other aspects. For instance, a wide range of initiatives are used to promote sustainable public procurement. Collaboration is seen as a vital link between the public procurement process and the development of sustainable business practices, where the experience gained in the collaboration process serves as the basis for suppliers and procurers in improving their sustainable management (Witjes & Lozano, 2016).

Moreover, Europe's public authorities can use their purchasing power to choose environmentally friendly goods, services and works. This way they can make an important contribution to sustainable consumption and production. In a handbook the European Commission's suggestions for green public procurement are documented to help public authorities to buy goods and services with a lower environmental impact (European Commission, 2016).

Non-governmental organizations (NGOs)

In addition to governments, more and more NGOs or civil society activists have growing influence on global CSR practices. The UN claims that there are hundreds of thousands of international NGOs today. Well-known examples are the WWF (World Wildlife Fund), Amnesty International, Greenpeace, World Vision, Save the Children, and Oxfam (Pedersen, 2015). Sandra Waddock (2008) tried to list and categorize the various organizations and initiatives and build a new institutional infrastructure for CSR. The following types of NGO groups were identified:

- Principles, standards and codes, for example OECD Guidelines for Multinational Enterprises or UN Global Compact Principles.
- Accreditation, reporting and certification organizations, for example Forest Stewardship Council, Fair Trade Labelling, AccountAbility or Global Reporting Initiative.
- CSR consulting organizations, for example PricewaterhouseCoopers Sustainable Business Solutions, Corporate Citizenship, Institute for Global Ethics or SustainAbility,
- Business membership organizations, for example Business for Social Responsibility, Business in the Community, Ethics Resource Center or CSR Europe.

Even consumers can be active in a form of NGO as the following example of a carrotmob buycott shows:

So-called buycotts as a form of consumer activism are based on the use of social media where a community buys a lot of goods from one company in a short period of time. A carrotmob is a temporary buycott in the form of a purchase flashmob by a group of consumers organized by activists. The name carrotmob is derived from the carrot and stick idiom, which refers to a policy of offering a combination of rewards (carrots) and punishment (sticks) to induce behavior. Carrotmob is a nonprofit organization based in San Francisco that uses buycotts to reward a business's commitment to making socially responsible changes to the business. Carrotmob also refers to a global movement of community organizers who use the carrotmob tactic of consumer activism as a way to help businesses in their communities. In a carrotmob buycott, businesses compete to be the most socially responsible business, and then a network of consumers spends money to support the winner. The first carrotmob campaign happened in March 2008 in San Francisco. Brent Schulkin, the founder of Carrotmob went to 23 convenience stores with a plan to transform one of the stores into the most environmentally friendly store in the neighborhood. He promised to bring a "mob" of consumers to one store to spend money on one day. The response was overwhelming, which shows the consumer power and the motivation to participate in a carrotmob (Hoffmann & Hutter, 2012).

CSR

After having discussed the contents for sustainability and legal responsibilities when teaching strategic management, the concept of CSR should be delineated. The expression CSR is commonly used in international businesses, whereas some European companies still use social or corporate responsibility as a synonym. The Danish shoe producer Ecco, for example, use corporate responsibility including policies about corporate govern-ance, animal welfare, community relations, environmental and human rights (Ecco, 2019).

This subsection investigates the concept of CSR, starting with a short explanation of the historical development of CSR. The following section examines leadership and human resource management (HRM) of CSR which represents the internal stakeholder group in Figure 3.1. In the two-levels perspective of CSR, Hollensen (2019) exhibits the ethical behavior of an organization toward internal and external stakeholders. The roles, activities and responsibilities toward external stakeholders were described in the Legal Responsibilities section, where suppliers, consumers, share-holders, governments and NGOs were included.

The responsibility a company has toward the environment and society is shown in Figure 3.1, and will be discussed in the section on CSR Standards and Social Accounting.

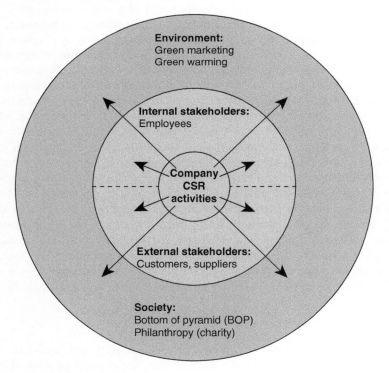

Source: Hollensen, 2019, p. 337.

Figure 3.1 The company's two levels perspective of CSR

Historical development of CSR

The first scholar to write about the topic of CSR was Clark (1916). In his article on "The changing basis of economic responsibility" he discussed that large parts of social responsibilities belong to businesses. Since Bowen and Johnson (1953) wrote the book *Social Responsibility of the Businessman*, a debate on CSR and ethics has taken place. There has then been a shift in terminology from social responsibility of businesses to CSR.

As a reaction on the debate, companies started to respond to ethical concerns. In the mid-1980s all US Fortune 500 companies had "code of ethics" which could resemble a mission statement, a set of values or codes that looked more like operating policies (Ciulla, 1991).

More recently, scandals like the Exxon Valdez oil spill (in Alaska 1989), Mattel toys including lead, obesity from McDonald's food and Nike Asia raised the need for business ethics. Therefore, internal CSR activities became more and more important, but laws and regulations are the most important external drivers for CSR (AMA, 2006).

Leadership and HRM for CSR

The impact of CSR activities on the internal stakeholder level (see Figure 3.1) in companies is complex. The challenges are associated with, for example, human rights, discrimination, health and safety for employees as well as corruption and ethical marketing.

When looking at leadership and CSR, topics such as executive compensation, humility and authority can be raised. The public perception of good leadership differs, and global corporations seem to contribute more to problems than to solutions of social and environmental challenges. Could this be a failure in leadership and what can leaders do to support CSR in their company?

Management and leadership begin with asking questions about CSR challenges and follow suggestions of employees. The following steps for practicing leadership in CSR are recommended (Pedersen, 2015):

- Asking questions to identify CSR issues.
- Raising awareness of the CSR issue with key stakeholders.
- Developing potential responses to the CSR issue.
- Appropriately implementing a response to the CSR issue.
- Continually engaging with the issue.

Additionally, humility is a key personality trait for practicing leadership in CSR where partnerships are built on mutual respect. This applies not only to business partners but also to employees and other stakeholders.

When looking at HRM, there are three different levels or spheres to be considered to support CSR (Pedersen, 2015):

1. The internal professional sphere: HRM is here concerned with work-related tasks such as workforce planning, recruitment, training, reward, health and safety.
2. The internal cultural sphere: HRM can influence the interactions and organizational culture through "greening" the business, ethical conduct, managerial culture, diversity and social inclusion.
3. The external professional sphere: HRM can help businesses to interact with external stakeholders in issues such as human rights, customer education or employee volunteering.

CSR standards and social accounting
The institutional framework for CSR such as initiatives, standards, labelling schemes, reporting systems help companies to find ways to organize and integrate CSR into business processes. CSR standards and practices differ among countries and industries. Practices are mostly dominated by large companies because they are more visible and under pressure from stakeholders. SMEs have less resources and need methods or tools to make CSR operable with regards to certification standards, labels and sustainable development.

Examples of CSR standards are the Global Reporting Initiative, various ISO standards, the Carbon Disclosure Project, Fairtrade Labelling and the UN Global Compact. The UNGC is a leadership platform for the development, implementation and disclosure of responsible corporate practices and policies. Launched in 2000, it is the largest corporate sustainability initiative in the world, with over 8,000 companies and 4,000 non-business signatories based in 160 countries. The 10 principles of the UNGC include regulations for human rights, labor rights, environment and anti-corruption (UNGC, 2015).

Eco-labels as a type of CSR standard are mostly a mixture of environmental and social focus. At a national and international level, eco-labels such as Demeter, Blue Angel, Eco Mark, Dolphin Safe Tuna, EU Ecolabel, Green Seal or Rugmark exist.

CSR reporting and accounting becomes more common especially when larger companies report on CSR activities, making it a more standardized business practice. A sustainability or CSR report conveys disclosures on an organization's impact on the environment, society and the economy (see Figure 3.1) which can be positive or negative. The Global Reporting Initiative (GRI) is a leading organization in the field of sustainability and CSR. GRI promotes the use of sustainability reporting as a way for organizations to become more sustainable and contribute to sustainable development. (Global Reporting Initiative, 2013).

The future development of corporate social responsibility reporting and mainstream CSR reporting depends on several factors (Maguire, 2011):

- Reporting must become more standardized to improve comparability.
- CSR reporting regimes need to limit greenwashing and raise confidence in the disclosures.
- CSR reporting needs to be extended to more firms.
- Information disclosed through CSR reports needs to be centralized and made widely available to stakeholders.

EXERCISES AND CASE STUDY

After a theoretical explanation and discussion of the concepts of sustainable management, a practical part will follow in this section. Firstly, with the "journal paper exercise" students on Bachelor and Master level will understand how scholars discuss different perspectives of sustainable management from an academic perspective. Students will then be able to include appropriate sources in their theses and understand the different contributions of each journal article. Second, the case study helps students to connect the theoretical and practical perspective. The questions should be answered by students having read the case and investigated websites regarding the case study.

Journal Paper Exercise

The students' task in the exercise is to choose one or more articles from a list of relevant academic journal papers and write a one-page journal paper summary for each of them. This will help students understand how sustainable management has developed over time and what different perspectives are discussed by scholars. The view into the research on sustainable management and CSR provides them with skills to investigate a research field intensively by taking the theoretical perspective into consideration.

Following instructions for the one-page journal paper summary should be taken into account:

- Title: Full reference of the chosen journal paper.
- Journal evaluation: Relevance, impact factor, publisher, theoretical/ practical focus.
- Author/s: Reputation in the field, citations, previous publications.

- Methodology: Empirical/theoretical, applied model/theory, survey or case study based etc.
- Aim and main results: Hypotheses/research questions and outcome.
- Implications for businesses or theory.

The students can obtain the impact factor (IF) of an academic journal by searching the journal's webpage. It should be explained to the students that the IF is a measure reflecting the average number of citations to recent articles published in that journal. It is frequently used as a proxy for the relative importance of a journal within its field, where journals with higher impact factors are considered to be more important than those with lower ones.

By evaluating the difference in relevance of the journal paper as well as investigating the aim and main results, the student should be able to explain the implications for business and theory. Table 3.1 provides a list of journal papers that can be considered.

Case Study of Bestseller and its Activities in China

The case of Bestseller was developed to show students how difficult it can be to control the entire supply chain of a multinational manufacturing company. Setting up a CoC does not mean that CSR issues are solved on internal and external levels (see Figure 3.1).

Bestseller, a family-owned company, was founded in 1975 in Denmark by Merete and Troels Holch Povlsen, with now more than 15,000 employees. Fashion wear and accessories are designed and sold in 70 countries with brands like Jack & Jones, Only, Vero Moda, or Vila. They cooperate with selected suppliers in China, Bangladesh, India, Turkey, and Italy. The CoC ensures a sustainable approach in cooperation with suppliers and subcontractors. Bestseller state that CSR comes from within the spirit of the company: "If we are able to help others, then we have an obligation to do so. It is about having that extra surplus to help other people" (Bestseller, 2019).

Bestseller Fashion Group China is an independent company owned by the Holch Povlsen family and two Danish business partners in China. They design their own collections for approx. 7,000 stores in China.

The vision of Bestseller can be summarized as follows (Bestseller, 2019):

- One World: built on fairness and opportunities. Cultural differences are an advantage which will promote quality, good results and values.
- One Philosophy: We make the 10 Principles come alive by being humble and working hard. We base our cooperation on trust, partnership and honesty. We treat all people as individuals but act as a team. Therefore, we succeed.

Table 3.1 *Journal papers for evaluation*

Author/s:	Year:	Journal name:
Carroll	1991	*Business Horizons*
Elkington	1998	*Environmental Quality Management*
Frederick	1998	*Business & Society*
McWilliams/Siegel	2001	*Academy of Management Review*
Joyner/Payne	2002	*Journal of Business Ethics*
Marrewijk	2003	*Journal of Business Ethics*
Garriga/Mele	2004	*Journal of Business Ethics*
Matten/Crane	2005	*Academy of Management Review*
Morsing/Schultz	2006	*Business Ethics*
Porter/Kramer	2006	*Harvard Business Review*
Pedersen	2006	*Business and Society Review*
Matten/Moon	2008	*Academy of Management Review*
Cruz/Boehe	2008	*Management Decision*
Waddock	2008	*Academy of Management Perspectives*
Baden/Harwood/Woodward	2009	*European Management Journal*
Carroll/Shabana	2010	*International Journal of Management Reviews*
Rasche	2010	*Business Ethics*
Cheung/Tan/Ahn/Zhang	2010	*Journal of Business Ethics*
Epstein/Buhovac	2010	*Organizations Dynamics*
Gilbert/Rasche/Waddock	2011	*Business Ethics Quarterly*
Porter Kramer	2011	*Harvard Business Review*
McWilliams/Siegel	2011	*Journal of Marketing*
Lis	2012	*Management Revue*
Flammer	2013	*Academy of Management Journal*
Chin/Hambrick/Trevino	2013	*Administrative Science Quarterly*
Korschun/Bhattacharya/Swain	2014	*Journal of Marketing*
Campopiano/de Massis	2015	*Journal of Business Ethics*

● One Family: Our backbone is the family feeling. We help each other and have unlimited faith in our relatives. We show our identity in the good examples we set for one another. We are proud of our family, it is our link to our past and future.

Bestseller have worked with their CoC since 2002 and it clarifies to employees, suppliers and other stakeholders the expectations and demands for the working and environmental conditions in their supply chain. The Bestseller CoC describes ethical behavior that they wish to promote throughout the supply chain and it is directed at any supplier and subcontractor who manufactures products for Bestseller. Working with the Code, Bestseller wants to increase the level of transparency in their supply chain as well as enable suppliers to take further ownership for the conditions at the factories.

The Bestseller CoC includes the following areas: Human rights and labor rights, Health and safety, Environmental protection, and Ethics. To support suppliers and local colleagues, Bestseller launched a number of written guidelines and policies which work as tools on how to implement their CoC (Bestseller 2019).

Questions

Besides the case itself, the journal paper exercise can help students to find answers to the questions. More recent information, articles and books should be considered as well. Examples of where to start looking are given below.

1. How can Bestseller ensure that the CoC is followed by their suppliers?
   - Baden et al. (2009). The effect of buyer pressure on suppliers in SMEs to demonstrate CSR practices: an added incentive or counter-productive?
   - Epstein and Buhovac (2010). Solving the sustainability implementation challenge.
2. Is it possible to adapt the Danish understanding of sustainable management to China?
   - Cheung et al. (2010). Does corporate social responsibility matter in Asian emerging markets?
   - Chin et al. (2013). Political ideologies of CEOs: The influence of executives' values on corporate social responsibility.
3. How can more than 7,000 stores in China be controlled with regards to CSR?
   - Korschun et al. (2014). Corporate social responsibility, customer orientation, and the job performance of frontline employees.
   - Cheung et al. (2010). Does corporate social responsibility matter in Asian emerging markets?

DISCUSSION QUESTIONS

The following discussion questions can be used in a final discussion round at the end of the course or as exam preparation. The comments below each question indicate how to answer them.

1. How did the concept of sustainable management and CSR evolve over time?
   - Journal paper exercise
   - Intensive reading and evaluation of the academic journal papers
   - Historical development of the field
2. Which scholars had the biggest impact on the research field of sustainable management?
   - Journal paper exercise, especially IF and citations will help here
3. What concepts of sustainability and CSR are relevant for strategic management?
   - The four dimensions of Löbel et al. (2005), sustainability reporting
   - The two-levels perspective of Hollensen (2019)
4. Which stakeholders are involved in the sustainable development of businesses?
   - All internal and external stakeholders (see section on CSR)
5. How do the stakeholders act to contribute to sustainable management of companies?
   - Stakeholders' contribution in various ways (see section on Legal Responsibilities)
6. Is CSR different in the Asian context?
   - Information on the differences can be found on companies' webpages and reports
   - See case study of Bestseller.

HOW TO TEACH THE CONCEPTS

Summarizing the chapter on teaching sustainability in strategic management, the ways in which the different concepts can be taught are presented below:

- **Sustainability**: This part serves as an introduction to the topic of sustainability in strategic management. Teachers should discuss how the term sustainability evolved and what it means to provide the students with a fundamental knowledge about sustainability.
- **Legal responsibilities**: Regarding the roles of external stakeholders, teachers could select a number of stakeholders, depending on the focus of the course. Students could be asked to find examples of how companies manage challenges regarding external stakeholders.
- **CSR**: The teacher should present the concept of CSR from an internal stakeholder perspective and discuss with the students practi-

cal problems that can occur. Regarding the internal stakeholder perspective, students can usually identify several examples of how companies manage problems. Further, the need for standards and social accounting can be discussed to ensure sustainability in strategic management.

Referring to the last part of this chapter, the journal paper exercise needs to be included when teachers expect a critical evaluation of the literature. This would be especially relevant for graduate students that work toward their Master thesis. The case study of Bestseller serves as an example of how a multinational company tries to adapt its sustainable strategic management in other cultural environments.

REFERENCES

Accenture, 2011. A new era of sustainability: UN Global Compact–Accenture CEO Study 2010. Accenture, accessed January 7, 2020 at https://archive.epa.gov/wastes/conserve/tools/stewardship/web/pdf/accenture.pdf.

AMA, 2006. The ethical enterprise: doing the right things in the right ways, today and tomorrow, American Management Association, accessed March 15, 2019 at www.amanet.org.

Baden, D.A., Harwood, I.A. and Woodward, D.G., 2009. The effect of buyer pressure on suppliers in SMEs to demonstrate CSR practices: an added incentive or counter-productive?. *European Management Journal*, 27(6), pp. 429–441.

Bestseller, 2019. About Bestseller, accessed January 7, 2020 at https://www.bestseller clothing.com/pages/about-bestseller.

Bowen, H.R. and Johnson, F.E., 1953. *Social Responsibility of the Businessman*. London: Harper.

Boyd, B., 2010. Sustainable management in long-lived family businesses: a resource-based analysis of northern German builder's providers. *International Journal of Entrepreneurship and Small Business*, 11(3), pp. 308–321.

Brundtland, G. H., 1987. Report of the Brundtland Commission: Our common future. World Commission on Environment and Development, Oxford University Press.

Campopiano, G. and de Massis, A., 2015. Corporate social responsibility reporting: A content analysis in family and non-family firms. *Journal of Business Ethics*, 129(3), pp. 511–534.

Carroll, A.B., 1979. A three-dimensional conceptual model of corporate performance. *Academy of Management Review*, 4(4), pp. 497–505.

Carroll, A.B., 1991. The pyramid of corporate social responsibility: Toward the moral management of organizational stakeholders. *Business Horizons*, 34(4), pp. 39–49.

Carroll, A.B. and Shabana, K.M., 2010. The business case for corporate social responsibility: A review of concepts, research and practice. *International Journal of Management Reviews*, 12(1), pp. 85–105.

Cheung, Y.L., Tan, W., Ahn, H.J. and Zhang, Z., 2010. Does corporate social responsibility matter in Asian emerging markets?. *Journal of Business Ethics*, 92(3), pp. 401–413.

Chin, M.K., Hambrick, D.C. and Treviño, L.K., 2013. Political ideologies of CEOs: The influence of executives' values on corporate social responsibility. *Administrative Science Quarterly*, 58(2), pp. 197–232.

Ciulla, J.B., 1991. Why is business talking about ethics?: Reflections on foreign conversations. *California Management Review*, 34(1), pp. 67–86.

Clark, J.M., 1916. The changing basis of economic responsibility. *Journal of Political Economy*, 24(3), pp. 209–229.

Crane, A. and Matten, D., 2016. *Business Ethics: Managing Corporate Citizenship and Sustainability in the Age of Globalization*. Oxford: Oxford University Press.

Cruz, L.B. and Boehe, D.M., 2008. CSR in the global marketplace: Towards sustainable global value chains. *Management Decision*, 46(8), pp. 1187–1209.

Ecco, 2019. Corporate Responsibility, accessed January 7, 2020 at https://group.ecco.com/en/responsibility.

Elkington, J., 1994. Towards the sustainable corporation: Win–win–win business strategies for sustainable development. *California Management Review*, 36(2), pp. 90–100.

Elkington, J., 1997. *Cannibals with Forks: The Triple Bottom Line of 21st Century Business*. Oxford: Capstone Press.

Elkington, J., 1998. Partnerships from cannibals with forks: The triple bottom line of 21st-century business. *Environmental Quality Management*, 8(1), pp. 37–51.

Elkington, J., 2013. Enter the triple bottom line. In Elkington, J. *The Triple Bottom Line* (pp. 23–38). London: Routledge.

Epstein, M.J. and Buhovac, A.R., 2010. Solving the sustainability implementation challenge. *Organizational Dynamics*, 39(4), pp. 306–315.

Ethical Consumer Research Association, 2019. Ethical Consumer Markets Report 2018, accessed January 7, 2020 at https://www.ethicalconsumer.org/research-hub/uk-ethical-consumer-markets-report.

European Commission, 2016. *Buying Green! A Handbook on Green Public Procurement*, 3rd edition, accessed January 7, 2020 at http://ec.europa.eu/environment/gpp/pdf/Buying-Green-Handbook-3rd-Edition.pdf.

Flammer, C., 2013. Corporate social responsibility and shareholder reaction: The environmental awareness of investors. *Academy of Management Journal*, 56(3), pp. 758–781.

Frederick, W.C., 1998. Moving to CSR: What to pack for the trip. *Business & Society*, 37(1), pp. 40–59.

Friedman, M., 1970. A Friedman doctrine: the social responsibility of business is to increase its profits. *The New York Times Magazine*, 13(1970), pp. 32–33.

Futerra, S.C.L., 2005. The rules of the game: The principles of climate change communication. Department for Environment, Food and Rural Affairs: London, UK.

Garriga, E. and Melé, D., 2004. Corporate social responsibility theories: Mapping the territory. *Journal of Business Ethics*, 53(1–2), pp. 51–71.

Gilbert, D.U. and Huber, K., 2017. Labour rights in global supply chains. In: Rasche, A., Morsing, M. and Moon, J. (Eds.), *Corporate Social Responsibility: Strategy, Communication, Governance* (pp. 451–472). Cambridge: Cambridge University Press.

Gilbert, D.U., Rasche, A. and Waddock, S., 2011. Accountability in a global economy: The emergence of international accountability standards. *Business Ethics Quarterly*, 21(1), pp. 23–44.

Global Reporting Initiative, 2013. Sustainability Reporting Guidelines, accessed January 7, 2020 at https://www.globalreporting.org/resourcelibrary/GRIG4-Part1 -Reporting-Principles-and-Standard-Disclosures.pdf.

Harland, D., 1987. The United Nations guidelines for consumer protection. *Journal of Consumer Policy*, 10(3), pp. 245–266.

Hoffmann, S. and Hutter, K., 2012. Carrotmob as a new form of ethical consumption. The nature of the concept and avenues for future research. *Journal of Consumer Policy*, 35(2), pp. 215–236.

Hollensen, S., 2019. *Marketing Management: A Relationship Approach*, 4th edition, Amsterdam, the Netherlands: Pearson Benelux.

Joyner, B.E. and Payne, D., 2002. Evolution and implementation: A study of values, business ethics and corporate social responsibility. *Journal of Business Ethics*, 41(4), pp. 297–311.

Korschun, D., Bhattacharya, C.B. and Swain, S.D., 2014. Corporate social responsibility, customer orientation, and the job performance of frontline employees. *Journal of Marketing*, 78(3), pp. 20–37.

Lis, B., 2012. The relevance of corporate social responsibility for a sustainable human resource management: An analysis of organizational attractiveness as a determinant in employees' selection of a (potential) employer. *Management Revue*, 23(3), pp. 279–295.

Löbel, J., Schröger, H.A. and Closhen, H., 2005. *Nachhaltige Managementsysteme*. Erich Schmidt Verlag GmbH & Co KG.

Loew, T., Clausen, J. and Westermann, U., 2005. Nachhaltigkeitsberichterstattung in Deutschland: Ergebnisse und Trends im Ranking 2005, Hannover.

Louche, C. and Lydenberg, S., 2017. *Dilemmas in Responsible Investment*. London: Routledge.

Maguire, M., 2011. The future of corporate social responsibility reporting, accessed January 7, 2020 at http://www.bu.edu/pardee/files/2011/01/PardeeIIB-019-Jan-2011.pdf.

Mamic, I., 2005. Managing global supply chain: the sports footwear, apparel and retail sectors. *Journal of Business Ethics*, 59(1–2), pp. 81–100.

Matten, D. and Crane, A., 2005. Corporate citizenship: toward an extended theoretical conceptualization. *Academy of Management Review*, 30(1), pp. 166–179.

Matten, D. and Moon, J., 2008. "Implicit" and "explicit" CSR: A conceptual framework for a comparative understanding of corporate social responsibility. *Academy of Management Review*, 33(2), pp. 404–424.

McWilliams, A. and Siegel, D., 2001. Corporate social responsibility: A theory of the firm perspective. *Academy of Management Review*, 26(1), pp. 117–127.

McWilliams, A. and Siegel, D., 2011. Creating and capturing value: Strategic corporate social responsibility, resource-based theory, and sustainable competitive advantage. *Journal of Management*, 37(5), pp. 1480–1495.

Morsing, M. and Schultz, M., 2006. Corporate social responsibility communication: Stakeholder information, response and involvement strategies. *Business Ethics: A European Review*, 15(4), pp. 323–338.

Newholm, T. and Shaw, D., 2007. Studying the ethical consumer: a review of research. *Journal of Consumer Behaviour: An International Research Review*, 6(5), pp. 253–270.

OECD, 2006. The UN Principles for Responsible Investment and the OECD Guidelines for Multinational Enterprises: Complementarities and Distinctive

Contributions, accessed January 7, 2020 at http://www.oecd.org/investment/mne/38783873.pdf.

Pedersen, E.R.G., 2006. Making corporate social responsibility (CSR) operable: How companies translate stakeholder dialogue into practice. *Business and Society Review*, 111(2), pp. 137–163.

Pedersen, E.R.G. (Ed.) 2015. *Corporate Social Responsibility*. London: Sage.

Porter, M.E. and Kramer, M.R., 2006. The link between competitive advantage and corporate social responsibility. *Harvard Business Review*, 84(12), pp. 78–92.

Porter, M.E. and Kramer, M., 2011. Creating shared value. *Harvard Business Review*, 89(1/2), pp. 62–77.

Rasche, A., 2010. The limits of corporate responsibility standards. *Business Ethics: A European Review*, 19(3), pp. 280–291.

Smith, A.D., 2008. Corporate social responsibility practices in the pharmaceutical industry. *Business Strategy Series*, 9(6), pp. 306–315.

UNGC, 2015. Supply chain sustainability – a practical guide for continuous improvement, accessed January 7, 2020 at https://www.unglobalcompact.org/library/205.

United Nations Climate Change, 2019. Process and meetings – Paris agreement. accessed March 15, 2019 at https://unfccc.int/process/conferences/pastconferences/paris-climate-change-conference-november-2015/paris-agreement.

Van Marrewijk, M., 2003. Concepts and definitions of CSR and corporate sustainability: Between agency and communion. *Journal of Business Ethics*, 44(2–3), pp. 95–105.

Waddock, S., 2008. Building a new institutional infrastructure for corporate responsibility. *Academy of Management Perspectives*, 22(3), pp. 87–108.

Witjes, S. and Lozano, R., 2016. Towards a more circular economy: proposing a framework linking sustainable public procurement and sustainable business models. *Resources, Conservation and Recycling*, 112, pp. 37–44.

World Commission on Environment and Development, 1987. *Our Common Future*. Oxford and New York: WCED.

PART II

Methods for teaching strategic management

4. Service learning in strategic management: opportunities, challenges, and examples

Candace M. TenBrink and Krysti Turnquest

4.1 INTRODUCTION

Teaching strategy is rewarding, yet challenging. The enjoyment for many faculty lies within the flexibility and applicability of the material. As for challenging, given that strategic management tends to be commonly deliberated, executed, and assessed at the executive level, it is fairly difficult for many students to grasp. Master's level students commonly state that they "know" strategy and yet they frequently lack the skillset required for strategic analyses and decisions. Dissimilarly, undergraduate students frequently appear overwhelmed with the concepts. They tend to have no experiential bank from which to draw and have had little exposure to strategy. In this chapter we explore how strategic management may be taught with the adoption of an experiential pedagogy – service learning – that offers both levels of students an opportunity to engage with the material.

Experiential learning, of which service learning is a part, has been found in the university setting for decades. It is commonly housed in or endorsed by academic learning centers where it can be centrally promoted across colleges and departments. Intuitively, the idea of experiencing education sounds logical when we think of the more physically oriented courses such as chemistry, art, and medical sciences. Imagine teaching piano without striking the keys or engaging in medical courses without the lab work and one may understand the need to engage in a more physical model of learning. What may be surprising to some, is that even in the social sciences, research indicates experiential pedagogies are more engaging than a text and lecture model (Piercy and Caldwell, 2011). Research reveals that engagement with course concepts has been associated with the foundation of education – greater learning (Kolb, 1984; Michel, 2009). The box highlights many forms of experiential learning. While we discuss service learning in this chapter, there are many other methods for faculty to fortify student engagement and education via non-traditional pedagogies.

Experiential Learning Examples

Clinical work and fellowships*

Fundraisers and awareness campaigns*

Internships, apprenticeships, co-ops and volunteering*

Practicum

Research and field work*

Service learning

Simulations and cases*

Study abroad*

*Easily converted into service learning

Experiential learning in the business school may take on a host of forms. It may involve internships, co-ops, or vocational training. It may also include work within student clubs such as an accounting club that assists low-income community members with their tax returns. Another example is found within study abroad programs that incorporate course work into the trip.

Regrettably, experiential options are infrequently available in the realm of strategy due to its complex processes and amorphous outcomes. Experiencing strategy, similar to experiencing many challenging feats such as ballet dancing and creating financial statements, takes time and is learned with practice. One method to experience strategy is to offer service-based learning. Service learning may cost nothing to deploy and may be deployed in private or public institutions in big or small cities with deep or sparse financial resources across a variety of modalities and class sizes.

4.2   SERVICE LEARNING BACKGROUND

With roots in experiential learning, some say that service learning has been around as long as people have been helping others. Yet, many credit John Dewey (1933) with the foundational concept when he encouraged a linkage between education, experience, democracy, and social change in the middle of the last century. If asked to define the term, you are likely to receive as many unique replies as people that you query. The National Service-Learning Clearinghouse, the largest online library for service learning related resources in the United States, provides a civic-minded definition. They argue that service learning is "a teaching and learning strategy integrating meaningful community service with instruction and reflection to enrich the learning experience, teach civic responsibility, and strengthen communities" (n.d.). Service learning scholar, Andrew Furco (1996), suggests that service learning is about the combination of community benefit and student learning through critical reflection.

In terms of this chapter, we define service learning as a teaching and learning method that applies knowledge from the course to benefit a third party. Thus, service learning is useful; it is not an exercise without beneficiaries. It is also a method to teach, therefore it must bridge course topics with the activity. Finally, we submit that service learning requires a contribution to an external entity. That is, it offers needed output. Without this third party product, the student activity may be seen as inconsequential or typical classwork. We purposefully chose to not include a boundary condition of community or civic benefit as (a) the designation of a community is ambiguous, (b) helping organizations grow, succeed, and navigate issues is a benefit to many stakeholders, and (c) many business schools incorporate ethics into their program, rather than civics, which has a tighter connection with business.

Where is the service learning? For the newcomer the nomenclature may be confusing. The words *"service learning"* may refer to a pedagogy, to a project, and to assignments. A service learning course is one that integrates a service learning project into the course. Ideally, at least some of the learning objectives are incorporated into the project. For instance, a strategy class may learn about food science while participating in a project that examines the scope and scale of a baby food manufacturing start-up. The knowledge that service learning leverages is that of the course; in this example it is the strategic decisions involved with scale and scope. If the students learn about food science, that is fine, nevertheless the food science knowledge is secondary. As for a "service learning project," it is the central component of the course. Likewise, service learning assignments are those that are tied to the service learning project.

Service learning often fits into the university landscape by fulfilling a broader mission of knowledge exchange. While teaching has always been a key focus of education, universities are beginning to incorporate an objective of knowledge and skill sharing with their communities (Langworthy, 2007; Shore and McLauchlan, 2012; Zomer and Benneworth, 2011). In Europe and spreading quickly, this expanded mission is often referred to as the "Third Mission" or "knowledge exchange" (Zomer and Benneworth, 2011; Shore and McLauchlan, 2012). The United States has a long-standing history with prioritizing, at least in theory, democratic or civic learning to promote democratic ideals (see: 1993 Defense Authorization Act; Edward M. Kennedy Serve America Act of 2009; National and Community Service Act of 1990; The National and Community Service Trust Act of 1993; USA Freedom Corps of 2002; National Task Force on Civic Learning and Democratic Engagement, 2012). At the core of each of these philosophies is the central idea that higher education is not meant to operate in a vacuum. As universities search for opportunities to engage with communities, service learning offers a viable opportunity for cost-effective implementation.

An interesting note about the vague nature of terms like "Third Mission" or "civic learning" is that the implied communities with which universities are meant to engage is up for interpretation (Pinheiro et al., 2015). This latency leaves the door open for practitioners to develop their own constructs for community engagement. In the case of service learning, community can often be defined geographically, or by some other commonality such as a business community.

One unique aspect of service learning in upper education is that it is open to all. Community colleges may participate at the same level as research-focused institutions; there is no need for deep financial resources or extensive research capabilities to be successful with this teaching style. Similarly, these experiences may be undertaken by all student levels.

Service learning projects vary widely. They may include endeavors with for-profit or non-profit organizations, with government bodies or privately owned entities, with religious or secular institutions, with small, local businesses or global conglomerates. The caveat is that the project and timeline mesh with your students' capabilities and your learning objectives.

In spite of the multitude of service learning definitions, research indicates service learning is beneficial to the students. A recent meta-analysis (Celio et al., 2011) compared empirical studies of hundreds of service learning programs to determine if courses with a strong grounding in the core principles of service learning (tied to academic content, incorporation of student perspective, leveraging the serviced communities as partners, and intentional student reflection) showed stronger linkages to positive student outcomes. This study found that student outcomes in the areas of self-attitude, attitude toward learning, civic engagement, social skills, and academic achievement were all significantly, positively impacted by the incorporation of these service learning principles (Celio et al., 2011). Furthermore, the National Association of Colleges and Employers found that experiential educational activities, such as service learning, helped to increase students' employability post-graduation (2008).

4.3   OPPORTUNITIES FOR SERVICE LEARNING IN BUSINESS SCHOOLS

Prospects for positive change with the adoption of service learning abound. These benefits incorporate deepening the impact of learning, expanding career opportunities, and cultivating the ability to creatively think. Business schools have incorporated service learning opportunities, although they have not been widely embraced. For example, service learning has been applied to study abroad projects (Sachau et al., 2010), human resources projects (Madsen and Turnbull, 2006), and social entrepreneurship (Litzky et al., 2010) to list a few. Some colleges, such as Bentley University and the Ross School of Business at the University of Michigan (Salimbene et al., 2005) have taken steps to institutionalize service learning into their curricula. However, these examples are in the minority.

First, regardless of one's view about the role of business schools – to educate or to prepare for a career – business schools may offer greater learning with the adoption of more experientially-based pedagogy choices. When the majority of business school courses are taught with a traditional method, combining reading and lectures, this leaves the students with two gaps. One gap presents itself in the surface-level understanding of the material, a product of the traditional or "hands off" pedagogy that dominates the classroom (Godfrey et al., 2005). This traditional and functionally oriented pedagogy often leaves business school alumnae unable to distinguish themselves upon entering the workforce. An empirical study by Casile et al. (2011) showed that service learning helped students obtain a better grasp of content knowledge in an undergraduate management course than their peers assigned to a research paper. Interestingly, they also noted that the results were more favorable for female students than for male.

A second gap is that students are often not only unprepared to solve complicated, real-world problems that deviate from coursework (Godfrey et al., 2005; Papamarcos, 2005) but also, they have not had a tangible experience with the tools that professionals in their field use. Service learning is a viable method for fulfilling the need to solidify content knowledge, to produce more employable graduates, and on a broader scale, to increase the democratic capacity of students (Abdullah and O'Steen, 2018; Astin and Sax, 1998; Friedman, 1996).

In addition, research indicates that students involved in service learning may improve their critical thinking capability or their degree of care and understanding. These are both critical in business. Evidence shows that students' critical thinking processes may improve when there is a self-reflection and analysis aspect of the service learning project (Giles and Eyler, 1998; Palmer and Short, 2010; Sedlak et al., 2003). However, some suggest that deep, substantial change is rare in the average undergraduate student or in an educational setting (Chen et al., 2018). Instead, they argue that the more common and more relevant type of outcome is a "schema transformation," characterized by students' newfound ability to understand issues and place them within real-world contexts (Chen et al., 2018). Schema transformation also emphasizes caring about issues versus rote understanding.

Finally, we suggest that business schools are not just tools to promote winners in the global landscape of competition. Business schools may serve as an incubator to introduce students to caring about change, a concept that many stakeholders find appealing (Sobczak et al., 2006). A study for the United Nations found that young professionals "appear unconvinced over the materiality of most environmental, social, and governance issues to business; unable to consider them because of inadequate information, training, or tools; and unwilling to depart from business as usual because of conflicts with remuneration, career advancement, or culture" (World Business Council for Sustainable Development Young Managers Team and United Nations Environment Programme Finance Initiative, 2005, p. 1).

4.4 CHALLENGES FOR SERVICE LEARNING IN BUSINESS EDUCATION

Service learning can be incredibly complex and time consuming, at least initially. In fact, a leading deterrent for deploying service learning in a course is the time and logistical effort required to successfully construct, manage, and complete a project (Abes et al., 2002). Another deterrent for faculty engaged in service learning is the reluctance of some institutions to include it in rank and tenure decisions (Morton and Troppe, 1996). In many instances there is a greater emphasis on publication quality and quantity than on collaboration or community engaged scholarship.

Students also face impediments to engaging in service learning opportunities. One formidable consideration is their motivation to participate in service learning. Chapdelaine et al., (2005) point out that for adult learners, the time spent completing the "service" part of a service learning course may place an undue burden on their already long priority list as they often have outside commitments to which they are beholden. This could be an exceedingly limiting factor for faculty and students at institutions with a large population of commuter or graduate students. Despite this potential obstacle, Phillips (2013) found that adult students were interested in pursuing service learning opportunities through their degree programs despite the inherent outside-of-class time commitment. In addition to time constraints, Hagan (2012) points out that the varied backgrounds of students, particularly at the MBA level, increase the probability that many are also distance learners. Hagan acknowledges that the popularity in online education is growing but that it also presents challenges for faculty to provide experiential learning opportunities for remote students (2012).

This leaves a question about the depth of service learning in strategy. While we were unable to find many scholarly articles that emphasized the implementation of service learning within strategic management (Angelidis et al., 2004; Graham, 1996; Robinson et al., 2010) that does not mean it is not occurring. Via our social network we know that universities across the world are engaging in service learning within the strategy realm. Perhaps the lack of articles says more about balancing research choices than it does about the popularity of this domain.

4.5 INTEGRATING SERVICE LEARNING WITH STRATEGIC MANAGEMENT

Service learning offers a method to associate the ephemeral nature of strategy with a grounded, real-life experience. As discussed, undergraduates rarely have non-academic exposure to the material covered in strategic management courses, let alone direct contact with the field. Service learning bridges the gap, enabling students to learn by doing. In terms of higher education, it provides an occasion to understand how aspects of the strategic process or strategy tools are selected, deployed, and measured. Graduate students often find their view of strategy expanding as they progress through the project. However, unlike their junior peers, they often leverage their previous work experiences (Levoke et al., 2014).

While service learning offers the benefits of helping others, it also promotes thinking about learning. Faculty that have been active in the experiential learning environment are familiar with the reflection stage, a staple of this pedagogy. This learning and thinking process may also serve to promote critical thinking, design thinking, and other aspects of how one grapples with learning (Palmer and Short, 2010; Sedlak et al., 2003; Vogelgesang and Astin, 2000).

With service learning there is the opportunity for students to create value that may change the direction for an organization. In low-risk scenarios, like academic service learning, it is critical that the students have the opportunity to manipulate pieces of the strategy toolkit, process, or analysis. Having access to faculty with frequent check-ins offers an added degree of assistance while mitigating the wrong application of strategy tools. The students need an arena that is safe from judgment and suitable for thought experimentation.

Student benefits. Students may reap benefits aside from the more obvious ties to knowledge creation and helping others. They have an opportunity to experience business challenges that matter to a third party. When the organizations offer positive feedback to the students during or post the project, the students are often pleasantly surprised that their input was helpful.

Students are able to explore and display creativity in business. While creativity is frequently associated with the arts, it is a facet of many other aspects of business. Creativity appears in innovation and entrepreneurship, but it also is needed in solving firm, product, and project hurdles. With a service learning project, students have the ability to not only grapple with developing solutions for real entities, but also to experience the integration of strategy content in the context of the ambiguity of the current business environment.

We note that students have an opportunity to leverage this experience in several ways. Most commonly we find that students weave the service learning experience into their resume or into interview discussions. Savvy students with an aim to build relationships also have an excellent opportunity to use their service learning experiences to stay in touch with the hosting firm. This relationship may provide several benefits such as internships, job possibilities, and long-term network strengthening.

4.6   FACULTY CONSIDERATIONS

Your teaching modality may impact your service learning project and your learning curve. The majority of the faculty with whom we have spoken began with some degree of face-to-face teaching. There are three primary considerations related to modality. First, consider in which area you have the most experience or comfort. Launching a service learning project is time intensive and takes much preparation and guidance as the term progresses. Adding the stress of teaching in a new modality, or in an unfavored one, may not be the best choice for the uninitiated faculty. Second, an online modality may prevent some group camaraderie that tends to emanate from class discussions. A face-to-face component also serves as a source of real-time feedback from student to faculty and vice versa. Third, if the service learning project is complex or takes an unexpected turn, be prepared to take the time to address it. Speaking from experience, this appears to be quite effective and efficient when students are near each other.

Universities may also differ in how they support service learning. Some may offer a faculty stipend, workshops, or access to other funds, to name a few benefits. Many universities offer specialized training in service learning. You may be able to find support from others. Keep in mind this support may come from outside the business school. Thus, tip sharing will likely be more generalized to common issues.

The benefits to engaging in service learning opportunities may be intrinsic for faculty. On the other hand, in schools that place more significance on research or in universities that require a high level of service, service learning may not yield an extrinsic benefit to the faculty member.

The faculty must be comfortable and adept at managing client relationships. The client may struggle with how much information to share, with trust, and with time management. Deciding how much data to share and what is sensitive is often a struggle for organizations. A non-disclosure agreement may suffice for a small group of students but often is unwieldy for larger groups. Clients also need to build trust with the faculty. It takes time and a track record to convey how the service learning process will work between the faculty, the client, and the students. A big challenge for the faculty and the client will be controlling the information flow. The amount of time the client has to spend on the project will vary considerably.

Faculty may want to think about a few factors as they contemplate engaging with service learning:

- Service learning has a steep learning curve for the faculty. It is time consuming to learn the process let alone to design a course that integrates best practices. Faculty will want to consider how this pedagogy fits in with their other time commitments.
- Service learning doesn't have to be mutually exclusive from your other academic responsibilities. Some of the most successful faculty find ways to tie service learning projects, particularly multi-term projects, into their research.
- Students may be confused as to why they are helping others; some may even question why there is no remuneration. Be prepared to share your philosophy of why your class will incorporate service learning.
- Pre-plan what you will do if a student has an issue with your external partner. You may want to consider back-up options for the project. For example, some students may have religious objections to your external partner's general mission, or some may face logistical barriers to meeting with the client or in completing project-related activities.
- When dealing with external entities there is always a risk that your project may not proceed as planned. You may encounter transportation issues, student issues, and random problems with the client. If the faculty is in a school or department that penalizes mistakes, service learning may be a difficult pedagogy to adopt.

- Consider your aptitude for handling the unknown. There are a myriad of factors and variables that may impact the success and efficiency of the project. Faculty may want to consider how their tolerance for ambiguity may impact the project.
- If the faculty member receives funding or support for a service learning initiative there may be "strings attached," such as pedagogy papers or conference presentations.

4.7 MAJOR STEPS IN LAUNCHING A SERVICE LEARNING COURSE

These steps may occur in a variety of paths, with some steps happening simultaneously and some being fine-tuned as you learn.

Determine what assistance your university or college may offer and what you are required to do. Some universities will designate courses as service learning. Make sure you understand the responsibilities that you and your students will have if you begin your foray with an official designation. It may be tempting to run your service learning course outside of the university's formal program, but consider the value-add students may experience by receiving official university recognition for their participation in the course.

Find a partner. Similar to an entrepreneur planning a start-up, in our experience, the development of a service learning course may easily begin with the identification of an unmet need in a community. For example, Jones et al. (2018) suggested that the growth of financial literacy service learning courses in business schools was spurred on by the lack of basic personal finance understanding made apparent by the 2008 US financial crisis.

Plan your project. Determine what you want the students to learn, what the outcomes might be, and how you will successfully manage the project.

Revise and review your plans/output with your client. This may take several iterations. Make sure that you tie some course modules to the project. We suggest that you choose an important concept or tool that would benefit from the experiential component. Discuss how and when the students will interact with the client. Also identify sensitive data and information that may or may not be shared.

Research any help that you may need. Reach out to those that have launched service learning at your school, or beyond. What works well for one faculty member may not work well for another, given different resources or personalities.

Ask students to reflect on the service learning process. Research indicates that a reflective assignment or task is essential to learning. This will also help you gauge the depth of your students' learning and to make future adjustments.

Keep in touch with the client about expectations. In our experience there are always modifications. As in the world of business, there will be unforeseen obstacles that must be addressed. Communicate with the client and your students throughout the project to alleviate negative surprises.

4.8 SERVICE LEARNING EXAMPLES

This section offers a variety of ideas and options for easing into service learning:

- Begin with finding a project. Contact a local organization and ask if they need help with a strategy issue. Also, find out how much they want to be involved and if they want to attend a final unveiling.
- Once you have a project in mind, ascertain that you can map some of your learning objectives to the project. If your project expands beyond your course objectives, that is fine.
- In our experience, the client tells us what their problem is, or in the words of consultants, they communicate what their challenge is and we provide solutions. While the client has a need, they are typically unfamiliar with some strategy concepts. We offer several options in everyday language and listen for their interest. You may assign more than the client requests.
- As you progress with your projects you may want to consider the output that is best for your client. It may be a report, a white paper, a presentation, or a slide deck, to name a few options.
- We frequently ask the students to turn in each component of the project. We offer feedback to help the students pinpoint areas of misunderstanding, to resolve issues with depth or strategy techniques, and to strengthen quantitative or qualitative support.

4.8.1 Example 1 – Accelerator Sponsorship

No experience needed; no funding required; travel optional.
Class format: hybrid, MBA; face-to-face, BBA.
Level: any, ideal for a capstone project.
Output: Slide decks and presentations (per group).
Groups: I used small groups.

I am involved with many local start-ups and have used that access to tap into strategy-based consulting work for my students. In reality, there is much need for strategy help, especially in small and not-for-profit firms. One of my first projects involved producing a plan that could be used by one of the world's largest accelerators to increase sponsorship for their largest fundraiser. While this may not be relevant to some strategy classes, I incorporated strategy tools and processes into the project scope. I selected the strategy concepts that I believed would help guide the project.

Project requirements:
1. PESTEL analysis.
2. Five forces analysis.
3. Industry drivers that impact the health of the firm and fundraiser.
4. Local competitive analysis.
5. A plan to increase sponsorship (based on the research and analysis compiled in steps #1-4).

The students worked in conjunction with the accelerator and within their groups to devise what they thought would be a good plan as supported by data and the first four requirements.

Pros: This type of project lends itself to a variety of functional backgrounds as it included not only strategy, but also marketing concepts. In hindsight, the students appeared motivated to help the non-profit. However, I think the students' interest may have been driven by creative freedom and their interest in social media rather than by the accelerator's mission, job hunting prospects, or even the opportunity for networking.

In this project there was no need to work face-to-face with the firm. For non-traditional students this proved to be a benefit. The firm offered feedback to the students that was positive and appreciated; the output was useful to the organization. Both MBA and BBA classes did well; there was no major difference in output creativity. Although, the MBAs generally offered more depth.

Cons: For students wanting more client contact, they had to take the initiative to make it happen. Also, this project incorporated a marketing plan, a topic that is not covered in our strategic management course. For faculty that are uncomfortable with output that is not directly tied to their experience or course, they will need to be careful to limit the scope of the project and to be mindful of requisite skills and knowledge.

4.8.2 Example 2 – MenuGenie Market Launch

No experience needed; no funding required; travel optional.
Class format: hybrid (could also easily be face-to-face).
Level: MBA. This could be done with BBAs if they are able to embrace the breadth and depth of the project.
Output: Paper, slide deck, and presentation.
Groups: I used small groups.

This project involved a for-profit start-up that I will call MenuGenie. This firm asked for a market entry plan. Recall, it is important to set expectations up front. My discussion with the firm evolved from a laundry list of what they would like to what I felt my students realistically could deliver. MenuGenie's business purpose was to create meal plans for those needing special diets as dictated by the individual's medical profile.

Project requirements:
1. Complete a PESTEL (in this example I asked for a table format to reduce page count).
2. Industry analysis:
    a. What industry is this? With whom are they competing?
    b. Complete a five forces analysis.
    c. Identify the competitive group(s) in which the firm will operate/ compete.
    d. Complete a SWOT.
3. Market entry strategy:
    a. How do you advise them to enter the market? Why?
    b. Where should they enter?
    c. How do you advise them to deploy and leverage social media? Which types are best?
    d. How would you implement and evolve the product after market entry?
    Student note: you may introduce several options. For example, you may have two or three choices for market entry. Additionally, you may support your case while showing that other options are less favorable. Support your ideas with data.
4. Pricing strategy:
    a. Do you advise changes to their current pricing model? For example, would you suggest an alternative such as subscription-based pricing? Why?
    b. Are there any complimentary services they should provide? Discuss how these services may impact the model.

Note that the focus is on applying tools from the course: external analyses, competitive strategy, and business pricing strategy. I did not attach all the learning modules of the course. Choose what fits with your course schedule and see if it will work in the time you have allotted for the project. For example, I cover international strategy at the end of the course. Therefore, I would not consider an international project without modifying my course schedule.

Pros: This was a complex project for MBAs. I would not use it for BBAs at my university as they would find #3 and #4 cumbersome within the time allotted for the course. The MBAs found several issues with the start-up's model that needed to be addressed.

Cons: This project benefitted a for-profit firm. I have no problems with this as my definition of service learning is to assist others rather than focus solely on not-for-profit community service. My concern is that the students learn strategy while providing a service to others; this raises the stakes for the students and indicates how real firms need and use strategy. You may feel differently about the entity that receives the benefit.

4.8.3 Example 3 – Mapping Course Content with a Local Organization that Needs Strategy Assistance with a Tangible Payoff

Requirements: an organization that needs strategy help. Prize or award for the best output.
Experience: varies, more service learning experience is desirable; funding may be required; travel optional; award or tangible prize optional but preferred.
Class format: any depending on your experience level and client needs.
Level: any, ideal for a capstone project.
Groups: I prefer small groups to enhance idea generation and knowledge sharing.

Your project may involve endeavors such as a product launch, a move to a new city, or a decision to expand. Use your imagination and network to create a project. The major difference between this case and the others in this chapter is the payoff for the students. The payoff could be a grant, a job or internship, or a certain grade, to name a few ideas. The payoff could also include an intangible award such as recognition by the client or the business school.

4.9 FACULTY POINTS TO PONDER PRIOR TO IMPLEMENTING SERVICE LEARNING

1. What challenges may you encounter in large or small classes?
2. What challenges may you encounter when teaching in an online format?
3. What challenges may be presented in hybrid classes?
4. What might the challenges be in an elite institution, in a community college, or in a rural setting?
5. How does service learning align with your institution's mission?
6. How will you manage the process?
7. How will you create the groups and what size will optimize the trade-off between learning and relationship management?
8. Are there other faculty at your institution with whom you can collaborate to share the workload?
9. What is your back-up if a student elects to not participate (dissent)?
10. How might you handle a major disruption in the project? For example, what will you do if your sponsor backs out at the last minute or there is a natural disaster (both have happened to us)?
11. How will you acclimate to service learning?
12. Is this a good fit for your personality and work–life balance?
13. How will you approach service learning in a resource rich or constrained environment?
14. How will you manage risk-taking when administration is not in favor of new pedagogy styles?

4.10 STUDENT REFLECTION QUESTIONS

1. How might your view of the organization's mission and vision alter your interest in this project? For example, would you feel more compelled to help a non-profit?
2. Reflect back to a time when you learned a new concept and then tried to engage in it. This could be a new swim stroke, language, math concepts etc. What were the challenges that you encountered when you actually did (experienced) it? Compare and contrast that with your experience in this course.
3. Compare your pre-project expectations with your post-project thoughts. How do they differ?
4. Considering your service learning project, how did the project outcome impact (or not impact) the organization?

5.   What surprised you (or was unexpected) about the project and why do you feel surprised?
6.   What role or expertise did the client contribute to your project (if any)?
7.   Compose a paragraph about how the collaborative experience impacted the project. Was it difficult to work with others outside of the university? Did you learn from them?
8.   Reflecting on your service learning project, what role do you think strategy has in improving society at-large?
9.   What would you change if you were to join another service learning project in the future? Why?
10.   Appraise your efforts and reflect on your weaknesses and strengths.
11.   Many academics believe that service leaning should be attached to democratic growth. Do you agree or disagree? Defend your position.

REFERENCES

Abdullah, M.S. and B. O'Steen (2018), 'Volunteering engagement through service-learning community-based youth critical participatory action research: Evidenced in reflection writing,' *Journal of Applied and Fundamental Sciences*, **10** (4S), 1541–1563.

Abes, E.S., G. Jackson and S.R. Jones (2002), 'Factors that motivate and deter faculty use of service-learning,' *Michigan Journal of Community Service Learning*, **9** (1), 5–17.

Angelidis, A., I. Tomic and N.A. Ibrahim (2004), 'Service learning projects enhance student learning in strategic management courses,' *Review of Business*, **25** (2), 32–36.

Astin, A.W. and L.J. Sax (1998), 'How undergraduates are affected by service participation,' *Journal of College Student Development*, **39** (3), 251–263.

Casile, M., K.F. Hoover and D.A. O'Neil (2011), 'Both-and, not either-or: knowledge and service-learning,' *Education+ Training*, **53** (2/3), 129–139.

Celio, C.I., J. Durlak and A. Dymnicki (2011), 'A meta-analysis of the impact of service-learning on students,' *Journal of Experiential Education*, **34** (2), 164–181.

Chapdelaine, A., A. Ruiz, J. Warchal and C. Wells (2005), *Service-learning Code of Ethics*. Bolton, MA: Anker Publishing.

Chen, T., R.S. Snell and C.X. Wu (2018), 'Comparing the effects of service-learning versus nonservice-learning project experiences on service leadership emergence and meaning schema transformation,' *Academy of Management Learning & Education*, **17** (4), 474–495.

Dewey, J. (1933), *How We Think: A Restatement of the Relation of Reflective Thinking to the Educative Process*. Boston, MA: Heath & Co Publishers.

Friedman, S.D. (1996), 'Community involvement projects in Wharton's MBA curriculum,' *Journal of Business Ethics*, **15**, 95–101.

Furco, A. (1996), 'Service-learning: A balanced approach to experiential education,' in B. Taylor (Ed.), *Expanding Boundaries: Service and Learning*, 2–6. Washington, DC: Corporation for National Service.

Giles, D.E. and J. Eyler (1998), 'A service learning research agenda for the next five years,' *New Directions for Teaching and Learning*, **73**, 65–72.

Godfrey, P.C., L.M. Illes and G.R. Berry (2005), 'Creating breadth in business education through service-learning,' *Academy of Management Learning & Education*, **4** (3), 309–323.

Graham, J. (1996), 'Business plan proposals for inner-city neighborhoods: A strategic management assignment for MBA students at Loyola University Chicago,' *Journal of Business Ethics*, **15** (1), 87–94.

Hagan, L.M. (2012), 'Fostering experiential learning and service through client projects in graduate business courses offered online,' *American Journal of Business Education*, **5** (5), 623–632.

Jones, R., J. Petrie and A. Murrell (2018), 'Measuring impact while making a difference: A financial literacy service-learning project as participatory action research,' *Journal of Service-Learning in Higher Education*, **8**.

Kolb, D.A. (1984), *Experiential Learning: Experience as the Source of Learning and Development*, Vol. 1. Englewood Cliffs: Prentice Hall.

Langworthy, A. (2007), 'Education for the public good: Is service learning possible in the Australian context?' Paper presented at the Australian Universities Community Engagement Alliance, 70.

Levoke, C.Z., S. Brail and A. Daniere (2014), 'Engaged pedagogy and transformative learning in graduate education: A service-learning case study,' *Canadian Journal of Higher Education*, **44** (3), 68–85.

Litzky, B.E., V.M. Godshalk and C. Walton-Bongers (2010), 'Social entrepreneurship and community leadership: A service-learning model for management education,' *Journal of Management Education*, **34** (1), 142–162.

Madsen, S.R. and O. Turnbull (2006), 'Academic service learning experiences of compensation and benefit course students,' *Journal of Management Education*, **30** (5), 724–742.

Michel, N. (2009), 'Active versus passive teaching styles: An empirical study of student learning outcomes,' *Human Resource Development Quarterly*, **20** (4), 397–418.

Morton, K. and M. Troppe (1996), 'From margin to the mainstream: Campus Compact's project on integrating service with academic study,' *Journal of Business Ethics*, **15**, 21–32.

National Association of Colleges and Employers (2008), *Experiential Education Survey*. Bethlehem, PA: National Association of Colleges and Employers.

National Service Learning Clearinghouse (n.d.), *What is Service Learning?* http://www.servicelearning.org/what-service-learning (accessed February 20, 2019).

The National Task Force on Civic Learning and Democratic Engagement (2012), *A Crucible Moment: College Learning and Democracy's Future*. Washington, DC: Association of American Colleges and Universities.

Palmer, T.B. and J.C. Short (2010), 'Getting engaged: Factors enhancing perceived student benefits from service-learning in business education,' *Journal on Excellence in College Teaching*, **21** (2), 5–28.

Papamarcos, S.D. (2005), 'Giving traction to management theory: Today's service-learning,' *Academy of Management Learning & Education*, **4** (3), 325–335.

Phillips, L.A. (2013), 'Working adult undergraduate students' interest and motivation in service learning and volunteering,' *Journal of Continuing Higher Education*, **61** (2), 68–73.

Piercy, N. and N. Caldwell (2011), 'Experiential learning in the international classroom: Supporting learning effectiveness and integration,' *International Journal of Management Education*, **9** (2), 25–26.

Pinheiro, R., P.V. Langa and A. Pausits (2015), 'One and two equals three? The third mission of higher education institutions,' *European Journal of Higher Education*, **5** (3), 233–249.

Robinson, D.F., A.L. Sherwood and C.A. DePaolo (2010), 'Service-learning by doing: How a student-run consulting company finds relevance and purpose in a business strategy capstone course,' *Journal of Management Education*, **34** (1), 88–112.

Sachau, D., N. Brasher and S. Fee (2010), 'Three models for short-term study abroad,' *Journal of Management Education*, **34** (5), 645–670.

Salimbene, F.P., A.F. Buono, V.V. Lafarge and A.J. Nurick (2005), 'Service-learning and management education: The Bentley experience,' *Academy of Management Learning & Education*, **4** (3), 336–344.

Sedlak, C.A., M.O. Doheny, N. Panthofer and E. Anaya (2003), 'Critical thinking in students' service-learning experiences,' *College Teaching*, **51** (3), 99–104.

Shore, C. and L. McLauchlan (2012), '"Third mission" activities, commercialisation and academic entrepreneurs', *Social Anthropology*, **20** (3), 267–286.

Sobczak, A., G. Debucquet and C. Havard (2006), 'The impact of higher education on students' and young managers' perception of companies and CSR: An exploratory analysis,' *Corporate Governance: The International Journal of Business in Society*, **6** (4), 463–474.

Vogelgesang, L.J. and A.W. Astin (2000), 'Comparing the effects of service-learning and community service,' *Michigan Journal of Community Service Learning*, **7**, 25–34.

World Business Council for Sustainable Development Young Managers Team and United Nations Environment Programme Finance Initiative (2005), *Generation Lost: Young Financial Analysts and Environmental, Social and Governance Issues* (Executive Summary). WBCSD, Geneva.

Zomer, A. and P. Benneworth (2011), 'The rise of the university's third mission,' in J. Enders, H.F. de Boer and D.F. Westerjeijden (Eds.), *Reform of Higher Education in Europe*, 81–101. Leiden, the Netherlands: Brill Sense.

5. Experiential approach to strategy formulation

Richard R. Smith and Patrick Tan

INTRODUCTION

While strategy formulation is a topic of active research by strategy scholars, the methods for teaching strategy formulation are often left to conceptual frameworks and generic toolsets in the business school classroom. Many instructors use case-based approaches to apply constructs to analyze the strategic decisions and positions of firms in relation to others in strategic groups.

In fact, strategy scholars continue to question the very purpose of the core strategic management course and the best way to teach it. Many faculty members, because of their prior training, tend to lean toward either economics or organization theory in the treatment of course content (Greiner et al., 2003). While theoretical training is important and necessary, we remain concerned with the lack of integration across disciplines and the neglect of practical training in the teaching of strategic management. Rumelt states that "Strategy is about action" (2011, p. 87). Teaching strategy formulation involves the teaching of the nature and attributes of strategic formulation and decisions, and how to put those decisions into action. Experiential fieldwork learning experience has been recommended by many scholars as a useful approach to teach strategy (Kolb, 1984; Thompson and Koys, 2010; Klimoski and Amos, 2012; Association of American Colleges and Universities, 2013).

To address the learning associated with strategy formulation, we developed Master's- and undergraduate-level business practicum courses to allow students to learn through practical application. In this chapter, we will share the background associated with teaching strategy and experiential approaches, provide an overview of the concepts used to make teaching in an experiential format most effective, share a proven process for teaching in this method, and discuss several areas of consideration.

The specific goal of this chapter is to share our experiences, challenges and insights as we experimented with and taught these business practicum courses, in the hope that readers interested in teaching strategy formulation using the experiential approach may benefit from our learning.

BACKGROUND

As strategy scholars, we explore the underpinnings of firm growth through our research on innovation, resource attainment, alliances, and other growth models. We often teach the strategy formulation process as a set of interconnected analyses that provide considerations for decision-making at the top management team level. Yet, the teaching related to this process of finding growth opportunities is often unclear. While we frequently use cases to illustrate innovation through technology innovation, considering the actual management decision-making and influences is usually not within the scope of our lessons.

In their recent review of the strategy formulation process in entrepreneurial settings, Ott et al. (2017) highlighted the limited empirical research that brings the value of learning from experience together with an understanding of the overall process. One of the primary challenges of considering strategy formulation is the dynamic nature of a firm and the high-velocity environment of many industries (Eisenhardt, 1989). Therefore, executives are often in the position of learning by doing, experimentation, or other approaches that involve a high level of experience (Bingham and Davis, 2012).

While learning by doing provides one avenue for considering strategy formulation, others have suggested creating a more holistic understanding or cognitive approach (Kiss and Barr, 2014). Mental models or maps can help build an understanding of key variables that must be considered in strategy formulation (Gary and Wood, 2011). In Kolb's experiential learning cycle, concrete experience forms the first step, leading to observation and reflection, forming abstract concepts, and testing them in new situations (1984). The cycle combines experience, perception, cognition, and behavior. These and other strategizing by thinking approaches suggest that executives use various forms of vision, analogies, or blueprints for strategy formulation based on their experience. While these ideas have been predominant in research, these concepts have not yet enabled the process of teaching strategy formulation.

Other areas of research focus on the political nature of strategy formulation (Dess, 1987). While decision-making by a single executive may be somewhat straightforward, several levels of complexity are added due to the multiple stakeholders in top management, company stakeholders, and board members. This is complicated further when considering the nature of country-based interests and other potential constituencies (Hillman and Hitt, 1999). While team dynamics and stakeholder management are generally part of the curriculum for business students, the strategy formulation education tends to focus more on analysis techniques rather than achieving buy-in from others.

The streams of research in strategy formulation highlight several challenges when it comes to teaching strategy formulation. A common challenge in business school education is creating an application-oriented learning environment related to strategy. While the case-based learning approach can provide valuable lessons, the view of the student remains as a third-party perspective. When considering how we might bring the learning related to strategy formulation and an entrepreneurial orientation to the Master's level curriculum, some schools have started to introduce "Practicum" or "Consulting" courses in programs as an experiential approach.

Experiential courses allow students to basically work with a live company as consultants to develop a new idea for business growth. This application-based approach helps bring together the experience of applying knowledge, taking a learning approach, and experiencing potential political dynamics. It is similar to many entrepreneurial application courses, but with an existing business where the students must choose where they would make strategic investments for the future and then develop a business plan. We therefore find good evidence to support an experiential approach to strategy formulation and find success in delivering in this approach.

CONCEPTS

Experiential learning through a business practicum provides students with an opportunity to experience working with a live company to solve large, unstructured problems in a classroom setting. It prepares students for the complex business environment of today by emphasizing the application of academic knowledge accumulated in prior core courses to solve real-world problems. Unlike teaching a case study, this can be a messy process as there are many variables to consider that are rather dynamic in nature.

Experiential learning has been defined as "the process whereby knowledge is created through the transformation of experience. Knowledge results from the combination of grasping and transforming experience" (Kolb, 1984, p. 41). For this chapter, we will address experiential learning in the context of strategic management by considering the business practicum approach. A business practicum is a pedagogy specifically designed to engage students in an active process of learning that involves integrating of theoretical knowledge and skill development. It involves the students in reconciling different ways of seeing and acting in the world, interacting with their environment and reflecting on their learnings and knowledge gained.

A key characteristic of a business practicum course is its multi-disciplinary approach to problem solving. Working in multi-disciplinary teams, students are required to develop solutions leveraging on their knowledge and skills from multiple courses. It develops in students an ability to identify and frame problems and develop solutions by analytic review and abstract idea generation through the development of innovative solutions to real client projects. Taking students out to meet and work with a business on strategic challenges may not be exactly straightforward. Over the past five years, we have run a variety of business practicum courses for students at both the Master's and undergraduate level and will share our experiences from Singapore Management University and others from around the world who have taken up similar teaching pedagogies related to strategic management.

There are a number of specific, important goals that a business practicum has for student learning. By the end of the course, students should be able to:

- Assess a business problem and/or opportunity from the current business environment, including new and untapped markets.
- Design interdisciplinary solutions to address the business challenge or future opportunities by considering strategy, marketing, operations, organization, finance, and communication.
- Reason critically through the solution process with appropriate modes of analysis.
- Describe the solution's implementation plans and processes with regards to the firm's existing strategy, market, and organization.

At the same time, students develop critical management skills related to teamwork, leadership, project management, stakeholder management, client communication, and presentation skills through the process of the business practicum course. While we would find these topics elsewhere in the curriculum, the business practicum tends to bring out multiple challenges for student teams due to the complexities and ambiguity of a real business situation and real business leaders.

Across universities, we note that there are several ways business practicum courses may be designed and taught based on the objectives in the curriculum. However, it seems that there are a set of certain design features that commonly enhance the effectiveness of the program. Following are descriptions of some of the more popular features.

1. *Clear Vision for the Business Practicum* – Although this sounds obvious, it is not uncommon for schools to fail on this dimension. A good business practicum program requires the support of the school, faculty, business clients and students. It is therefore crucial that the vision and philosophy of the business practicum is clearly articulated and understood by all the stakeholders.

2. *Instructor as Guide and Facilitator* – In a business practicum course, the instructor plays different roles. Besides providing the lectures, the instructor is expected to act as mentor, facilitator, advisor, and coach to the student teams (Bruhn and Camp, 2004; Manuel et al., 2008) and as manager (Stanfill et al., 2010). It can be a challenge to find instructors who are able to play these different roles well in a variety of contexts.

3. *Business Executives as Mentors* – Although any faculty member can teach the latest management and organizational behavior theories, a business practicum requires the integration of multi-disciplines to address a real business issue. Faculty members that are domain experts in their respective fields are likely to have superficial knowledge of subjects outside of the specialization. In such cases, it is best to have a practitioner teach or co-teach as a mentor. Using current business leaders as instructors or mentors ensure that the learning for the students is grounded in the reality of the business world.

4. *Clear Client Selection Guidelines and Process* – Finding business leaders with a genuine interest in student learning along with an openness to share their business challenges can be a tricky combination. While there seem to be many large multi-national business leaders who are interested in supporting students, it is often difficult to create meaningful student projects with large firms due to the business complexities and data restrictions. We have found that medium-sized firms with a keen interest in growth are a strong potential partner in the student learning. Often times, these firms do not have access to consulting solutions and welcome the chance to work with an external group to gain new perspectives and potential insights on their business or industry.

5. *Overall Process and Anchors for Students* – Taking on a business challenge may sound straightforward but managing the student teams through the constraints of the university academic term can be difficult. Providing clear milestone targets for the student teams along with standard frameworks for the process become critical. To help anchor the team solutions in a common format for both the client and the instructor, we use the Business Model Canvas (BMC), developed by Osterwalder and Pigneur (2010), as the organizing framework across

all disciplines (marketing, strategy, finance, communication, operations, organizational behavior and human resources, accounting, etc.).
It becomes important that all class sections have the same frameworks
and guidelines to help ensure consistency and clarity of expectations
for the students.

6.　*Teaching Assistant* – The amount of administrative and coordination
work involved in successfully running a business practicum course
cannot be under-estimated. It is recommended that instructors have a
teaching assistant to manage all the administrative and coordination
work, as well as assist with out-of-classroom consultation, where
appropriate. To minimize any inconveniences to the client, the teaching assistant acts as the liaison person between the client and the
students.

These business practicum features provide good parameters for conducting
a successful business practicum course. However, there are several other considerations related to the type of business clients, nature of projects, involvement of the instructor, method of assessment, positioning with students,
and support from the school. As we designed variations of the business
practicum, there were several questions that emerged around these topics.

Should we provide the business client or let the students find their own
projects? In one of the early versions of the course, we asked the students
to find their own projects. In a class of 45 students we had nine student
teams – each with a different business they were addressing. The students
were resourceful in finding businesses (e.g. uncle's cleaning business,
friend's start-up venture, father's multi-national employer), but it became
quite challenging for the instructor to really understand each business
and evaluate the student work. In addition, it was not possible to create
a meaningful lesson for the entire class using this divided approach. We
therefore migrated to a model where the entire class section has one client
and the student teams work separately within the context of the same
business and industry.

The type of client partners we seek are those that understand the
importance of putting learning first. It is important that the leaders from
the organization understand the focus on learning – secondarily they may
find some good business ideas from the teams. A sponsor from the client
partner is appointed to support the team. Ideally, this sponsor should have
some significant influence within the organization and could ensure that
some of the proposed ideas may be implemented. From our experience,
we have found that a client is constantly looking for new ideas and different perspectives to their business. Properly structured and managed, it is
common for clients to adopt some of the ideas from the students.

Where do you find the business clients? We generally start looking for potential business clients about three months ahead of the start of the class by using university networks, alumni, and referrals. In some universities, there is a coordinated process for identifying and selecting clients as these courses are part of "Consulting Services" provided by students. It is important to note that it can take several attempts to find the right business that fits with the course plans as well as with the background of the instructor. The lead time in this process should not be under-estimated. We found that there is a long lead time needed to onboard a client and to constantly build a pipeline of potential clients that can be used for the business practicum course in future terms.

What type of business project is ideal for student learning? The type of projects we seek must be significant enough and address practical business problems, to be completed by a team of four to five students or a class consisting of seven to nine teams over fourteen weeks. The majority of projects involve a growth opportunity. This allows students to explore ideas and think about new business models in an innovative way to deliver a value proposition. The most valued types of projects are those involving student teams initiating a strategic shift in the client's business model or a new venture that the client is committed to launch. These are the most challenging to handle as students have to grapple with lots of ambiguities and complexities. The success or failure of any project is much dependent on the way the project is structured. It is thus crucial that projects are properly scoped and organized to ensure success. In several cases, the client challenge was regional growth or expansion. This allows each student team to tackle the international entry strategy for a country (e.g. Myanmar, Vietnam, etc.) while also considering various adaptations to a business model.

How do you set expectations with the business client? When working with smaller businesses, it is particularly important to set clear guidelines and expectations. We have had some small business owners that get overly excited about working with the students that they offer them employment or try to implement ideas prior to the conclusion of the class! As mentioned above, we strive to find business clients with a strong interest in growth. When focused on external market opportunities, we find that the students do not require as much data from the client business. Often times, client business leaders are hesitant to disclose data and sensitive information to student teams – even with a non-disclosure agreement (NDA). This can be frustrating for the students and a growth project becomes less invasive for the business client as the student teams do not require as much detailed knowledge of the business. Throughout the project, we continually reinforce that our primary objective is on student learning. The business client must put learning first – this is essential to have the right engagement expectations. The outputs from the student teams may present interesting ideas for the client. More about the specific client expectation management is outlined in the process for teaching section that follows.

What is the ideal class size and class dynamic? While some universities run a business practicum in a large-scale format with hundreds of students, we find that a class of 40 to 45 works well. This allows us to assign students into 8 or 9 teams. We typically assign them based on business major, so we have various disciplines represented by the team members. While we allow the students to scope their own project, the instructor coaches the teams in different directions to avoid direct competition of the same ideas between teams – and to allow the business client to receive multiple solution ideas. In the context of our course in Singapore, the student teams tend to be a bit competitive and hold their scope and ideas in close confidence. By working with a single client, we can provide general updates to the class and discuss any common challenges that the teams are facing. Facilitating the teams in a way that allows them to scope a meaningful, yet manageable project is a bit of an art that comes with some experience. Allowing each of the student teams to maintain their confidential project through the term creates some anticipation for the final presentations where all the solutions are presented to the client, instructor, and student peers.

How do the teams generate new strategies? As a business practicum, we know that the students have had all the basic business subjects, including strategic management. Most have also had some courses on innovation and design thinking as well. After the students consider project scope ideas, they typically struggle with developing a business strategy. This demonstrates the value of an experiential approach as the students question how to leverage strategic management frameworks (e.g. SWOT, Five Forces, PESTEL, etc.). What we find is that they have learned and memorized the frameworks, but have no experience in using them – this course creates real learning through this application of strategic management. Students are expected to develop creative solutions to the client's problems. During each stage of the process through the course term, the instructors will coach and remind students about creative processes and ideas but will take care not to create new approaches or break into lecture-mode. Whether it is designing a better product, service or improving the internal processes for the client, we encourage students to focus on the people they are creating the solution for by adopting a human-centered view. Some instructors use the Stanford Design School videos to allow the students to have access to resources and approaches for reference.

How do we create learning without lectures and lessons? For those instructors who come from an approach of giving lectures during the term followed by an examination, this course is rather unsettling. At the same time, it is also unsettling for students as they cannot sit back in the lecture hall each week and then cram for an exam at the end of the term. This course requires consistent work for both the instructor and the student. During the first week, we set the stage and describe the process. After the client is introduced, the instructor may only provide some announcements or reminders at the start of the class session (10–15 minutes). The remainder of the class time is used for working in teams with the instructor rotating around to visit with each of the teams to understand their process, progress, and any issues. Given that much of what occurs in a business practicum course is through discussion, the instructor needs to keep the students focused. From our experience, we found that the instructor playing an informal managerial role monitoring the team's progress, helping the team to resolve any issues, and keeping the team on track to achieve the course objectives, is more effective than a hierarchical approach.

How do we assess the students in an experiential learning course? The majority of the assessment for a course like this is typically on the final team report and presentation. However, this can often lead to free-riding within the teams. To address this, we have a peer evaluation along with instructor assessment of participation/engagement each week. We find that the course is also an opportunity for student reflection and encourage them to not only keep a journal, but consider what aspects of the project or business sparks interest for their future careers. For the business practicum, we have the following assessments:

Class participation/Engagement = 20 percent
Team Mid-term Presentation = 20 percent
Individual Reflection = 15 percent
Final Presentation and Report = 35 percent
Peer Evaluation = 10 percent

How do we make this a positive experience for students? Several universities have similar courses to the business practicum and will often leverage external consultants as mentors to help highlight the importance of the effort. We work hard to make this course one of the highlights in the curriculum and celebrate the successes of the student teams in the media, internal communication, and poster events. In general, we communicate that this course is a "CV Worthy Experience" and encourage students to put this on their resume to enhance their experience for employers. Since the nature of the projects are cross-discipline, we find that the nature of the project works well to showcase student accomplishment as well as furthering the reputation of our graduates.

PROCESS FOR TEACHING

While there are many approaches, we outline a process in this section that is designed for the standard 14-week term that is commonly found in many business schools. The program can be modified to accommodate any variations in the term. We will take a chronological view.

Three months prior to the commencement of term, we start to identify and select the client organization for the course. Sufficient lead time is required to identify the right client organization. If the selection of the client and the project are a critical first step, then preparing the client for the project is the next crucial step.

The instructor for the course needs to work closely with the client to scope out the project and develop the problem statement. It usually takes several iterations to get it right. The success or failure of any project is much dependent on the way the project is structured and managed. It is thus crucial that the project is properly scoped and structured to ensure success. It is important that the problem statement and the project deliverables are extremely clear. Problems can arise later if the problem statement or project deliverables are not clear, too broad or too narrow.

Just as there are different ways to design and teach business practicum courses, there are a variety of ways in managing the client relationship. Cognizant that the client is providing a platform for our students, we are mindful of minimizing any inconveniences to them. We found certain design features enhance the effectiveness of our client management. Following are descriptions of some best practice features.

1. Clearly defined role for the client and client sponsor – to have the right engagement with the business, the client needs to understand its role and that the primary objective of the business practicum project is student learning. Any interesting or good business idea that comes out of it is a secondary benefit. This can sometimes be difficult for clients who come with pre-conceived ideas about the outcome or what they want the solution to look like.
2. Non-Disclosure Agreement – to protect the client's interest, we require all instructors and students in the course to sign a Non-Disclosure Agreement with the client.
3. Confidential Information – notwithstanding the signing of a Non-Disclosure Agreement, certain information in listed companies remains confidential and cannot be publicly released. We would ask the client to either mask or omit the data. Students should still be able to complete the project by making assumptions.

4. Handling Questions – to minimize any inconveniences to the client, we limit the number of times the students are allowed to ask questions of the client. Questions from the different groups are consolidated by the instructor or teaching assistant, sieved through for duplicates and redundant questions before sending them to the client. The client is usually given forty-eight hours to respond to the questions. The number of times the client is prepared to answer questions from the students depends on the client. Our experience suggests that three to five times during the fourteen weeks is the optimal range. Limiting the number of times the students can ask questions forces them to be sharper and more focused in their questions.
5. Company Visit – to help the students better understand the client's business, we sometimes arrange for the students to visit the client's business premises.

The 14-week program is broadly divided into three stages, with a one-week recess in Week 8.

Part 1 – Assess Business Challenge Stage – Week 1 to 3
Part 2 – Develop Ideas Stage – Week 4 to 7
Part 3 – Design Business Model and Plan – Week 8 to 14

ASSESS BUSINESS CHALLENGE STAGE

Week 1 – Introduction and Getting Organized

The course kicks off with an introduction to the course requirements, the Business Model Canvas (Osterwalder and Pigneur, 2010) and organizing students into their teams. Students are randomly organized into teams of 5 to 6 per team. We found that 5 to 6 per team is an optimal size. It provides students adequate opportunity to be actively engaged in the project and minimizes free-riders in the team. Too small a number, and the team lacks diversity. Too large a team, inefficiency creeps in, and some students may free-ride on the process.

We recommend that the instructor or teaching assistant assign students to teams, instead of letting students form their own teams. Teams should have members with different majors or specializations, experience and background. We found that students that form their own teams tend to congregate with friends who have similar majors or specializations. Such teams have a tendency to struggle most as the project progresses because of a lack of diversity and are often caught in groupthink.

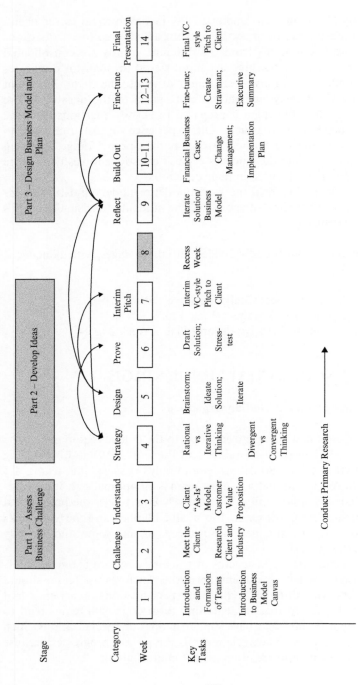

Source: Singapore Management University.

Figure 5.1 Structure of business practicum course

As teamwork is crucial for the success of the project, team members are encouraged to have some social activity during the first week to bond. We encourage them to consider their team roles and how they might leverage their experiences and study areas to the project.

As with any types of projects, close monitoring and reporting is crucial to ensure the teams stay on track and are progressing well to deliver on the objectives. Teams are required to submit a Weekly Report to the instructor. This Weekly Report provides a status update on progress, issues encountered, and actions taken. The instructor or mentor provides feedback and guidance to help the teams move along.

Week 2 – Meet the Client

The client is invited to present to the class on their business, industry, and the business challenge for the students to tackle. Preparing both the client and students in advance on what to expect, and to ask questions is important. It helps them clarify and better understand the project.

During the week, students will conduct secondary research on the client and the industry using strategic frameworks, such as Porter's five-forces, PESTEL, and so on that they have been taught in strategy courses. We have found that while students may have learned and memorized the frameworks, they have no experience in actually using them. This is where they learn the value of applying strategy and strategic thinking in a live environment.

At this stage, students probably still have lots of questions about the business challenge and the client's business. Having access to the business mentors helps the students clarify and frame any questions they may have. The teaching assistant helps to collate and vet through the questions before forwarding them to the client.

Week 3 – Understand

To understand how the client creates value, delivers value and captures value in its business, the students are asked to complete an "As–Is" Business Model of the client's business. This is the first time for most students in using the Business Model Canvas. Most of them will need help to understand the linkages between the nine building blocks and the gaps in the client's business.

Depending on the problem challenge, students are usually required to conduct primary research through surveys, focus group discussions, and other methods to gain deeper insights of the customer. Teams start preparation work for primary research.

Students also learn how to gather insights around the needs of people through different research techniques, often involving observation, interviewing and immersive empathy. Generally, the research can be classified as:

- Validating research – which helps to understand what is currently happening.
- Generative research – which helps to explore needs and identify new opportunities.
- Evaluative research – which helps to iterate forward from feedback gathered on experiments.

To prepare students for Part 2 – Develop Ideas Stage, students may be taught design thinking or other relevant creative thinking concepts and methods, understanding customers' needs through "the job to be done," "gains" and "pains" during Week 3. Students learn how to turn problems into questions so as to get to the root of the challenge.

Week 4 – Strategy

In Week 4, we discuss topics on rational versus iterative thinking, divergent and convergent thinking, to prepare students to brainstorm ideas and ideate solutions. Students are encouraged to think out of the box and to consistently challenge assumptions as they go through the iterative process.

Students continue with their primary research and start drawing insights from their observations. As information is not perfect in the real-world, students will struggle to deal with the lack of complete information, ambiguity and uncertainty.

Week 5 – Design

Teams start to brainstorm and ideate solutions in Week 5. Brainstorming and ideating solutions is an iterative process and involves moving back and forth between the challenge, the ideas and solution. Frustration starts to set in for some teams as they struggle with the process, and deal with ambiguity and uncertainty.

Some teams will approach the instructor hoping the instructor will provide them with the right answer. Tempting as it may be, instructors must resist the urge to provide any answers to the teams. Students need to discover the path forward and learn to make decisions. We found that the best way to help the students is not by providing them with answers, but by asking them questions to guide them in their self-discovery.

Instructors and mentors need to be mindful and watch out for teams that are stuck in a rut to guide them forward, and for students that dominate the discussion, to the exclusion of other viewpoints.

Week 6 – Prove

Come Week 6, a draft solution is born. The draft solution will have to be stress-tested and its assumptions challenged. At this stage, teams start putting together their presentation slides and rehearsing for the mid-term presentation or Interim Pitch.

As the reality of the presentation deadline approaches, panic may start to set in as some teams may realize that they present to the client in a week's time – especially if they are not fully confident in their proposal. Some teams may need guidance on how to present in a "venture-capital" pitch style.

Week 7 – Interim Pitch

At Week 7, the teams present their proposal to the client with a "venture-capital" pitch style, seeking the client's authorization to proceed with the project. Each team is given 15 to 20 minutes to present. This is followed by 5 minutes of Questions and Answers. This forces the teams to be sharp in their presentations.

What happens next is like the real-world. Three possible outcomes follow from the presentation. The client may approve for the team to proceed with the proposal as is, the client may request for some amendments to be made to the proposal, or the client may reject the proposal outright.

Teams may come out of the meeting feeling elated or rejected. The instructor should set aside time for consultation and counseling with the teams. Teams will be looking for feedback on their mid-term presentation. Some will need counseling and coaching to recover from the client's response to their proposal.

Week 8 – Recess Week

Week 9 – Reflect

Students return from their term break and reflect on their proposed business model and the client's feedback received during the Interim Pitch in Week 7. The teams continue to iterate and refine the business model for the client. In some cases, the feedback from the presentations requires a bit of re-thinking in some teams – this may require special attention by the instructor.

Week 10 and 11 – Build Out Stage

The teams start to build out the financial business case, change management and implementation plan, considering the impact on the various stakeholders.

To have students reflect on their learning journey, we have the students write an Individual Self-Reflection Paper. This paper is usually due by Week 11.

Week 12 and 13

With the proposal built out, the teams work on fine-tuning the proposal, creating the strawman, and rehearsing for the final pitch. Panic will once again set in as teams rush to finalize their proposal and rehearse for the final pitch.

Week 14 – Final Presentation and Celebration

The teams are brought together to present to the client with a "venture-capital" pitch style. For the final presentation, we have all the teams attend so that they can listen to and learn from the other teams. Broadly, teams are assessed on the following criteria:

- Assessment of Environment and Context
- Innovative and Compelling New Ideas
- Value BMC Prototype (Customer Segment/Customer Relationship/Channels)
- Business Operations Prototypes (Key Activities/Key Partners/Key Resources)
- Cost and Revenue Prototypes
- Presentation Quality and Teamwork.

Following the final pitch, we invite the client to provide feedback to the teams on their proposal. This marks the end of the 14-week Business Practicum course.

HOW LEARNING TAKES PLACE

The two goals in the experiential learning process are: (1) To learn the specifics of a particular subject, and (2) to learn about one's own learning process (Kolb and Kolb, 2009). Learning takes place when knowledge is created through the transformation of experience involving a creative tension among four learning modes of: (1) Concrete Experience (CE), (2) Abstract Conceptualization (AC), (3) Reflective Observation (RO), and (4) Active Experimentation (AE) (Kolb and Kolb, 2009).

In the business practicum course, students learn through each of these modes by experiencing, reflecting, thinking and acting in a recursive process that is responsive to the learning situation. For example, to solve the problem effectively, the four steps students typically apply to problem management correspond to the four learning modes.

1. Situation Analysis (CE).
2. Ideas Generation (AC).
3. Information Gathering (RO).
4. Implementation (AE).

The iterative process of moving back and forth between opposing modes of action, reflection and thinking, which students must go through in generating ideas and developing the solutions for the client, helps drive the learning process. Students often struggle with the differences, conflict and disagreements between the opposing modes of action, reflection and thinking. It takes time for students to recognize that what drives learning is the resolution of conflicts between dialectically opposed modes of adaptation to the world and learning how to adapt to them.

STUDENT REFLECTIONS: LEARNING STRATEGY FORMULATION IN THE REAL WORLD

- Reflecting on the value of Business Practicum
  Collections of quotes from students' feedback

  - *It was a good way to incorporate different disciplines for a real-life client-based project > It made us envision the life of being a consultant > Valuable life lessons > Applying what we learnt in theory to a practical setting was really challenging yet truly memorable. (Business Practicum Student 2018)*

  - *This is one of the best courses in the program. It helps us put into practice all the other modules we have learnt. It is really helpful for me as I aspire to be a consultant. (Business Practicum Student 2018)*

  - *The course was challenging but learned a lot, especially since we were given the chance to work on a real-life project and present to a real life client. Able* to link the course material to the project. Overall gained a lot of insights. *(Business Practicum Student 2018)*

- *Very challenging course, loved it and learnt the most in this course so far; especially, the team dynamics. (Business Practicum Student 2018)*

- *A very challenging course. Our brains were literally drop dead by the end, but somehow we knew we had to sail through. (Business Practicum Student 2018)*

- *I think the Business Capstone is an excellent way for us to understand the differences between academic requirements and real-world business requirements. More often than not, we are focused on pursuing the "A" grade and do things the academic way. But at the workplace, expectations are different. Businesses look out for different things. For example, in most academic projects, we can simply present the front facing aspects of the strategy (i.e. execute a digital marketing strategy). However, in real world businesses, it is important to show the operational, financial and other aspects as well. I think this course gives us that kind of exposure. (Business Capstone Student 2018)*

- Reflecting on the limitations of Business Practicum

  - *The course lacked a structure to it. We found this very inconvenient and couldn't work systematically. There were very few client meetings scheduled and to give our client the best possible solutions, we need to get more time with them. (Business Practicum Student 2018)*

  - *The client wouldn't provide any internal information. (Business Practicum Student 2018)*

  - *The course duration could be stretched to accommodate for the requirements that it possesses. (Business Practicum Student 2018)*

INSTRUCTOR REFLECTIONS: TEACHING STRATEGY FORMULATION IN THE REAL WORLD

In the undergraduate Business Capstone class, I derive the greatest joy from seeing the students transform from "unconscious incompetence" to "conscious competence." Eventually, most teams will deliver a stellar proposal that will pleasantly surprise me, the client and even themselves. However, underpinning that transformation is often a painful metamorphosis that involves a paradigm shift from "Prof/Client/Google/somebody else knows the right answer" to "We need to justify our own recommendations by stepping into the shoes of the business owner." I believe this mindset shift is the most critical for students to maximize their learning in this course, however, it is also the most difficult to "teach" because they need time and space to internalise what the shift in perspective means to them. (Adjunct Faculty)

Teaching the Business Practicum course is like leading several teams of new consultants on their first project! It can be a lot of work, but if it is set-up well with the client it can be great fun as a collective shared experience and challenge. I still keep in touch with many of my capstone students since our time together was so meaningful. (Professor of Strategic Management)

One of the key challenges in teaching Capstone is to switch from a controlling style to a coaching style, because Capstone is about problem definition and idea generation through teamwork. There is no textbook. Instructors need to relinquish their control in the classroom and foster a conducive environment for students to collaborate, share ideas, and facilitate discussions. Teaching Capstone is definitely more challenging than teaching a traditional class, but after teaching Capstone, I wouldn't go back to traditional teaching anymore. I began to incorporate activities and drills in all my other classes for students to be active and engaged in their projects. (Assistant Professor, Strategy & Organization)

When teaching a Business Practicum, you have to be prepared to make quick decisions and adjust the plans along the way. Once when the entire class was discouraged with a challenging client situation, I called the client in the middle of our class session and broadcast the call in the room by using Skype to help bring clarity and the reality of the project to life. Keeping the project real with real impact is not always easy. (Professor of Strategic Management)

AREAS OF CONSIDERATION

1. What are the potential pitfalls of this approach?
   Potential pitfalls of this approach include: (1) the alignment of client expectations and the learning objectives of the course; (2) the student expectations being out of line with the goals of the course; (3) instructor familiarity with an applied multi-disciplinary approach; and (4) instructor ability to manage ambiguity while juggling the expectations of client and students.
2. Can any instructor teach using this approach? What skills and experience are needed?
   Any instructor can teach using this approach. However, our experience suggests that practice-based instructors tend to perform better in teaching business practicum courses. Their skills and experience in the business world allows them to apply a multi-disciplinary approach to problem-solving, and play the different roles of lecturer, mentor, facilitator, advisor, coach and manager. Research-based instructors without real-world business experience are best advised to partner with another to co-teach the course.

3. What about free-riders in the team projects?
    Certain measures can be put in place to manage free-riders. We control the number of members in each team to around 5 or 6. From our experience, we found that this is an optimal size for the teams to work together as it requires everyone to pitch in. There is little room for free-riders in a team of this size. We also included peer evaluation, along with instructor assessment of participation/engagement each week, as part of the assessment. When noted by the instructor or in peer evaluation, free-riders are significantly marked down in their grades.
4. How to manage the client who has high expectations?
    Managing a client's expectations starts with identifying and selecting the right client organization to work with, the client organization needs to understand the primary focus of business practicum courses is on learning. This needs to be communicated clearly at the beginning and reinforced during the course. Generally, if this is well communicated and expectations managed upfront, clients are usually very supportive of the learning objectives.
5. How much extra effort does it take for teaching using an experiential approach?
    Unlike teaching a traditional course, teaching business practicum courses using an experiential approach requires extensive planning and preparation. Things are very dynamic as we are dealing with various stakeholders in the process and no one class is the same. Ample lead time is required to identify and select the right client organization, and to scope out the project. Most of the work that the students will be doing will be outside of class hours. Instructors and mentors should also factor in time for mentoring and coaching teams outside of class hours.
6. How might this approach create different results from that of a simulation?
    A simulation is a model of a set of problems or events that can be used to teach someone how to respond or do something in a given situation or event. The situation or event may seem real, but is not real. With simulation, there is usually a prescribed way of dealing with the situation or event, and the result is usually known at the end of the simulation.

    With business practicum, the students are dealing with a real client with a live problem. There is no prescribed way to deal with the situation and students have to deal with lack of information, ambiguity and uncertainty. The result is not immediately known.

SUMMARY

While strategic management scholars debate the nature and teaching of strategy courses in business schools, we continue to see value providing students with the tools and approaches through traditional classroom approaches. However, we find great value when these courses are followed by an experiential learning opportunity to apply their knowledge. We have described an approach that has been fine-tuned over several years – and we continue to work to improve on our outcomes.

To date, we have discovered significant impact in our student experience and hope that our experiences provide value to others considering how to create impact with strategy formulation. While we teach strategy formulation in the traditional strategic management courses, the actual process and challenge of considering strategy comes to life in the experiential business practicum course. By creating the right learning environment and making it real with a live client, suddenly the concepts become real and we are able to create a powerful experience that brings not only strategy formulation, but also other disciplines to life. As educators, we continue to look for ways to make impact in the student learning journey and we have found this course to be particularly rewarding for both students and faculty.

REFERENCES

Association of American Colleges and Universities (2013). *Employers More Interested in Critical Thinking and Problem Solving Than College Major*. https://www.aacu.org/press/press-releases/employers-more-interested-critical-thinking-and-problem-solving-college-major (accessed January 10, 2020).

Bingham, C. and Davis, J. (2012). Learning sequences: Their existence, effect, and evolution. *Academy of Management Journal*, 55(3), pp. 611–641.

Bruhn, R. and Camp, J. (2004). Capstone course creates useful business products and corporate-ready students. *ACM SIGCSE Bulletin*, 36(2), pp. 87–92.

Dess, G. (1987). Consensus on strategy formulation and organizational performance: Competitors in a fragmented industry. *Strategic Management Journal*, 8(3), pp. 259–277.

Eisenhardt, K. (1989). Making fast strategic decisions in high-velocity environments. *Academy of Management Journal*, 32(3), pp. 543–576.

Gary, M. and Wood, R. (2011). Mental models, decision rules, and performance heterogeneity. *Strategic Management Journal*, 32(6), pp. 569–594.

Greiner, L., Bhambri, A. and Cummings, T. (2003). Searching for a strategy to teach strategy. *Academy of Management Learning & Education*, 2(4), pp. 402–420.

Hillman, A. and Hitt, M. (1999). Corporate political strategy formulation: A model of approach, participation, and strategy decisions. *Academy of Management Review*, 24(4), pp. 825–842.

Kiss, A. and Barr, P. (2014). New venture strategic adaptation: The interplay of belief structures and industry context. *Strategic Management Journal*, 36(8), pp. 1245–1263.

Klimoski, R. and Amos, B. (2012). Practicing evidence-based education in leadership development. *Academy of Management Learning & Education*, 11(4), pp. 685–702.

Kolb, A. and Kolb, D. (2009). Experiential learning theory: A dynamic, holistic approach to management learning, education and development, in *The SAGE Handbook of Management Learning, Education and Development*. Edited by: Steven J. Armstrong & Cynthia V. Fukami. London: Sage Publications, pp. 42–68.

Kolb, D. (1984). *Experimental Learning: Experience as the Source of Learning and Development*. Englewood Cliffs: Prentice Hall.

Manuel, M.V., McKenna, A. and Olson, G.B. (2008). Hierarchical model for coaching technical design teams. *International Journal of Engineering Education*, 24(2), pp. 260–265.

Osterwalder, A. and Pigneur, Y. (2010). *Business Model Generation*. Hoboken, NJ: Wiley.

Ott, T., Eisenhardt, K. and Bingham, C. (2017). Strategy formation in entrepreneurial settings: past insights and future directions. *Strategic Entrepreneurship Journal*, 11(3), pp. 306–325.

Rumelt, R. (2011). *Good Strategy Bad Strategy*. New York: Random House US.

Stanfill, R., Moshin, A., Crisalle, O., Tufekci, S. and Crane, C. (2010). *The Coach's Guide: Best Practices for Faculty-Mentored Multidisciplinary Product Design Teams*. Washington, DC: American Society for Engineering Education.

Thompson, K. and Koys, D. (2010). The management curriculum and assessment journey: Use of Baldrige criteria and the occupational network database. *Journal of Leadership & Organizational Studies*, 17(2), pp. 156–166.

6. Writing and using your own case study for strategy teaching

Uwe Stratmann

6.1 THE PURPOSE AND VALUE OF TEACHING CASE STUDIES IN THE FIELD OF STRATEGY AND MARKETING

Teaching strategy needs to find an effective balance between theory and practice. It is a challenging task for teachers because of the variety of questions, corresponding theories and management concepts. Due to their lack of real-life experiences, students (e.g. Bachelor level) often struggle to transfer theoretical knowledge into practice. However, one main teaching purpose of business education should exactly be about that: the pragmatic application of know-how and teaching content.

Therefore, it is not a surprise that case studies represent a very effectful teaching concept. The initial use of case studies was about this objective: to enhance the ability of business students to solve practical problems. The integration of case studies supports the motivation and activation of students as well as their problem-solving competence. According to Volpe (2002) students learn best through self-learning and through practical experiences rather than traditional teacher- and pure theory-centric didactical concepts. Furthermore, case studies build up a very effective link between academic research and classroom teaching (e.g. Neuman, 1994; Brew, 2003; Strach and Everett, 2008).

Writing and using your own case study can create further benefits compared to the use of existing case studies (e.g. such as Harvard Business School case studies). If you work on your own teaching case (including conceptualization of the case, collection and analysis of data, definition of teaching questions etc.) this can automatically increase your own motivation and credibility during the process of teaching the case. These factors are again important for the didactic success and effective integration of cases (e.g. Chakrabarti and Balaji, 2007). You can furthermore adapt the case individually to your script and content. The teacher is in the best position to assess the existing knowledge of students and to define the focus of the content, including the alignment of the teaching case.

However, existing literature deals in particular with the preparation and development of research case studies (e.g. Yin, 2014), but not with the preparation and use of your own cases. Due to that there is still a research gap in the field of developing and producing your own teaching case (e.g. Jennings, 1996; Cockburn, 2000; Strach and Everett, 2008).

This chapter focuses especially on the question: what is the best way to write, use and integrate your own case studies for business and management courses? After a brief introduction into case studies, the following sections deal with core questions linked to the development and production of your own teaching cases, in particular:

● How do you select and write up a teaching case study to activate and motivate business students in the discipline of strategy?
● What are effective ways to integrate the case study into the lecture concept, to link theory, research and didactic elements?
● Which specific requirements are vital to design a teaching case for a strategy class?, and
● What are the core benefits of producing your own teaching case?

I will use my own case study about Nespresso's business and marketing strategy to exemplify the didactical concept and the overall writing and teaching process. The Nespresso case study was conceived for a class on strategic marketing (Bachelor program). It demonstrates personal experiences and outcomes according to the different didactic objectives.

6.2   INTEGRATION OF CASE STUDIES INTO THE TEACHING CONCEPT

6.2.1   Didactic Concept and Integration of Students

This section deals with appropriate didactic methods to integrate case studies into the teaching concept and to align the case with the overall content. Common ways of using cases are (see Peterson, 1996; Chakrabarti and Balaji, 2007):

● "Case-to-Concept"
● "Concept-to-Case" and
● "Case-to-Case."

Case study integration in your lecture content

"Concept-to-Case" is the prevailing method for using cases as a teaching strategy for management courses (Chakrabarti and Balaji, 2007, p. 16). This method builds on the process of first introducing the theory and concepts and then discussing the case. The core teaching objective is the reinforcement of the lecture content by using the case as a real-life example. Abstract theoretical models and concepts can be transformed into practical examples. The Concept-to-Case approach supports understanding and motivates students to discuss certain models and theoretical approaches. It also shows the practical relevance of supposedly irrelevant textbook knowledge and theories.

The "Case-to-Concept" approach is based on a reverse order: first the case study is introduced and discussed. The lecture is then linked to the case and involves those theories and models which are discussed in the case study before. However, the case study analysis and discussion could be problematic due to the reverse order (compared to the "Concept-to-Case" approach). Students might not have the necessary knowledge for analysing and discussing the case and it could also lead to a lower attention to work with the case study. For a similar teaching success students might analyse the case study again after they have read it the first time. Didactic effectiveness could therefore be lower compared to the "Concept-to-Case" method. Even worse, students might not understand the case study and the teaching benefits could be inferior.

Teaching certain theories and concepts is not in focus of the "Case-to-Case" method. This case study integration concept is not built on any theoretical background but rather on a pragmatic learning approach which is built on real-life examples. It could be an appropriate approach for teaching practitioners with both, experiences in business and some basic understanding of relevant theories. Therefore, it is not the most effective didactical approach for Bachelor and Master courses. The "Case-to-Case" model is more useful for executive management courses.

Case study format

In terms of the case study format, the dominant type is still print (e.g. based on comprehensive notes or rather summarized slides/case study presentation). The production of a video case could overcome first motivation barriers on the students' side, but this requires a professional concept and a sophisticated video production. One core issue is the timeliness of data. Updating video material could require much more effort or even the production of a completely new video case. The production of comprehensive teaching notes (e.g. an instructor's guide) is normally necessary to publish the case study and make it available to other faculties.

Integration of students

Another question is about the integration of students themselves. Corresponding questions are: should the case study be presented foremost by the teacher, by the students, or should students and the teacher share this job? If the teacher decides to keep the control about the case study, there is lower risk of wrong interpretation of the case study content, which is important to deliver the right messages. However, this could lead to a lower general involvement and insufficient motivation. Based on my own experiences, it could be most effective to work on the case study jointly, with the teacher in the role of moderator for solving questions and misunderstandings.

Evaluation of case study analysis

As part of the overall teaching concept, the case study presentation and discussion are evaluated and feed the overall semester grade (besides a written exam). The evaluation is linked to the preciseness, correctness and profoundness of the given answers as well as the overall discussion and way of presentation (for general evaluation criteria see Hawes, 2004; and Chakrabarti and Balai, 2007, pp. 17 and 22).

Table 6.1 provides an overview about the core didactic levers according to an effective case study integration in your teaching concept.

6.2.2   Nespresso Case Study: Applied Didactic Concept

In the following the didactic levers mentioned in section 6.2.1 will be exemplified by the Nespresso case. The Nespresso teaching case is integrated by the "Concept-to-Case" approach. The class receives the whole case study in the first lecture, including a brief and general introduction into the case

Table 6.1   Vital decisions for an effective integration of case studies

Didactic levers	Possible solutions
Integration of case study into the lecture content	Transfer of lecture content on teaching case or vice versa?
Integration of case during the semester	From single events up to complete semester accompaniment
Involvement of students	Teacher lead on teaching case, student lead or combination?
Case study format	Analogue (summarized case study presentation or paper) or digital (blended learning)
Evaluation of case study analysis	Based on different evaluation criteria (problem statement, analysis, etc.)

(here a brief introduction about Nestlé and Nespresso). The case study is structured according to the teaching content and accompanies the class during the whole semester. By that students experience the evolutionary strategy process model – from a white piece of paper to a complete strategy concept. Another approach would be the integration of different, shorter case studies on certain topics. However, this could mean longer preparation and set-up time (e.g. as students need to dive into different case study examples) and perhaps could lead to lower identification with single cases.

Students are integrated through working in teams (e.g. three to four students per team). They are expected to work on certain questions and exercises during the whole semester. These questions are linked to the respective lecture and case study sections. It is very important that you formulate the questions as precisely as possible. The questions should lead the students to the right messages. It is important that the class processes the case study content in the right way and learns the core messages. Each team must prepare a brief presentation about their topics and present these in front of the class. Teams in charge need to solve any kind of potential misunderstandings and questions beforehand and need to ensure the correctness of their material. This is important to avoid misinterpretation and mistakes among the team members as well as in the whole class. The presentation itself should be concise (e.g. about 20 minutes) as it will take place during the lecture hours.

During or after their presentation it is important to allow an open and lively participation and discussion with the rest of the class. By that students are teaching the case study content themselves and they are involved in the overall teaching process. The teacher moderates and leads the case study discussion and should have questions for the presenting group as well as for the class.

Table 6.2 summarizes the didactic concept of the Nespresso teaching case, including the core challenges and questions.

6.3 THE CHALLENGE OF SELECTING THE RIGHT TEACHING CASE FOR STRATEGY AND MANAGEMENT COURSES

The selection of the teaching case is vital for your didactic success – which is about an efficient (e.g. in terms of time and lecture resources) and effective knowledge transfer between the teacher and the classroom. Skill enhancement depends on the extent of attention and initiatives undertaken by the students in terms of preparation for the case analysis and discussion and the general active involvement during and after the class (Chakrabarti

Table 6.2   Didactic approach of the teaching case example (Nespresso)

Didactic levers	Example Nespresso teaching case
Integration of case study into the lecture content	Concept-to-Case approach: case study is applied on given lecture content.
Integration of case during the semester	Complete semester accompaniment: teaching case is designed according to the lecture content and chapters.
Involvement of students	Combined analysis and presentation: student teams need to work on certain case study chapters and questions. Teacher as the moderator.
Case study format	Students receive a summarized presentation with core content. E.g. additional information needs to be analysed and researched by students plus certain questions on single case study chapters.
Evaluation of case study analysis	Students need to present their analysis and results in front of the class, followed by a discussion (led by the teacher).

and Balaji, 2007). Hence, important selection criteria will be discussed, and success factors will be highlighted in the following sections.

6.3.1   Case Study Selection Criteria to Increase Involvement of the Class

What aspects should be considered for the case selection from a student's point of view? First, the case study should be stimulating and activating. Here it is important that there is a certain identification of the students with the case. A basic level of awareness and knowledge about the case is useful as well. This generates a certain level of attention which is important for the overall teaching success. Besides that the case study should incite emotions to support the overall involvement and participation. With regard to the cognitive and learning processes students should recognize a clear and real story which is relatively easy to understand. Figure 6.1 outlines the overall teaching concept and vital aspects.

If a large number of students have basic knowledge about the case example this again will support identification with the topic and overall attention. Attention and involvement are important factors supporting students' willingness to work intensely with the case and to participate actively during the class. Knowledge about the case can be based on, for example, their own experiences with the brand and product. For the general acceptance the emotional aspects are important as well. For example, teaching strategy in the area of marketing should not ignore gut feeling. It can support the didactic outcome if you address students' emotions and

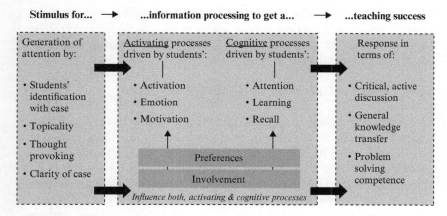

Figure 6.1   Case study teaching concept

if you attract empathy for the case study. Besides that, the case should be thought provoking and initiate controversial debates in the class.

From the teacher perspective, several aspects should be considered to prepare a teaching case efficiently and to reach an additional teaching success, such as:

- identification with the topic,
- data availability and confidentiality,
- overlap between teaching case and general teaching content,
- concepts and theories can be illustrated in a clear and precise manner.

Data availability and confidentiality is a vital aspect for the case study writing process, for example, a case study built on your own experiences and knowledge about your former company/employer could be the most authentic way to integrate it in your class. However, there is often the dilemma between using deep insider knowledge on the one hand and confidentiality issues on the other. The transfer of research into a teaching case study could be confronted with the same problem – the publication of primary, confidential data. The availability of enough secondary data could therefore be helpful. This is also true with regard to frequent data updates and the integration of students into the research process (e.g. students can develop the case further with additional data and information).

For the teaching success it is additionally important to find a case study which provides a strong overlap with the general teaching content. The more convincing the strategy concept is, the easier it is to transfer the core messages and content (e.g. a clear brand and product positioning which again is linked to a certain pricing and communication strategy). If you choose a case with a misfit between strategy decisions, this can lead to confusion and misunderstandings in the class.

6.3.2   Nespresso Case Study: Applied Selection Criteria

The aspects mentioned above (see Figure 6.1) shall be explained again by the selected Nespresso case study. General brand and product awareness about Nespresso are very high, and this is supporting the general involvement and participation of the class. A large number of students have direct (e.g. by consuming Nespresso) or indirect (e.g. by social interaction with Nespresso customers or by advertising) experiences with the product and therefore feel prepared to contribute to the topic. The critical public opinion and press about Nestlé is generating additional attention and provides emotional and motivational benefits. Even if this involves many negative aspects (e.g. the environmental harmfulness of Nespresso's capsule system) it is generally supporting the attention and is provoking discussions. In other words, the Nespresso case produces a certain level of basic attention and this again is the underlying starting point for the resulting teaching success. Overall the Nespresso case shows rather unusual strategic decisions which help raise interest and provoke critical questions and comments. Table 6.3 gives an overview about elements of Nespresso's business strategy.

Anyhow, the integration of students into the case study analysis generally leads to a higher level of activation. This is particularly true compared to a typical teacher and pure content focused lecture concept. In summary, the Nespresso case involves a naturally inspiring momentum and therefore is very suitable for teaching purposes. The resulting teaching success is very positive in terms of lively discussions and active debates about Nespresso's chosen strategies and practices. The general motivation to work on the case is high and it removes the pressure to get students' involvement and attention. They understand and learn about Nespresso's success formula on their own.

6.4   DESIGNING A CASE STUDY ALONG THE STRATEGY PROCESS MODEL

6.4.1   General Considerations for the Case Study Design and Content

This section introduces the process, core aspects and requirements of preparing a teaching case study in the field of strategy. In the first step,

Table 6.3   Profile of Nespresso's business strategy

Business Model Idea	Target customers	Unique strategy
Launched in 1986, a kind of platform concept for coffee products (i.e. internet side as key brand showcase and sales channel). Relaunch in 2000, with a new corporate identity and branding concept (premium strategy). Today: market leader in the market segment for coffee capsules and pads.	First focus on business/ office sector. With relaunch (in year 2000) a wider customer segment including private and business customers was reached.	Nespresso consequently implemented a premium brand/differentiation strategy. Nespresso's business model design and strategic decisions are very useful to teach state-of-the-art strategy concepts.

the case study should transport an understanding about the term and core elements of strategy. Even if the term "strategy" is inflationary used in management courses, students are often struggling to define and explain strategy in a clear and precise manner. The "big strategy picture" builds the framework for the overall strategy process model. Various analysis steps are necessary to assess, select and implement certain strategies. These steps will be outlined in the following.

Strategic analysis of the external market environment
The first analysis step should focus on the market conditions and require-ments. According to the market-based view, strategy should reflect certain market conditions and requirements. A core teaching aim is about the definition of the overall market, the market segment in question and the underlying customers, competitors and important stakeholders. The resulting questions and answers build the framework for the case study content and structure.

Experiences with management and marketing courses show that students underestimate the market research step. Without the application of real-life examples, many students do not see the challenges and complexity of a market definition and market segmentation. This supposedly easy task and question often leads to a lot of confusion and problems. One of the case study's teaching aims is about the clarification of this phenomenon: those questions which appear very simple in theory can be very difficult in reality.

Internal company analysis
External market analysis should be completed by the internal company view: for example, what resources need to be possessed, effectively integrated and protected to reach and sustain competitive advantages? The resource-based view identifies firm-specific resources as the main source of sustainable competitive advantage (Barney, 1991). Here the VRIO concept turns out as a pragmatic analysis framework to identify core strategic advantages of an organization (Barney and Hesterly, 2011). This analysis step offers a very good opportunity to integrate students in an active way (see the section "Analysing strategic competitiveness: effective integration of students" for a more detailed example). Integration of students is supporting their involvement and active participation.

Development and definition of strategic objectives
Teaching strategy is about understanding and anticipating the future. Strategic objectives are vital for the selection of both, the selection of strategies as well as of management and marketing instruments. A case study helps to explain the function and application of complex and rather abstract forecasting methods. Quantitative (sales) objectives are particularly vital for strategic marketing objectives. Hence different quantitative and qualitative forecast concepts are applied to anticipate the market size and finally the definition of specific company sales objectives.

The interrelationship between single steps of the analysis can be highlighted: for example, the anticipation of the future market size is linked to the definition and quantification of the current market. Students understand the complexity of strategy and the coherence of strategical questions and analytical steps. The application of forecasting models requires solid market data. This underlines the importance of data availability and validity, mentioned and discussed in the section about the selection of a teaching case (see section 6.3).

Design of a strategic business and marketing concept
An effective strategy concept builds on a complex system comprising various coherent decisions. The teaching case should make clear that there is not just one single strategy decision. A business strategy needs to find answers on, for example, business model design, brand positioning, the application of effective marketing tools as well as on international strategy questions. The interrelationships between strategy decisions are important to teach as well. Students often struggle to see the consequences of a single decision as they do not realize direct and indirect links to other strategic elements. A core teaching objective is about: what strategy decisions should be considered and how far are these decisions

Table 6.4   Lecture topics along the strategy process model

Strategy process step:	Core research question:
A general introduction into strategy.	What is strategy about and what dimensions of strategy are relevant (corporate and business levels)?
Strategic analysis of the external market environment.	What is the focused product segment? What market structures (customers, competitors, stakeholders) can be identified and how attractive is the industry?
The research step about the internal company analysis.	The competitiveness of a company – how can this be measured, how well is a company prepared to succeed in a given market?
Development and definition of a system out of strategic objectives.	What objectives play a strategic role, how to define and link them with each other?
The design of a strategic business and marketing concept.	This step is about following questions: a. What business model design should be used? b. How to build up a brand? c. What marketing tools are appropriate to feed the branding concept?, and d. What is the international marketing strategy about?

linked with each other. Table 6.4 shows the chosen entire strategy process model.

6.4.2   The Nespresso Case: Learning Objectives and Core Messages

Strategy! What is strategy. . .?
In the beginning, the teaching case draws the big picture of Nestlé's corporate and business strategies. Here it is important to show that there is a central corporate strategy of Nestlé which is the framework for different business units and divisions (see Figure 6.2). Nespresso itself is a business division within Nestlé's business unit "powered and liquid beverages" (Nestlé, 2018, pp. 14–15). This should highlight the differences between the levels of corporate and business strategy and the purpose of developing single business units and divisions. Nespresso's business units show a clear focus on certain market, product and customer types, which is important to establish a precise business and marketing (customer centric) strategy.

The Nestlé/Nespresso case is very beneficial to show the complexity of steering such a diversified (e.g. in terms of brand, product and international portfolio) company. A strategic triangle can be drawn up: Nestlé's

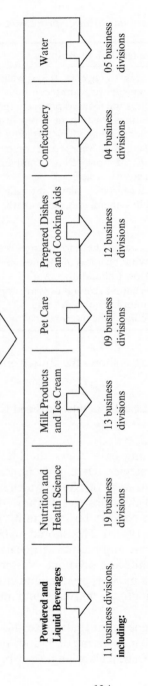

Source: Own figure based on Nestlé, 2018, pp.14–15.

Figure 6.2 Nestlé's business units and divisions within the units

corporate strategy provides the direction for seven business units, which cover 73 business divisions with more than 2,000 single brands.

The Nespresso case also shows how different single business units can be defined, positioned within the market, and managed. For example, whereas Nespresso is positioned as a premium brand within the business area of powered and liquid beverages, the positioning of Nescafé is different (rather in the middle/lower price segment). This exemplifies the benefit of well-defined business units and divisions. It is the basis for the development of strategic concepts and tools according to specific customer and market segment requirements. Contrarily, a vague distinction of business units can lead to an inaccurate strategy and marketing concept.

What is the product, the market and the industry about? How simple questions can turn into very difficult ones

The initial question of the market research step is: what is my underlying market, what customer requirements are focused by my products and finally what are my strategically important competitors? During the market definition process, students get an idea that there are multiple possible solutions. For example, a very coarse-grained market definition would start to look at hot beverages (see Figure 6.3). Of course, this is

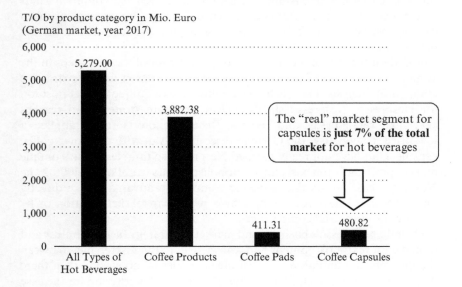

Source: Based on Statista, 2019.

Figure 6.3 From a coarse-grained down to a precise market definition

very unspecific as it would consider coffee, tea and other hot beverages. Different to a pure product-focused market definition, the case follows a definition approach which is focused on the core customer requirements. What is the core customer value of Nespresso and the underlying coffee capsule concept? Students need to answer the question of what kind of consumer problem is solved, and which customer needs are satisfied by Nespresso? Based on the market and segment definitions students have to identify the core customer and competitor groups.

Again, the supposed easy question about customer needs normally turns into a lively discussion in the classroom and it clarifies that market boundaries are linked to individual definitions. For example, should Nespresso's market segment include coffee pad systems and traditional espresso machines, or should they just consider the market segment for coffee capsules? There is no right answer to this question. It depends on the individual company, their brand positioning and self-understanding.

Students may see the question about the market definition as rather trivial for the strategy development process. But during the case study discussion it becomes clearer that the definition is linked to the question: what is my market size and potential and who are the core customers and competitors? Different segment definitions lead to different sales potentials, to different customer target groups as well as to different kinds of competitors. In this context the so-called "marketing myopia" problem can be discussed, which is the result of a pure product-centric market definition.

Based on the market definition and quantification, the next steps in the strategy process model involve customer segmentation and the strategic competitor analysis. The teaching case illustrates a unique market position for Nespresso. Nespresso shows a clear premium strategy and reaches very high retail prices and returns. Recent followers rather applied a low-price strategy (e.g. the German discounter Aldi with their own coffee capsules) but have not really harmed Nespresso so far. Nespresso's unique market position is the basis for monopolistic rents (e.g. Porter, 2006). The Nespresso case shows that strategic competitive advantages are directly linked to uniqueness, for example by a particular market position or by specific resources and competences.

Overall, Nespresso's business and marketing strategy facets are clear and in line with textbook content and knowledge. If the discrepancy between the theoretical foundation and real-life examples is too strong, then there is the risk of misunderstandings. This is an important criterion for the case study selection.

Analysing strategic competitiveness: effective integration of students
How to assess the strategic competitiveness of Nespresso? The case study
is built on a resource analysis. For the application of the VRIO concept,
students need to assess the value of Nespresso from a customer's point of
view. Most students know or are even customers of Nespresso. Therefore,
they can assess the value and benefit of the product. After the evaluation of
certain product criteria (e.g. taste, design of machine, branding, etc.), students need to analyse how far competitors dispose of those resources which
are very important and valuable for customers. Thus, students conduct their
own consumer research and reply to their own questionnaire. Parallel, they
understand and learn about the reasons and secrets for Nespresso's success:
the very effective marketing and branding (as one of the core competences
and resources). The question of imitability underlines the value and strategic
advantage of intangible resources such as the brand. The very size of Nestlé
and the performance of the marketing organization is thematized in terms
of the effectiveness of the company and organizational facets and structures.
Table 6.5 shows the application of the VRIO concept on the case study.

**Strategic objectives: looking into a crystal ball or analytical anticipation of
the future?**
Different forecasting concepts are applied to the Nespresso case, for
example different quantitative trend forecast models (linear, exponential

Table 6.5   VRIO concept and integration of students

VRIO variables	Questions to assess and debate by the class
Valuable resources	From a customer perspective: what core costumer value is provided by Nespresso? Students take over the role of the researcher AND consumer.
Rare resources	Comparison with strategic competitors of Nespresso: is the value provided by Nespresso unique or are other competitors able to provide a similar value? Again, this can be discussed out of a consumer perspective.
Imitable resources	Do Nespresso's competitors without the resource or capability face a competitive disadvantage in developing it versus Nespresso (that already possess it)? Discussion is about the costs to develop similar resources (e.g. brand image).
Organizational implementation	Does Nespresso have an effective organization (control systems, processes, incentives, reporting) to exploit those valuable, rare and inimitable resources?

Source: Based on Barney, 1991.

and logistic trend concepts) complemented by qualitative scenario approaches. In this context you can often recognize a kind of enlighten-ment on the student side. Students often assume a strong correlation between quantitative, mathematical methods and the validity of forecasts. However, the simple selection of a different trend analysis concept (e.g. exponential instead of linear trend model) can have substantial impacts on the forecasting result. The same effect for scenario models – the result depends on the selection and weighting of factors influencing the market size. By that students learn about analytical bias. This is particularly true for the strategy discipline.

Strategic decisions: the complexity of strategy
Core strategic decisions and their alignment are exemplified by the Nespresso case. A core benefit of Nespresso is about the uniqueness and distinction of certain strategic facets and decisions. The teaching case highlights Nespresso's business model design, the brand and marketing concept as well as the international business strategy.

Business model design　A first question is about the business model design. According to that question, the Nespresso case offers an innovative strategic element: the platform business model concept. Platform concepts "... provide the infrastructure and rules for a market place that brings together producers and consumers. The players in the ecosystem fill four main roles but may shift rapidly from one role to another" (Van Alstyne et al., 2016, p. 6). A key aspect of platform products is about network effects, that is, the willingness-to-pay of one market side of the platform increases with the size of the other market side of the platform (Beckmann and Royer, 2016, p. 8). Examples for such two- or more-sided platform markets can often be found in the online world, for example, Uber, eBay or the video game industry.

Even if Nespresso is a tangible product, the business model shows ele-ments of a platform concept: Nespresso is a system out of coffee machines and complementary products (i.e. the coffee capsules) and services (i.e. sales and repair services). Core questions on Nespresso's business model are: what network effects can be identified, what kind of market sides play a role, who is supplying the platform product and complementary products/services, and how are rents generated and distributed between the participation players.

Brand positioning　According to the brand positioning question, the Nespresso case is a very good example of a differentiation, premium branding strategy. Another special feature of Nestlé's/Nespresso's marketing strategy is about its multi-branding approach. Whereas Nespresso is positioned as a premium brand, Nescafé Dolce Gusto is rather positioned in the middle/low price market segment. Both products and brands are focusing on the coffee market. However, there is no real cannibalization as both concepts show a clear segment focus with a different customer-centric marketing approach.

Strategic marketing   The conception of the marketing toolbox is linked to the brand positioning. Again, it is a core teaching aim to show the necessity that marketing instruments must be aligned with the superordinated marketing strategy. A coherent marketing strategy requires certain product, pricing, communication and distribution concepts. For example, a misaligned pricing strategy can disturb brand image and therefore the overall brand positioning. The Nespresso toolbox is consistent and coherent with a premium brand concept. Table 6.6 illustrates core characteristics of Nespresso's marketing mix.

After studying the case study, it becomes clear how far the premium pricing, the product conception and design as well as the communication and unique sales approach are meshing with each other. This again is the backbone of the branding concept and finally one major element of Nespresso's strategic advantage. Students should discuss the unique marketing approach and the strategic consequences, including a debate of alternative solutions.

Table 6.6   Nespresso's unique and consequent marketing concept

Product	Price	Distribution	Communication
• Ecosystem which compromises capsules and coffee machines (plus further complementary services and products). • Sophisticated product and packaging design. • Irradiation strategy to communicate quality leadership.	• Premium pricing strategy. • Strong control on retail pricing. • High price stability.	• Integrated distribution strategy (control and operation by Nespresso). • Effective multi-channel management and control. • High customer loyalty through "Nespresso Club" concept.	• Very successful testimonial strategy with George Clooney. • Very sophisticated communication concept. • Successful differentiation and premium brand strategy.

International business strategy Another strategy puzzle piece is the international business approach. Core teaching questions are: how international marketing strategy can be systematized and analysed (i.e. based on the integration-responsiveness framework), what strategy approaches can be applied (i.e. standardization or differentiation of marketing tools), and finally be implemented. As mentioned before, students need to discuss these questions with regard to the overall strategy framework and business objectives. Like other successful premium brands (such as BMW, Apple or Hugo Boss), Nespresso applies a high level of international standardization of marketing tools (e.g. uniform product, sales and communication approach) with some local adjustments (e.g. pricing).

Finally, all strategic decisions and characteristics of the teaching case (here decisions about the business model, branding, marketing instruments and international approach) are building up a consistent strategy model. It is important to draw this comprehensive picture, to explain the links between single strategy decisions and to build up understanding about the interrelationships.

6.5 REFLECTION AND CONCLUSION

What are the benefits and advantages of the integration of case studies into the teaching concept, especially the use of your own case studies? Benefits could appear in terms of: the level of active student participation and involvement during the semester, the level of knowledge transfer and the development of competences to solve strategic and practice-orientated business problems.

The feedback is consistently positive regarding the course evaluations. Students appreciate the strong link between teaching content and praxis. Feedback indicates that a case study can reduce the abstractness of textbook concepts and theories, and is supporting tangibility. This again is linked to the didactic goal of reaching a high level of clarity and comprehensibility. Furthermore, students are building up problem-solving competences by their active integration into the case study analysis and research process.

In general, students like the didactic concept of teaching strategy by case studies. They appreciate those methods which lead to a stronger interaction between the class and the teacher. A teaching case obviously supports this interaction in an active and lively way. Students expect the use of case studies as a didactical concept – this has obviously become a basic requirement for a contemporary teaching concept.

In addition, the comparison between the use of existing cases and the production of your own case shows the following benefits: very focused alignment of the case study with the teaching content and target group (here students) plus a stronger identification of the teacher with the content, which again supports authenticity. This improves the involvement and motivation levels on the student side. Therefore, writing your own case study is a longer-term investment into your teaching concept and needs to be well prepared. However, positive feedback and teaching results can justify these efforts.

REFERENCES

Barney, J.B. (1991), Firm resources and sustained competitive advantage, *Journal of Management*, Vol. 17, 99–120.

Barney, J.B. and Hesterly, W.S. (2011), *Strategic Management and Competitive Advantage*, London: Prentice Hall, 4th edition.

Beckmann, O. and Royer, S. (2016), *Business Models and the Impact of Different Market Contexts: Towards an analytical framework for researchers and practitioners*, Sønderborg/KoldingFlensburg / Sønderborg/Kolding, Danish-German Research Paper No. 5, International Institute of Management and Economic Education (IIM), Europa-Universität Flensburg and Department of Entrepreneurship and Relationship Management, University of Southern Denmark.

Brew, A. (2003), Teaching and research: new relationships and their implications for inquiry-based teaching and learning in higher education, *Higher Education Research and Development*, Vol. 2, No. 1, 3–18.

Chakrabarti, D. and Balaji, M.S. (2007), Perception of faculty on case study method of teaching in management education: An empirical study, *The Icfaian Journal of Management Research*, Vol. VI, No. 10, 7–22.

Cockburn, A. (2000), *Writing Effective Use Cases. Addison-Wesley*, Upper Saddle River, NJ: Prentice Hall.

Hawes, J.M. (2004), Teaching is not telling: The case method as a form of interactive learning, *Journal of Advancement of Marketing Education*, Vol. 5, 47–54.

Jennings, D. (1996), Strategic management and the case method, *Journal of Management Development*, Vol. 15, No. 9, 4–12.

Nestlé (2018), *Annual Review 2018: Nestlé. Enhancing quality of life and contributing to a healthier future*, accessed November 24, 2019 at www.nestle.com/sites/default/ files/asset-library/documents/library/documents/annual_reports/2018-annual-rev iew-en.pdf.

Neuman, R. (1994), The teaching–research nexus: Applying a framework to university student's learning experiences, *European Journal of Education*, Vol. 19, No. 3, 323–338.

Peterson, H.C. (1996), Integrating decision cases into the design of courses, *Journal of Agribusiness*, Vol. 14, No. 2, 183–196.

Porter, M. (2006), *Wettbewerbsstrategie: Methoden zur Analyse von Branchen und Konkurrenten* = Competitive strategy, Frankfurt am Main: Campus Verlag, 11th edition.

Statista (2019), *Statista-Dossier zum Markt für Heißgetränke*, accessed October 24, 2019 at https://de.statista.com/statistik/studie/id/41262/dokument/heissgetraenke -statista-dossier.

Strach, P. and Everett, A.M. (2008), Transforming research case studies into teaching cases, *Qualitative Research in Organizations and Management: An International Journal*, Vol. 3, No. 3, 199–214.

Van Alstyne, M.W., Parker, G.G. and Choudary, S.P. (2016), Pipelines, platforms and the new rules of strategy, *Harvard Business Review*, accessed February 29, 2020 at https://hbr.org/2016/04/pipelines-platforms-and-the-new-rules-of-strategy.

Volpe, G. (2002), *Case Studies. The Hand Book for Economic Lecturers*, accessed October 24, 2019 at www.economicsnetwork.ac.uk/handbook/printable/case studies_v5.pdf.

Yin, R.K. (2014), *Case Study Research, Design and Methods*, London: Sage Publications, 5th edition.

7. Interactive exercises, peer coaching, and videos in strategic management education

Sabine Reisinger

7.1 INTERACTIVE METHODS IN STRATEGIC MANAGEMENT COURSES

The skills and learning characteristics of students have changed vastly over the last two decades that I have been teaching strategic management. The traditional classroom formats in their own way no longer correspond to the preferences and learning needs of the students of the twenty-first century (Generations Y and Z). Nor does the Nth edition of textbooks with overused models and cases support students to develop the strategic competences needed to run a business in today's digitized, highly connected, globalized world (Eason et al., 2019; Swanzen, 2018) without adequate adjustments and extensions. With the aim of aligning my courses more closely with the characteristics of today's students and the demands of the business world, I have integrated interactive methods into all my strategic management courses (Bachelor's, Master's and Leadership).

Grant and Baden-Fuller (2018) recommend that the emphasis of a core strategic management course should be on application, which is based on theories, concepts and analytical tools. In this chapter I describe two interactive teaching designs for strategic management courses (section 7.2) which follow this advice (see Figure 7.1). They combine theory, concepts and interactivity in a form that makes it easier for students of the twenty-first century to dive into the complexity of strategic management. In addition, I present an interactive toolbox (section 7.3) which contains a number of methods to adapt existing courses to the learning styles of Generation Y and Z.

Teaching strategic management is a challenging task that is often insufficiently handled, as shown by the numerous calls for more relevant and practicable strategic courses (Albert & Grzeda, 2015; Grant, 2008; Mintzberg, 2004; Ungaretti et al., 2015). By integrating interactive

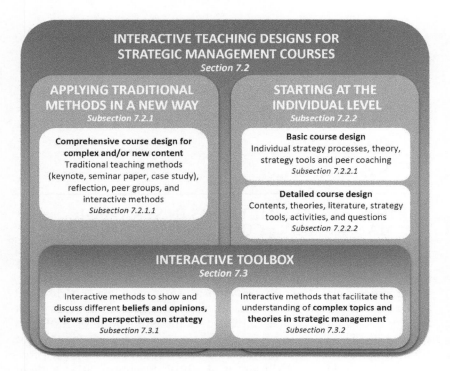

Figure 7.1   Interactive teaching designs for strategy classes

methods and cutting-edge research, such neglect of practical relevance can be overcome. This does not necessarily require radical changes or large expenditure; in many cases, the thoughtful use of interactive methods and the inclusion of new concepts and theories is sufficient to enable students to acquire the required competencies. For this purpose I present tried and tested interactive methods that can be integrated in an existing strategy course to show and discuss different beliefs and opinions, views and perspectives on strategy (subsection 7.3.1) or to facilitate the understanding of complex issues in strategic management (subsection 7.3.2).

Modern technologies allow the use of most interactive methods in the classroom and/or online. However, when designing a strategic management course, the advantages and disadvantages of presence and online activities should be taken into account. For example, interactive exercises in a presence session allow direct contact and a more diverse perception. The classroom enables personal contact that allows the teacher to supervise teamwork and push students forward (Jaskari & Jaskari, 2016).

Alternatively, online activities are not restricted to a certain place or time and may provide anonymity. Their effective use, however, requires motivation, commitment and initiative. As Jaskari and Jaskari (2016, p. 180) report, "students who are not motivated in the classroom do not become motivated on the Web, especially when the focus is on complex and uncertain matters." Since complexity is inherent in most strategic issues, interactive presence activities are often better than interactive online activities. Notwithstanding this, current students have a high technical literacy (Hunter-Jones, 2012; Swanzen, 2018). Integrating current technology, smartphones, social media and social networks into interactive learning is commensurate with the learning styles of digital natives.

In addition, the current student generation mostly access their information online, they are active on social networks, and trust their peer communities. Therefore, peer-to-peer exchange of information is an appropriate learning form for Generation Y and Z. Peer-to-peer exchange can be used as an alternative form to teacher–student exchange (Bell et al., 2018). It can enhance students' engagement, social development, and critical thinking (Jaskari & Jaskari, 2016; MacGregor et al., 2000). In particular, when students spend a whole term in one peer group, interacting, working and reflecting together, mutual trust grows and a safe learning environment emerges (Hooker, 2015; Ladyshewsky, 2007). In such a peer group, students can freely express their views, test ideas, apply strategy tools, articulate observations and reflect on them. Thereby, they develop the listening and communication skills essential for strategy work, especially when it comes to enacting strategies successfully (Grant & Baden-Fuller, 2018; Lindsay et al., 2018). Section 7.2 describes two strategic management course designs employing peer groups. In the first, peer groups complement traditional teaching methods, ensuring that even in large classes all students can be (inter)active. The second course design uses peer groups for peer coaching within the framework of individual strategy processes. In this setting, each student takes on different roles (coach, coachee, reflecting partner) in order to support each other, practice together and reflect with each other. Critical success factors for the peer coaching relationship are confidentiality, mutual respect, trust, honesty, communication skills as well as the students' background knowledge and their social competencies (Hagen et al., 2017; Hooker, 2015).

Peer coaching can be used to enhance the depth of learning and expand communication and reflection skills (Ladyshewsky, 2006, 2007). Benefits of peer coaching result from the non-judgmental nature of a peer coaching relationship (Hooker, 2015; Ladyshewsky, 2007), shaping a safe learning environment in which students can verify and grow their own knowledge base and expand their skills and competences. However, the efficiency and effectiveness of peer coaching can be limited by lack of experience (Hooker, 2015), prejudice, or advice from the coach (Hagen et al., 2017). For inexperienced groups, it may therefore be advantageous to teach basic coaching skills in advance of actual peer coaching experiences with strategy tools. After all, this course should allow students to make strategy tools useful for themselves and their strategies.

If students can apply concepts, frameworks and strategy tools in a context that is relevant to them, they not only gain initial experience, they also experience their benefits and limitations immediately. This makes comprehensive case studies, real cases, and online cases very popular in strategic teaching. Experience is a foundation of learning, or in other words, "all learning is experiential" (Bird, 2015, p. 3). Underpinning this experience with concise yet high-quality theoretical explanations can help students to reflect deeper on the power and restrictions of the applied strategy tools and the underlying theories (Bell et al., 2018; Grant & Baden-Fuller, 2018). Applying strategy tools for themselves makes the task even more relevant than learning and discussing it along with case studies or on a purely theoretical basis. Therefore, the motivation to learn and to take responsibility for their own learning is higher (Jaskari & Jaskari, 2016; Priem, 2018). The next section describes two interactive teaching designs in detail.

7.2   INTERACTIVE TEACHING DESIGNS

Interactive teaching designs for strategic management courses help students gain conceptual and analytical as well as procedural, metacognitive and affective knowledge. This is essential to diagnose strategic problems, generate and select among strategic options, or implement strategy (Bell et al., 2018). According to Grant and Baden-Fuller (2018), conceptual knowledge (theories, concepts, and strategy tools) has to be complemented by judgment, insight, intuition, creativity, and the capacity to interact with other people. In order to build up such strategic, personal and interpersonal competencies it is necessary to practice and to reflect on experiences with regard to theory. Interactive strategic management courses can support students to develop the required competencies (Albert & Grzeda, 2015; Grant & Baden-Fuller, 2018; Jaskari & Jaskari, 2016).

In this section, two interactive teaching designs for strategic management courses are described in detail. The first comprehensive course design is suitable to teach complex theories and concepts of strategy and/or new subjects like platform industries, value networks or business ecosystems. "Applying traditional methods in a new way" employs traditional teaching methods like keynotes, seminar papers, case studies in combination with reflection, peer groups, and interactive methods. The second course design "starts at the individual level" and allows students to use strategy tools for themselves. They discuss key perspectives of strategic management, gain experience in the context of their strategy processes and reflect upon them with regard to the underlying theory. Throughout this course, peer coaching is used as an interactive learning and reflection method. Both teaching designs use interactive methods, which are described in more detail in section 7.3.

7.2.1   Applying Traditional Methods in a New Way

This strategic course design is based upon well-known and proven teaching methods as well as interactive methods, peer groups, and reflection that effectively activate and guide students in their learning process. The overall objective is to make students better strategists. This is achieved by actively engaging students in a variety of ways with different theories, concepts and strategy tools and/or by addressing current and emerging issues in various ways. In combination with intensive reflection this experience helps students to develop their cognitive and behavioral skills relevant for strategy formulation and implementation (Albert & Grzeda, 2015; Priem, 2018).

Indeed, interactive activities, critical reflection and feedback are at the heart of learning in this course. Therefore, in-class time is reserved for students to actively engage in knowledge construction through interactions with peers and teachers (Bergmann & Sams, 2012, 2014; Priem, 2018). In class, students reflect theories, clarify concepts, and express different opinions, question perspectives and views of strategy. In order to make these activities worthwhile, students must come to class prepared (Kim et al., 2014; Priem, 2018), which is ensured by assignments such as written seminar papers or written case analyses.

7.2.1.1   Comprehensive course design for complex and/or new content
The learning objectives of this course design are to help students to develop:

- a knowledge base regarding the specific topic(s) of the course,
- analytical and critical thinking skills in order to apply them to strategic decisions,
- methodological skills, strategic and personal competences and social skills, and
- a basic understanding of the power and limitations of respective concepts and tools.

The tried and tested combination of different methods is based on the foundations of the flipped classroom (Bergmann & Sams, 2012, 2014), reflection-based teaching (Albert & Grzeda, 2015) and incorporates the benefits of peer groups (Jaskari & Jaskari, 2016; MacGregor et al., 2000). Table 7.1 explains the sequence of the individual steps, the use of the different methods and the respective learning objectives. The learning objective (first insights, theory and concepts, practice and experience, feedback & reflection), the task and group size (plenum, peer group, individual task), and the estimated time required (<15 minutes, 15–30 minutes, 30–45 minutes, >45 minutes) are described for each individual step.

This course can be used for working on fundamental topics of strategic management or for dealing with the very latest ideas from the business world and the scientific community. It also allows a combination of both. In this way, strategy teachers can include those topics that are relevant for making and executing strategy in today's digital, increasingly interconnected world.

This interactive course design uses a combination of methods that encourages students to bring theory to practice, to reflect on their own knowledge base, and to grow their strategy knowledge, skills and competencies. It acknowledges the importance of theory (Buckley, 2018; Grant, 2008), the relevance of practice and experience (Janasz & Crossman, 2018; Lindsay et al., 2018; Taras & Gonzalez-Perez, 2015), and the importance of reflection (Albert & Grzeda, 2015; Dyer & Hurd, 2016) to develop the strategic competences of students (Grant & Baden-Fuller, 2018).

7.2.2 Starting at the Individual Level

"Starting at the individual level" follows a learner-centric teaching philosophy in incentivizing and guiding students in their learning (Kim et al., 2014; Rotellar & Cain, 2016; Welsh & Dehler, 2012). The overall objective is to make the course valuable in manifold ways to every student. To achieve this, each student applies strategy tools for his or her own life, guides peers in the use of strategy tools and acts as a reflective partner for his or her colleagues. Through the repeated use of a strategy tool, students get to know the tool, its potential applications and its requirements. In doing so, they can expand their knowledge, develop their skills and critically question the theoretical foundations of a strategy tool.

7.2.2.1 Basic course design
The learning objectives of this specific course are to help students to develop:

Table 7.1 Applying traditional methods in a new way – comprehensive course design

Methods	Utilization in a course	Learning objectives	Task / group size	Time
		First insights	Plenum	<15 mins
		Theory and concepts	Peer group	15–30 mins
		Practice and experience	Individual task	30–45 mins
		Feedback and reflection		>45 mins
Introduction to a new topic	Opening: First short insights into a new and complex strategic management topic (theory, concept, view).			
	Individual question: What answers would I like to find on this topic?			
	Peer group discussion:			
	→ What do we already know?			
	→ What are our opinions, beliefs and experiences?			
	→ What else would we like to learn?			
	Closing: Discussion of central group results and open questions in plenary. Interactive methods like "opinion poll" or "opinion line" may be beneficial to visualize different point of views.			
Seminar paper (1)	Seminar paper: Building or expansion of knowledge base in relation to a topic through literature research and writing a seminar paper (first draft).			Homework
	Self-evaluation: Criteria-led reflection of the seminar paper (first draft).			

139

Table 7.1 (*continued*)

Methods	Utilization in a course	Learning objectives	Task / group size	Time
	Peer-evaluation: Peers give each other feedback on their seminar papers.			
	Fish bowl discussion (Option A) or market of possibilities (Option B): Main content of the seminar papers and findings from the self- and peer-evaluation process are presented and discussed.			
	Reflection: Relevance of the results from the evaluations and the fish bowl for the revision of the seminar papers.			
Strategy tool and case study (1)	Presentation: Explanation of the case study (and if necessary the case study method) with reference to the theory.			Homework
	Case study: Apply the theory/tools to the case study and write a report.			
Keynote regarding a complex topic	Presentation: Lecture on main aspects of the treated strategic management topic (theory, concept, view).			
	Peer group discussion (Option A) or World café (Option B):		Option A	Option A
	→ What did we learn from the presentation? What is interesting?			
	→ What else do we already know?		Option B	Option B
	→ Is the presentation relevant for the seminar paper or the case study?			
	→ Is there something we did not understand or that we still do not know?			

Homework

Depends on size of class and method

Closing: Reflection (thoughts, opinions and questions) on the presented content and its relevance for the seminar paper and the case study.

Seminar paper (2) Revision of seminar paper: Based on the feedback of peers and the insights from the discussion/ world café.

Self-assessment: Criteria-led self-assessment of the seminar paper.

Video and knowledge map: Peer-groups create a video and a knowledge map of the contents and arguments of their seminar papers.

Videos and knowledge maps: Three peer-groups combine their knowledge in one map. They select the best video and prepare a traditional presentation (Option A) of the map in plenary or in a more interactive form like a "market of opportunities" (Option B),

Presentation and discussion: Knowledge maps (topics, arguments, authors, etc.) and videos are presented (Option A) or exhibited and visited (Option B) and discussed.

Reflection and closing: Learnings from writing and assessing seminar papers. Evaluation of the usability and challenges of knowledge maps.

Strategy tool and case study (2) Peer self-evaluation: Criteria-led self-assessment of the case study paper.

Preparation of a pitch: Peer groups select their best arguments and prepare themselves to introduce them to a management board.

Note: 1–2 groups take on the role of the management board of the case.

141

Table 7.1 (continued)

Methods	Utilization in a course	Learning objectives	Task / group size	Time
	Pitch session: 3–5 minutes pitches of each peer group to the management board (1–2 peer groups).			Depends on size of class
	Peer-reflection:			
	→ Management board: evaluates presented arguments/ideas.			
	→ Pitchers: reflect on their pitch in comparison to other groups.			
	Closing: Management board informs about their evaluation.			
	Plenary reflection on pitches, with regard to strategy tool and theory.			
Summary and reflection on a topic	Individual question: What answers have I found on this topic?			
	Executive summary: Prepare an executive summary of the content and upload it to the learning platform.			
	→ What did we learn about the topic?			
	→ To what extent were the seminar paper, the case study, the keynote, the discussions and the other exercises interlinked?			
	→ Have our opinions changed throughout the learning process?			
	→ Is there something we have not understood or where we have not yet found an answer?			
	Award for the best executive summary: Assessment by students using voting software (e.g. www.mentimeter.com).			
	Closing: Summary and reflection of the learnings from the different course elements (seminar paper, case study, keynotes, discussions, reflections, and interactive exercises).			

- a fundamental knowledge base on key concepts of strategic management,
- critical and analytical thinking, in order to be able to use appropriate strategy tools,
- methodological skills, strategic and personal competences and social skills,
- a strategy for oneself, and a plan to implement it.

The course begins with a general introduction to strategy and basic information on peer coaching (see Table 7.2). After that, the actual strategy process starts with the strategic analysis, followed by strategy formulation, strategy implementation and strategic evaluation. Table 7.2 describes the basic activities in each session. The details for each step (theory, literature, strategy tools and useful questions) can be found in Table 7.3. The course ends with a comprehensive reflection of the entire strategy process and the experiences and insights gained throughout the process.

Table 7.2 provides the basic course description including learning objectives (experience first insights, theory and strategy tool, practice and experience, think and evaluate) and the estimated time required (<15 minutes, 15–30 minutes, 30–45 minutes, >45 minutes).

Experiencing the activities within the strategy processes enables students to develop an understanding and empathy for the micro-level complexity of strategy and how individual action and interaction can influence strategic outcome (Felin et al., 2015; Lindsay et al., 2018). Applying strategy tools in three different individual strategy processes encourages students to reflect deeply on their experiences with the strategy tools, the underlying theories and assumptions and the different contexts. Such a process allows for deep learning (Albert & Grzeda, 2015; Dyer & Hurd, 2016) and can motivate students to delve more deeply into strategic management (Priem, 2018).

7.2.2.2   Detailed course design

The strategic management community shares a broad consensus that there is no one best way to design a strategy process (Barney & Mackey, 2018; Mintzberg et al., 1998; Reisinger et al., 2017). Therefore, this course design uses a variety of theories, concepts, and strategy tools to help students formulate their strategy and prepare for its implementation. In order to cope with the complexity of strategic management, the course follows a planning-oriented approach without neglecting other important perspectives and insights.

During the process, students use a variety of strategy tools in their roles as coach, coachee and reflecting partner. The application enables first

Table 7.2   Starting at the individual level – basic course design

Starting at the individual level: course description		Learning objectives	Time
		✈ Experience first insights	◔ <15 mins
		📖 Theory and strategy tool	◑ 15–30 mins
		🕴 Practice and experience	◕ 30–45 mins
		✅❌❓ Think and evaluate	◔ >45 mins
General introduction to the individual strategy process	Opening: First insights on strategy (content, context and process) with regard to a firm and to an individual. First explanation of different forms of strategy processes (deliberate strategy and emergent strategy). Peer groups: Invite students to form peer groups with three students each. These peer groups stay together for the entire individual strategy process. It may be useful to address issues such as trust, heterogeneity and prior knowledge. First peer group discussion: → *What is your personal experience with strategy and planning?* → *Do you think that effective strategies are planned or that effective strategies evolve from day to day business? Why?* First plenary discussion: Results from peer group discussion, enriched with basic theories regarding strategy processes with regard to the upcoming individual strategy process. Interactive methods like "opinion poll" or "opinion line" may be beneficial to visualize different point of views.	✈ 🕴 📖	◔ ◑ ◔

144

Explanation of the individual strategy process:

Basic information about the main steps of the strategy process, the underlying theories, and the strategy tools to be applied.

↑ Strategic analysis (external and internal environment)
↑ Strategy formulation and evaluating strategies
↑ Strategy implementation and strategic change
↑ Strategic evaluation and performance measurement

Explanation of the peer coaching method:

Information about the coaching process, the different and altering roles (coach, coachee and reflecting partner) within the process, as well as supportive and hindering attitudes during the individual strategy process.

Activities in each session

Opening in plenary:

Brief explanation of a strategy tool and the respective theory. The focus of the explanation lies in the use of the tool in the individual strategy process and the specific procedure in the process. The students receive a handout with a brief explanation of the tool, the procedure and helpful questions.

Individual strategy process:

Application of a strategy tool on the individual-level (15–20 minutes each) guided by a peer coach and a peer-reflecting partner. The coach uses a handout to guide the coachee with helpful questions.

Each student will take each role (coach, coachee, and reflecting partner).

Round 1:	Round 2:	Round 3:
A = coach	A = reflecting partner	A = coachee (client)
B = coachee (client)	B = coach	B = reflecting partner
C = reflecting partner	C = coachee (client)	C = coach

Feedback and comparison of learnings and findings within the peer group.

145

Table 7.2 (continued)

Starting at the individual level: course description	Learning objectives	Time
Closing in plenary: 1. Reflection on experiences with the strategy tool on the individual level. 2. Discussion of potential benefits and pitfalls with reference to the theory. 3. Discussion of the suitability of the tool for different companies, situations, and environments.	☑ ☒ ?	◐
Reflection and Closing At the end of the final part of the strategy process, the students are invited to reflect on their experiences and learnings during the strategy process. → *What are our learnings from the individual strategy processes?* → *What benefits and pitfalls did we experience during the processes?* → *Which strategy tools are especially helpful in the individual setting? Why?* → *Which strategy tools and theories are particularly beneficial for which firms in which environments and in which situations?* A fish bowl discussion is a suitable format to summarize and discuss the experiences and learnings within the peer groups.	📖 ☑ ☒ ?	◕

experiences and allows their reflection in relation to strategic management theories. The role of the teacher is to support students in their interactive learning process. She or he gives basic information about the strategy tools, provides useful questions for the coaches, reflects on the findings and adds theoretical input. Table 7.3 provides suggestions for the whole process and the individual steps.

Working on their own strategy in peer groups motivates students to apply strategy tools, reflect on their experience and learn. Instead of dealing with theories, concepts and tools "only for school," they can use them for their own life. Thereby, they experience the advantages and disadvantages of various strategic instruments and learn about their effects and implications. They can reflect their experiences during the strategy process and the underlying theories and assumptions. This allows a deeper understanding of the fundamental differences and sometimes contradictory explanations within the strategic management literature (Barney & Mackey, 2018), a prerequisite to understanding which strategy tools are adequate for which organization and in which environment.

7.3   INTERACTIVE TOOLBOX FOR STRATEGIC MANAGEMENT COURSES

This interactive toolbox for strategy courses includes interactive methods to show and discuss different beliefs and opinions, views and perspectives on strategy (subsection 7.3.1) and interactive methods that facilitate the understanding of complex topics and theories in strategic management (subsection 7.3.2). Most of the methods can be used in class and/or online.

Interactive teaching methods allow students to engage emotionally and cognitively in their learning. Drawing on evidence from the field of neuroscience Grant and Baden-Fuller (2018) show that the development of cognitive capabilities is critically dependent on emotional development. Thus, the level of emotion present in an activity or experience affects the intensity and sustainability of the learning experience (Bird, 2015, p. 7). Therefore, it is worth the time and effort to integrate some of the interactive methods presented in this section in a strategy course.

7.3.1   Interactive Methods – Beliefs, Opinions, and Perspectives

Interactive methods can be helpful in identifying and discussing different beliefs, opinions and perspectives in class or online. They can be useful to gain insight into basic debates in the discipline of strategic management,

Table 7.3 Starting at the individual level – detailed course design

Content/Theory	Strategy tool	Procedure/Steps	Useful questions
Strategic analysis Internal and external environment Recommended Literature → The strategic position (Johnson et al., 2017) → The tools of strategy analysis (Grant, 2019) → The stakeholder approach (Carroll et al., 2016)	**Core competence analysis** Based on Prahalad & Hamel (1990) Alternative tool: **VRIO/VRIN** (Barney, 1995) **Stakeholder analysis** Based on (Carroll et al., 2016) Alternative tool: **Typology of stake-holder attributes** (Mitchell et al., 1997)	**Determine your situation** 1. Define the main elements of your individual competence tree. 2. Determine your core competences. 3. Check the ratio of roots and leaves/fruits. 4. Discover the potential of your core competencies. **Analyze your stakeholders** 1. Determine your relevant stakeholders. 2. Describe their respective demands toward you. 3. Identify potential opportunities and risks. 4. Define your own responsibility. 5. Discover suitable starting points and approaches.	→ What are your particular strengths? Do you have unique skills? What can you do especially well? → What are the results of your activities? Where are you successful? → What are your core competences? → How is the ratio of roots and leaves/fruits? → Can you use your core competencies in another way? → Who is important for you? Who has expectations of you? → What do the individual stakeholders want? → What are their claims on you? → How can you be supported or hindered by individual stakeholders? → What do you want to do for your stakeholders? What is your responsibility to your stakeholders? → What can you do to satisfy the needs of your stakeholders?
Strategy formulation Processes of generating strategic options Evaluating strategies and strategic decision-making processes	**Strategy journey to the future** Based on Hagen and Hauser (2008) Alternative tool: **Competence matrix** (Hamel & Prahalad, 1994)	**Imagine and formulate your vision/ strategy** 1. Make yourself comfortable and close your eyes. 2. Imagine we are beaming into a perfect future now. Everything worked great for you. You have	**Visualize the future image of yourself:** → Where are you? → How do you look? → How do you feel? → How are you living? → What is important to you in life? → Who is with you?

Recommended Literature	achieved more than you have ever dreamed of, professionally and personally.	→ What are you doing?
		→ What have you achieved?
→ Strategies choices and evaluating strategies (Johnson et al., 2017)	3. Describe your situation in this marvelous future.	→ What are you working on?
→ Strategy formulation (Wheelen et al., 2017)	4. Come back to the present and see how this image fits your vision/ strategy.	**Verify the image of the future:**
		→ Is the image of your future surprising to you?
		→ To what extent does the image fit your assumed vision/strategy?

SAFe +	**Assess your vision/strategy**	→ Can you capitalize opportunities and avert risks with this vision/strategy?
Based on Johnson et al. (2017)	1. Evaluate the suitability of your vision/strategy: does it address key opportunities and threats?	→ Can you best use your resources and skills through this vision/strategy?
Alternative tool: **Scenario analysis** (Schwenker & Wulf, 2013)	2. Assess the acceptability of your vision/strategy for your stakeholders.	→ What benefits do stakeholders have of your vision/strategy? Can you fulfill stakeholder expectations?
	3. Evaluate the feasibility of your vision/strategy: Can it actually work in practice?	→ Which stakeholders will actively support or hinder your strategy?
	4. Check if your vision/strategy is lawful and meets legal requirements.	→ Is the vision/strategy fundamentally feasible, can it work in practice?
		→ Is the information available to assess the vision/strategy sufficient?
		→ Do you have enough resources and skills to realize your vision/strategy, or can you acquire them?
		→ Can your vision/strategy be realized within the given legal framework?

Change Kaleidoscope (context factors)	**Analyze the context of change and learn about your scope for action**	Time: How much time is available? How soon is change needed?
Based on Balogun et al. (2016)	1. Identify the contextual factors (time, scope, preservation, diversity, capability, capacity, readiness, power) for your vision/ strategy.	Scope: What degree of change is required? How much has to change to realize your vision/ strategy?
Alternative tool: **8-Steps-Model** (Kotter, 2012)		

Strategy implementation
Strategic change: context, challenges, and levers of change
Change path, change targets, and activities

Table 7.3 (continued)

Content/Theory	Strategy tool	Procedure/Steps	Useful questions
Recommended Literature → Strategy in Action (Johnson et al., 2017) → Exploring Strategic Change (Balogun et al., 2016) → Leading Change (Kotter, 2012)		2. Define which factors are particularly noteworthy in your change kaleidoscope. 3. Find the bottleneck factors. They are of particular importance in determining the path of change.	Preservation: What has to be preserved? Which resources, skills, and characteristics need to be maintained? Diversity: How heterogeneous is your environment? Are you used to dealing with different people and situations? Capability: What experiences do you have with change? Do you have the capability to lead yourself and others? Capacity: How many resources do you have available for the change? Please consider needs in your daily life. Readiness: Are you ready for change? What is the level of suffering already? Power: What power do you have to impose change? Who are the powerful? Which persons (groups) can influence the process positively or negatively?
Change Kaleidoscope (change path) Based on Balogun et al. (2016) Alternative tool: **8-Steps-Model** (Kotter, 2012)		**Prepare implementation** 1. Define the change path from today to the day your strategy is to be realized. 2. Determine intermediate goals and define how you will celebrate them. 3. Define specific activities. Important: Plan the first steps to success in detail.	→ When should your vision/strategy be realized? → How much time to you need to implement it? → Are there important milestones? → Which intermediate goals do you want to reach when? → How do you celebrate the achievement of the intermediate goals? → What specific activities and measures do you take when?

Strategic evaluation
Performance targets and measurement
Recommended Literature
→ Measuring business strategy (Kaplan & Norton, 1996)
→ Evaluation and control (Wheelen et al., 2017)

Balanced Scorecard
Based on Kaplan & Norton (1996)
Alternative tool:
Intellectual Capital
(Roos & Pike, 2018)

4. Consider potential obstacles and disruptive factors and find alternative ways to fulfil your goals.
5. Review your change path with respect to the eight contextual factors.

Control implementation
1. Starting point: your vision/strategy.
2. Define the four perspectives of your balanced scorecard.
3. Derive strategic goals for each perspective.
4. Recognize cause-and-effect relationships.
5. Select measures and define targets for each perspective.
6. Define specific activities and measures in order to reach your strategic goals.

→ What are your first steps to success? What exactly will you do when?
→ What obstacles and disruptive factors can occur? What activities would then have to be undertaken?
→ Is the planned change path realistic in view of the given context factors?
→ What is your vision/strategy?
→ What are the four perspectives of your balanced scorecard?
  – What stands for stability/continuity?
  – What stands for change/learning?
  – Who are your key stakeholders?
  – What processes are important for you?
→ What strategic goals can guide you to realize your vision/strategy?
→ Can you identify cause-and-effect relationships?
→ How will you measure your progress and what targets do you want to achieve?
→ What activities do you plan to reach your strategic goals?
→ How do you and your stakeholders assess your current position?
→ What do you have to achieve so that your stakeholders are satisfied?

such as the source of competitive advantage and understanding which theory is suitable in which strategy context (Barney & Mackey, 2018).

Table 7.4 describes four interactive methods (opinion poll, opinion line, strategy debate, and fish bowl) and their potential application in a strategy course in detail. These include a short description, the specific procedure, the possible group sizes (<10, 10–30, >30), the learning objectives (experience first insights, practice and experience, repeat and learn, think and evaluate), and the estimated time required to use the method in class.

Interactive methods help strategic management teachers to engage all their students and encourage the reflection on controversial issues. Attention should be paid to the specific learning characteristics and requirements of Generation Y and Z (e.g. need for feedback, digital affinity).

7.3.2   Interactive Methods – Complex Topics

Complexity is inherent in strategic issues. Therefore, strategic management students need to develop an ability to cope with paradoxes and ambiguity in strategic decision-making (Bell et al., 2018) and the micro-level complexity of strategy implementation (Lindsay et al., 2018). The interactive methods described in detail in Table 7.5 (visualization, world café, knowledge maps, market of possibilities, explanation video, executive summary) allow a teacher to expand the students' knowledge of a comprehensive strategy topic or a comprehensive theory continuously.

The table shows the basic options to integrate these integrative methods in a strategy course. It offers detailed description of the procedure, informs about possible group sizes (<10, 10–30, >30), learning goals (experience first insights, practice and experience, repeat and learn, think and evaluate), and the estimated time required to use the method in class.

Interactive exercises (in class or online), contemporary forms of communication (social media, YouTube, videos), and information generation (Internet, Google) make it easier for students of the twenty-first century to get involved in the complex world of strategic management and to deal with the sheer amount of different theories, concepts and strategy tools. Therefore, if students are to become strong strategists, it is worthwhile to use interactive methods and new technologies in a course on strategic management. This is in line with the opinion of Bell et al. (2018), guest editors of the special issue of the *Academy of Management Learning & Education* regarding "Opportunities and Challenges for Advancing Strategic Management Education." They argue that management educators should explore the combination of different methods in their strategy courses to meet the new challenges resulting from rapid technological changes and the specific needs of today's students (Generations Y and Z).

Table 7.4 Interactive methods to show and discuss different beliefs, opinions, and perspectives

Interactive Methods: Description and procedure	Group size	Learning objectives	Time
	<10	Experience first insights	<15 mins
	10-30	Practice and experience	15–30 mins
	>30	Repeat and learn	30-45 mins
		Think and evaluate	>45 mins

Opinion poll (online or in class)

Lecturers and students immediately gain an understanding of the current range of opinion in the audience by using anonymous real-time polls. Interactive tools such as mentimeter.com help to make different opinions quickly and easily visible for everyone.

1. Prepare the online opinion poll in advance.
2. Start the presentation of the opinion poll online or in class.
3. Students are invited to vote anonymously on a voting website.
4. The results can be displayed in real-time or hidden until everybody is finished and then displayed to the audience.
5. Discuss the results of the opinion poll with the students and explain their relevance for the strategy topic covered.

The method can be applied as a starting point for an in-depth discussion of different views of strategy.

An opinion poll can also be used for a resume at the end of a session on different views or theories.

Opinion line (in class)

This holistic method allows a simple body-related demonstration of different points of view. An opinion line makes the range of opinions visible and tangible and shows the diversity of a group. The method helps to show that there are different perspectives or solutions.

The method is suitable to reveal presets and beliefs. It can be applied as a starting

Table 7.4 (continued)

Interactive Methods: Description and procedure	Group size	Learning objectives	Time

Students can discover where they stand compared to their colleagues regarding a specific topic. Lecturers immediately receive information about the extent of heterogeneity within the group.

1. Prepare two signs with opposing statements.
2. Position them at the opposite walls of the room and explain the two opposite poles. You can mark the middle of the room too.
3. Invite the students to position themselves physically along the line between the two poles according to their opinion.
4. Interview some of the students, why they have chosen a specific position. Start your interviews at one end of the line, continue at the other end and conclude in the middle of the line.
5. Discuss the homogeneity vs. heterogeneity of the group and its relevance in terms of perspectives and theories.

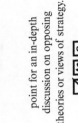

point for an in-depth discussion on opposing theories or views of strategy.

An opinion line can also be used to conclude such a session and visualize different views at the end of a session.

Strategy debate (online or in class)

Students have the opportunity to find arguments for and against a strategy perspective or theory. A debate can be held with or without reference to a particular company. Possible topics/questions could be, for example:

→ Is a specific strategic management theory suitable in a digitized and increasingly linked world (in general or for a particular firm)?

→ What strategy perspective (e.g. resource-based view (RBV)) vs. market-based view (MBV)) is for a (specific) firm better suited to stay competitive in a volatile, uncertain, complex, and ambiguous (VUCA) environment?

A moderator (lecturer or a qualified student) leads the debate. An open debate allows the students to discuss their views of a specific topic. A guided debate is led by prepared questions.

1. Divide the class in groups of 3 to 5 students.
2. Each group prepares their arguments and designates two people to participate in the discussion (20–30 minutes).

A debate allows students to think about a controversial topic and argue one of the two sides. In order to be able to discuss a specific theory or view of strategy, students should be familiar with its main aspects.

A controlled exchange of arguments allows the students

3. The moderator invites two groups (two persons each) to sit opposite each other at a table.

4. The moderator explains the rules (time restriction, should be between 30 and 60 seconds; rounds, should be between 5 and 10).

5. The debate starts when the moderator gives the floor to one side. After the predetermined period of time the other side can answer and so on. After the last round of arguments, the moderator ends the debate.

6. Reflection on the debate in plenary.

Fish bowl (in class)

A fish bowl is a simple but dynamic alternative to a panel discussion or strategy debate. It helps to structure a discussion and involve all students. The advantage of a fish bowl is that it allows the entire group to participate in a conversation.

1. Prepare the room: Arrange 4 to 6 chairs in an inner circle (fish bowl). Put the remaining chairs in concentric circles around it.

2. Invite 3 to 5 students to the fish bowl, who actively participate in the discussion from the beginning. In an open fish bowl, one chair is left empty. In a closed fish bowl, all chairs are filled.

3. The moderator (lecturer or a qualified student) introduces the topic and the inner circle students start the discussion. The students in the outer circle listen and take notes. In an open fish bowl, any member of the audience can, at any time, occupy the empty chair and join the fish bowl to formulate his thoughts, before leaving the inner circle again. In a closed fish bowl, a member of the fish bowl must voluntarily leave the inner circle.

4. The discussion continues with participants frequently entering and leaving the fish bowl. Everyone can express their own views, but should always justify them.

5. When time runs out the fish bowl is closed and the moderator summarizes the discussion.

6. Reflection on the discussion in plenary.

to follow the debate, learn and repeat. Several rounds of a debate result in repetitions but show also different nuances.

A fish bowl is suitable for the presentation and discussion of group results. It is also helpful to discuss contradicting theories and views of strategy.

All students can follow the discussion and have the opportunity to express their point of view. This helps to integrate knowledge of different aspects of a complex topic.

Table 7.5 Interactive methods that facilitate the understanding of complex topics and theories

Interactive Methods: Description and procedure	Group size	Learning objectives	Time
	<10	Experience first insights	<15 mins
	10–30	Practice and experience	15–30 mins
	>30	Repeat and learn	30–45 mins
		Think and evaluate	>45 mins

Visualization (in class)

Visualization allows students to understand quickly a complex situation, context or case study. This is based on the simultaneous activation of visual, auditive and kinesthetic perception channels. For this purpose, various materials (e.g. pencils, stones, shells) are used as symbols in order to represent a particular situation.

1. Prepare the room: Set up enough tables with 3 to 6 chairs each. Place enough material on each table to visualize a situation.
2. Divide the class into small groups (3 to 6 students) and invite them to sit at one of the tables.
3. The students use the material to visualize for example:
   – the key stakeholders of a firm and their relevance.
   – the current and/or future situation of a firm or case study.
      During this process, reflective questions can be helpful.
4. Reflection on the findings and the method in plenary.

The method can be used in the beginning, to get a quick first look at a complex situation or context.

Visualization is especially useful for learning about the specifics of a particular context or case study.

World café (in class)

A world café is a structured conversation for knowledge sharing in which groups of students discuss a topic at several tables. The discussants change at predetermined intervals (10–20 minutes) to another table, being introduced to the previous discussions at their new table by a table host.

1. Prepare the room: Set up enough tables with 5 to 7 chairs each in a café setting. Place a different set of questions regarding a topic on each table. Ideally, the questions of one table build on those of the previous one. Place enough material (paper, notes, and pens) on each table to document the results of the discussions.

2. Divide the class into small groups (5 to 7 students) and invite them to find one of the tables and define a table host.

3. The groups discuss the questions and document their results. After a predetermined time (10 to 20 minutes) participants move to the next table. The table host remains at the table, welcomes new participants and informs them about the discussion so far. Then the discussion will continue until the next change.

4. Reflection of the results of all groups in plenary. If necessary, the results will be supplemented by the lecturer.

Knowledge maps (in class or online)

A knowledge map is a method for gathering, exchanging and developing knowledge. Concept maps or mind maps can be easily started, extended, and restructured using interactive software applications such as CMAP (cmap.ihmc.us) or Mind42 (mind42.com). In class, guiding questions and electrostatically self-adhesive sticky notes can help to gather, organize and expand the knowledge of the students regarding a specific topic. In class the work with knowledge maps includes the following steps:

1. Prepare the room: Set up enough tables with 3 to 5 chairs each. Place the same set of questions regarding a specific topic on each table. Provide enough material (sticky notes and pens) on each table to document the results of the discussions.

A world café is helpful to introduce students to a comprehensive strategy topic or theory step by step. The knowledge of the group evolves with each discussion.

The method allows active participation of all students. With each discussion, they are continually expanding their knowledge.

Knowledge maps foster discussion and enhance understanding and comprehensible communication.

Knowledge maps enable students to share, integrate

157

Table 7.5 (continued)

Interactive Methods: Description and procedure	Group size	Learning objectives	Time
2. Divide the class into small groups (3 to 5 students) and invite them to share their knowledge regarding the topic. The questions should assist the group in creating their knowledge map (20–30 minutes). The notes are used to visualize their knowledge map. 3. In the next step, 2 to 3 groups analyze their maps with the aim of integrating the knowledge contained therein into one single map. This merging of knowledge can be repeated until a single knowledge map has been created. 4. Reflection of the knowledge map(s) in plenary. If necessary, the results will be supplemented by the lecturer.	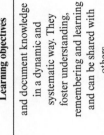	and document knowledge in a dynamic and systematic way. They foster understanding, remembering and learning and can be shared with others.	
Market of possibilities (in class or online) A market of possibilities is an interactive presentation method that allows students to present and explain previously acquired knowledge or the results of previous work in small groups. To this end, students prepare their information in a creative and compact way on "market stands" in class or online. The awarding of the best market stands at the end strengthens the engagement of the students. In class the market of possibilities includes the following steps: 1. Prepare the room: Set up enough tables with sufficient material (markers, flip charts, sticky notes, smileys, tablets, . . .). 2. Invite small groups (3 to 6 students) to find a table and arrange their knowledge or results of a previous project in an informative way (20 to 30 minutes). The stands become particularly interesting when different media (posters, films, visual objects) are offered. Ideally, visitors find a comprehensive and varied exhibition and enough space for their comments and questions.		The method allows students to interact with each other, to explain the results of their strategy project or presentation, to argue their point of view, and to question others.	
		The method is suitable for dealing with comprehensive information without boring the audience.	

158

3. One group member stays as an expert at the market table (can be alternating). The other group members visit the market place. Option A: The movement through the market takes place in fixed groups and fixed time intervals (between 10 to 20 minutes). An acoustic signal indicates when groups move to the next stand.
Option B: Free movement, driven by interests.
4. The evaluation of the market stands and the selection of the best is carried out by the students using voting software (e.g. www.mentimeter.com).
5. Reflection on the findings and the method in plenary.

Explanation video (in class or online)

Students produce and present (upload) a short (3 to 5 minutes) explanation video about a specific strategy topic.
Option A: The method can be used to lead to a specific topic. For this, all students receive the same task and guiding questions.
Option B: The method is also suitable to summarize and evaluate a complex topic. For this, the students receive different questions in order to cover the whole range of a strategy topic or theory.
1. Prepare the questions for the students and assure that students have suitable mobile devices that allow them to produce a video.
2. Invite small groups (2 to 4 students) to produce an explanation video (3 to 5 minutes) and upload it to a learning platform.
3. Ask all students to watch and evaluate the videos of their peers.
4. Option A: Show the best explanation videos in class and discuss them in plenary, using the videos as an introduction to the topic.
Option B: Show those explanation videos in class that are helpful to summarize/discuss and evaluate the topic.

Direct interaction and discussions in small groups are stimulated and students expand their knowledge continually.

The method allows students to introduce themselves to a new topic in a creative way. It helps the lecturer to assess and build on the knowledge base of the students.

To produce a video is a creative form of summarizing and evaluating a specific part of a complex strategy topic.

Table 7.5 (continued)

Interactive Methods: Description and procedure	Group size	Learning objectives	Time

Executive summary (in class or online)

To create an executive summary about a previously explained strategy topic or theory allows students to repeat, question, discuss and evaluate the information in small groups. An executive summary can be posted on a mutual learning platform or exhibited in class. Awarding the best executive summary fosters student engagement. In class, the following steps help in using the method.

1. Prepare the room: Set up enough boards with sufficient material (markers, notes, flip charts, . . .).
2. Invite small groups (3 to 6 students) to find a board to summarize the topic and to prepare a short (3 to 5 minutes) presentation (20 to 30 minutes).
3. Short presentations of the executive summaries in plenary. If necessary, the results will be amended by the lecturer.
4. Selection of the best executive summary by the students by means of voting software (e.g. www.mentimeter.com).
5. Reflection of the results of all groups in plenary. If necessary, the results will be supplemented by the lecturer.

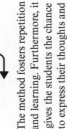

The method fosters repetition and learning. Furthermore, it gives the students the chance to express their thoughts and opinions.

An executive summary is useful to conclude a session and evaluate the presented and discussed theories or views of strategy.

REFERENCES

Albert, S., & Grzeda, M. (2015). Reflection in Strategic Management Education. *Journal of Management Education, 39*(5), 650–669. https://doi.org/10.1177/10 52562914564872.

Balogun, J., Hope Hailey, V., & Gustafsson, S. (2016). *Exploring Strategic Change* (4th edition). Harlow, UK: Pearson Education.

Barney, J.B. (1995). Looking Inside for Competitive Advantage. *The Academy of Management Executive (1993–2005), 9*(4), 49–61.

Barney, J.B., & Mackey, A. (2018). Monopoly Profits, Efficiency Profits, and Teaching Strategic Management. *Academy of Management Learning & Education, 17*(3), 359–373. https://doi.org/10.5465/amle.2017.0171.

Bell, R.G., Filatotchev, I., Krause, R., & Hitt, M. (2018). From the Guest Editors: Opportunities and Challenges for Advancing Strategic Management Education. *Academy of Management Learning & Education, 17*(3), 233–240. https://doi. org/10.5465/amle.2018.0213.

Bergmann, J., & Sams, A. (2012). *Flip Your Classroom: Reach Every Student in Every Class Every Day* (1st edition). Eugene, OR: International Society for Technology in Education.

Bergmann, J., & Sams, A. (2014). *Flipped Learning: Gateway to Student Engagement* (1st edition). Eugene, OR: International Society for Technology in Education.

Bird, A. (2015). Introduction: Experiencing the World. In V. Taras & M.A. Gonzalez-Perez (Eds.), *The Palgrave Handbook of Experiential Learning in International Business* (pp. 3–11). Dordrecht: Springer.

Buckley, P.J. (2018). How Theory Can Inform Strategic Management Education and Learning. *Academy of Management Learning & Education, 17*(3), 339–358. https://doi.org/10.5465/amle.2017.0076.

Carroll, A.B., Brown, J.A., & Buchholtz, A.K. (2016). *Business & Society: Ethics, Sustainability, and Stakeholder Management* (10th edition). Boston, MA: Cengage Learning.

Dyer, S.L., & Hurd, F. (2016). "What's Going On?" Developing Reflexivity in the Management Classroom: From Surface to Deep Learning and Everything in Between. *Academy of Management Learning & Education, 15*(2), 287–303. https://doi.org/10.5465/amle.2014.0104.

Eason, C.C., Mazzei, M.J., & Service, R.W. (2019). Teaching and Doing Strategy as an Intentional Strategic Innovation Mindset. *Journal of Strategic Innovation and Sustainability, 14*(4), 26–43.

Felin, T., Foss, N.J., & Ployhart, R.E. (2015). The Microfoundations Movement in Strategy and Organization Theory. *The Academy of Management Annals, 9*(1), 575–632. https://doi.org/10.1080/19416520.2015.1007651.

Grant, R.M. (2008). Why Strategy Teaching Should be Theory Based. *Journal of Management Inquiry, 17*(4), 276–281. https://doi.org/10.1177/1056492608318791.

Grant, R.M. (2019). *Contemporary Strategy Analysis* (10th edition). Hoboken, NJ: Wiley.

Grant, R.M., & Baden-Fuller, C. (2018). How to Develop Strategic Management Competency: Reconsidering the Learning Goals and Knowledge Requirements of the Core Strategy Course. *Academy of Management Learning & Education, 17*(3), 322–338. https://doi.org/10.5465/amle.2017.0126.

Hagen, M.S., Bialek, T.K., & Peterson, S.L. (2017). The Nature of Peer Coaching:

Definitions, Goals, Processes and Outcomes. *European Journal of Training and Development, 41*(6), 540–558. https://doi.org/10.1108/EJTD-04-2017-0031.

Hagen, M., & Hauser, E. (2008). Die Zeitmaschine: Ein Coaching-Tool zur Entscheidungsfindung. *Coaching Magazin*, 22–25.

Hamel, G., & Prahalad, C.K. (1994). *Competing for the Future*. Boston, MA: Harvard Business School Press.

Hooker, T. (2015). Peer Coaching: A Review of the Literature. *Waikato Journal of Education, 18*(2), 129–139. https://doi.org/10.15663/wje.v18i2.166.

Hunter-Jones, P. (2012). The Continuum of Learner Disengagement: Ethnographic Insights Into Experiential Learning in Marketing Education. *Journal of Marketing Education, 34*(1), 19–29. https://doi.org/10.1177/0273475311430801.

Janasz, S.C. de, & Crossman, J. (Eds.) (2018). *Elgar Guides to Teaching. Teaching Human Resource Management: An Experiential Approach*. Cheltenham, UK and Northampton, MA, USA: Edward Elgar Publishing.

Jaskari, H., & Jaskari, M.-M. (2016). Critical Success Factors in Teaching Strategic Sales Management: Evidence From Client-Based Classroom and Web-Based Formats. *Marketing Education Review, 26*(3), 171–185. https://doi.org/10.1080/10528008.2016.1209973.

Johnson, G., Whittington, R., Scholes, K., Angwin, D., & Regnér, P. (2017). *Exploring Strategy: Text and Cases* (11th edition). Harlow, UK: Pearson.

Kaplan, R.S., & Norton, D.P. (1996). *The Balanced Scorecard: Translating Strategy into Action*. Boston, MA: Harvard Business School Press.

Kim, M.K., Kim, S.M., Khera, O., & Getman, J. (2014). The Experience of Three Flipped Classrooms in an Urban University: An Exploration of Design Principles. *The Internet and Higher Education, 22*, 37–50. https://doi.org/10.1016/j.iheduc.2014.04.003.

Kotter, J.P. (2012). *Leading Change, With a New Preface by the Author*. Boston, MA: Harvard Business Review Press.

Ladyshewsky, R.K. (2006). Peer Coaching: A Constructivist Methodology for Enhancing Critical Thinking in Postgraduate Business Education. *Higher Education Research & Development, 25*(1), 67–84. https://doi.org/10.1080/13600800500453196.

Ladyshewsky, R.K. (2007). A Strategic Approach for Integrating Theory to Practice in Leadership Development. *Leadership & Organization Development Journal, 28*(5), 426–443. https://doi.org/10.1108/01437730710761733.

Lindsay, S., Jack, G., & Ambrosini, V. (2018). A Critical Diversity Framework to Better Educate Students About Strategy Implementation. *Academy of Management Learning & Education, 17*(3), 241–258. https://doi.org/10.5465/amle.2017.0150.

MacGregor, J., Cooper, J. L., Smith, K. A., & Robinson, P. (2000). *Strategies for Energizing Large Classes: From Small Groups to Learning Communities. New Directions for Teaching and Learning: Vol. 81*. San Francisco, CA: Jossey-Bass.

Mintzberg, H. (2004). *Managers not MBAs*. London: FT Prentice Hall.

Mintzberg, H., Ahlstrand, B.W., & Lampel, J. (1998). *Strategy Safari: A Guided Tour Through the Wilds of Strategic Management*. New York: Free Press.

Mitchell, R.K., Agle, B.R., & Wood, D.J. (1997). Toward a Theory of Stakeholder Identification and Salience: Defining the Principle of Who and What Really Counts. *The Academy of Management Review, 22*(4), 853–886. https://doi.org/10.2307/259247.

Prahalad, C.K., & Hamel, G. (1990). The Core Competence of the Corporation. *Harvard Business Review*, 79–91.

Priem, R.L. (2018). Toward Becoming a Complete Teacher of Strategic Management. *Academy of Management Learning & Education, 17*(3), 374–388. https://doi.org/10.5465/amle.2017.0237.

Reisinger, S., Gattringer, R., & Strehl, F. (2017). *Strategisches Management: Grundlagen für Studium und Praxis* (2., aktualisierte und erweiterte Auflage). Hallbergmoos, Germany: Pearson.

Roos, G., & Pike, S. (2018). *Intellectual Capital as a Management Tool: Essentials for Leaders and Managers*. London: Routledge.

Rotellar, C., & Cain, J. (2016). Research, Perspectives, and Recommendations on Implementing the Flipped Classroom. *American Journal of Pharmaceutical Education, 80*(2), 34. https://doi.org/10.5688/ajpe80234.

Schwenker, B., & Wulf, T. (Eds.) (2013). *Scenario-based Strategic Planning: Developing Strategies in an Uncertain World*. Wiesbaden, Germany: Springer Gabler.

Swanzen, R. (2018). Facing the Generation Chasm: The Parenting and Teaching of Generations Y and Z. *International Journal of Child, Youth and Family Studies, 9*(2), 125–150. https://doi.org/10.18357/ijcyfs92201818216.

Taras, V., & Gonzalez-Perez, M.A. (Eds.) (2015). *The Palgrave Handbook of Experiential Learning in International Business*. London: Palgrave Macmillan.

Ungaretti, T., Thompson, K.R., Miller, A., & Peterson, T.O. (2015). Problem-Based Learning: Lessons From Medical Education and Challenges for Management Education. *Academy of Management Learning & Education, 14*(2), 173–186. https://doi.org/10.5465/amle.2013.0245.

Welsh, M.A., & Dehler, G.E. (2012). Combining Critical Reflection and Design Thinking to Develop Integrative Learners. *Journal of Management Education, 37*(6), 771–802. https://doi.org/10.1177/1052562912470107.

Wheelen, T.L., Hunger, J.D., Hoffman, A.N., & Bamford, C.E. (2017). *Strategic Management and Business Policy: Globalization, Innovation, and Sustainability* (Global edition). Upper Saddle River, NJ: Pearson.

8. Tailored methods of strategizing in undergraduate education: from SWOT to the 6Ps of Business Strategy

Norman T. Sheehan

INTRODUCTION

This chapter describes a strategy formulation framework, the 6Ps of Business Strategy, which helps students overcome a key learning obstacle in strategic management: Ensuring that their proposed business strategies are comprehensive, coherent as well as profitable. The 6Ps of Business Strategy framework helps students overcome this common obstacle in two steps: It first directs students to formulate business strategies that contain each of the elements necessary to achieve organizational performance: purpose, product, people, process and path. It then asks students to test their business strategies before submitting them to their instructors for evaluation. The chapter outlines the 6Ps framework and the motivation for developing the framework. It then uses a worked example from the retail mattress industry to illustrate how strategy instructors can effectively apply the framework in their teaching.

CHALLENGES IN FORMULATING BUSINESS STRATEGIES

Business strategy is a set of inter-connected choices as to how to best serve an attractive set of customers (e.g. Porter, 1996). A key objective of undergraduate capstone strategy courses is for students to formulate business strategies that integrate the functional areas, such as marketing, production, supply chain, human resources and finance (Kachra & Schnietz, 2008; Inamdar & Roldan, 2013; Priem, 2018). This involves understanding the functional areas, how they are interrelated, and how they can be integrated to create profitable strategies. To accomplish this objective, instructors introduce students to strategy frameworks. Strategy frameworks help students to organize the disparate data about the firm and its competitive environment and thus simplify the task of formulating new business strategies (Wright et al., 2013). Given its simplicity and broad applicability, one of the most common strategic frameworks used to formulate integrative business strategies is the SWOT framework (Bell & Rochford, 2016; Bell et al., 2018; Bower, 2008; Gunn & Williams, 2007; Helms & Nixon, 2010; Madsen, 2016).

A typical SWOT-driven strategic formulation process involves students identifying internal factors that improve the firm's current profitability, such as an excellent design team, which are listed as strengths, and factors that harm current profitability, such as unreliable production processes, which are listed as weaknesses. Students then examine the firm's external environment to identify potential areas for the firm to increase its profitability, such as new markets for its products, which are listed as opportunities, and for factors that may decrease the firm's profitability, such as changes to regulations or tariffs, which are listed as threats. Once students have an extensive list of the firm's strengths, weaknesses, opportunities and threats, they attempt to generate alternative strategies that leverage the firm's strengths to capture the most profitable opportunities identified, while mitigating its weaknesses and avoiding any threats. After evaluating each of the alternatives proposed, students then write up their SWOT analyses and their recommended business strategy before handing it in for marking or presenting it to the class.

Effective business strategies need to be comprehensive in the sense that they include all the elements needed to succeed and coherent in the sense that the elements are aligned with each other (Grant & Baden-Fuller, 2018; Rumelt, 2011). The problem with using SWOT to generate new business strategies is that while it is an effective tool to categorize the firm's salient strategic factors, it does not go further than generating a long list of internal strengths and weaknesses and external opportunities and threats (Bell & Rochford, 2016; Grant & Baden-Fuller, 2018; Valentin, 2001; 2005). SWOT provides no guarantee that strategies generated are comprehensive, coherent and profitable. Thus even students who have performed a thorough SWOT analysis may still struggle to formulate business strategies that are comprehensive and integrate each functional area in a coherent fashion (e.g. Bell & Rochford, 2016).

While SWOT and other strategy frameworks, such as Porter's (1980) Five Forces, Porter's (1985) value chain, VRINE (Barney, 1991; Carpenter & Sanders, 2009) and PESTEL, should still be used to perform a thorough scan of the firm's internal and external environments, I believe a new strategic tool is needed to help synthesize the relevant strategic factors gleaned from the internal and external scans into a comprehensive and coherent framework. This chapter presents a strategy formulation tool to complement the traditional SWOT framework. The 6Ps of Business Strategy was developed based on years of experience teaching strategic management and coaching strategy case competition teams as a way to overcome the issues students face when using SWOT to formulate strategy.

As one would predict from Bloom's (1956) taxonomy, I find that my students can effectively apply SWOT and its underlying tools to analyze the firm's internal and external environments. However, they still struggle to synthesize its elements. Strategy formulation tools, such as Blue Ocean Strategy (Kim & Mauborgne, 2005) or Core Adjacencies (Zook & Allen, 2003), help students to formulate innovative and profitable strategies, but they still fail to address this shortcoming. The proposed tool, the 6Ps of Business Strategy, asks students to develop and then evaluate if their recommended business strategies are comprehensive, coherent as well as profitable. The 6Ps of Business Strategy framework presented below is based on a strategy consulting tool, and owes an intellectual debt to McKinsey's 7S framework (Waterman et al., 1980), Porter's (1985) value chain, Hambrick and Fredrikson's (2005) strategy diamond, and Kaplan and Norton's (1996) strategy map.

THE 6PS OF BUSINESS STRATEGY FRAMEWORK

The 6Ps of Business Strategy incorporates the key elements that affect organizational profitability: The organization's revenues are driven by the product's attractiveness, its price and the size of the target market, while the organization's costs are driven by the efficiency of its processes and people that produce and deliver its product (Sheehan & Powers, 2018). Profitable business strategies align the factors under firm control with factors in the firm's external environment to create value for its target customers (e.g. Porter, 1996). Placing the Ps together into one framework ensures students include all these elements in their proposed strategies and that the elements are aligned with each other. The six elements that make up the 6Ps are (adapted from Sheehan & Powers, 2018, p. 681):

Purpose * Product * Process * People * Path = Performance

- **Purpose** describes the reason the firm exists and its strategic direction. The firm's vision reflects its long-term aspirations and its mission broadly outlines how the firm will achieve its vision.
- **Product** is the value proposition the firm offers to its target customers, its price and marketing plans to reach those customers. It describes how the firm generates revenue (e.g. pricing model), its sales channels, and the marketing plans and capabilities of the firm's top rivals. It should also include an evaluation of the firm's value proposition relative to rivals' value propositions that target the same customers and review the potential impact of shifts in consumer preferences and industry trends on the firm's value proposition.
- **Process** refers to the activities that the firm undertakes to efficiently and reliably deliver the value proposition to its customers, such as production, supply chain, process and product innovation, and compliance activities. It should also outline the current and future impact of trends such as technologies and new regulations on the firm's production activities.
- **People** captures the capabilities that employees need to effectively complete the processes. It describes the desired culture, key employees, and includes a review of the skills of the executive leadership team.
- **Path** identifies the key initiatives, resources required for these initiatives, and the timing of the initiatives that the organization needs to implement if it is to achieve its proposed strategy.
- **Performance** reflects the outcome of the firm's ability to align its purpose, product, process, people and path with trends in its external environment. Company performance is typically assessed relative to budgeted expectations using measures of revenue, market share, profitability, return on investment, cash flow, stock price, and indebtedness. The discussion of a firm's performance should also include comparisons to key industry performance indicators, such as same store sales or sales conversion rates, as well as reviewing any macro-economic factors.

THE THREE TESTS TO EVALUATE BUSINESS STRATEGIES

To improve students' business strategy formulation skills it is important to encourage them to evaluate their own business strategies and then revise them as necessary. Therefore, after students use the 6Ps to formulate their strategies, they should be encouraged to evaluate the quality of their strategies prior to handing them in for assessment. The tool below, the three tests to evaluate a proposed strategy, ensures that students have formulated comprehensive, coherent and profitable strategies, which can be implemented (the three tests of strategy are based on Hambrick & Fredrikson, 2005, p. 61).

Test 1: Is There External Fit?

- Has the proposed strategy selected an attractive set of target customers and do these target customers see value in the proposed Product (i.e. customer value proposition)?
- Will the proposed Product (i.e. customer value proposition) win against rivals who are targeting the same set of customers?
- Does the proposed strategy address future threats to the Product (e.g. new rivals, substitutes, regulations or new technologies)?

Test 2: Is There Internal Fit between Product, Process, People and Purpose?

- Are the People and Processes aligned to efficiently deliver the firm's Product (i.e. its customer value proposition)?
- Does the proposed strategy fit with the firm's Purpose?

Test 3: Is the Proposed Strategy Implementable?

- Does the firm have the people and other resources, such as cash, to execute the proposed strategy?
- Can the proposed strategy be implemented at an acceptable level of risk?
- Will key stakeholders support the proposed strategy?
- Are the timing and resources needed to implement the initiatives outlined in the Path reasonable? Are any key initiatives missing?

When to Introduce the 6Ps of Business Strategy Framework

The 6Ps framework should be introduced to students during the session where the instructor reviews SWOT and the strategy tools that underlie it, such as using Five Forces and PESTEL to scan the external environment for key opportunities and threats, and using the Value Chain and VRINE to scan the internal environment for key strengths and weaknesses.

Instructors may use the following case assignment questions for cases that require students to formulate and evaluate alternative business strate-

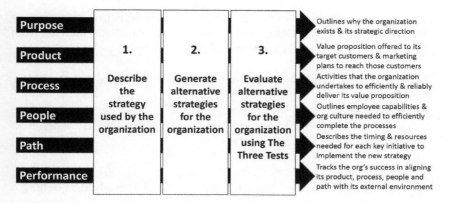

Figure 8.1   Using the 6Ps to formulate business strategies

gies for a company: (1) Describe the company's current strategy using the 6Ps; (2) Recommend a strategy that will allow the company to maximize its future profitability. Use the 6Ps (i.e. Performance = Purpose * Product * Process * People * Path) to describe your new business strategy in a comprehensive, coherent and profitable fashion; (3) Use the three tests of strategy to evaluate your recommended alternative. Figure 8.1 describes each of the Ps and the steps that students are to follow when formulating business strategies.

Intended Audience for the 6Ps of Business Strategy Framework

The framework is appropriate for all audiences. Undergraduate and MBA students without a business background will benefit from having a comprehensive framework to model and evaluate their proposed strategies. In my experience, executives also appreciate the guidance of how to meet instructors' requirements for preparing strategies that are comprehensive, coherent and profitable. The next section provides a straightforward example of how instructors can use the 6Ps of Business Strategy framework to improve their students' strategy formulation skills.

How to Use the 6Ps

The example provided below uses Sleep Country Canada to review the steps, suggested questions assigned to the students as well as providing a suggested solution. Sleep Country is Canada's largest retailer of mattresses, frames, sheets and pillows. It was formed in 1994 by four entrepreneurs and has since grown to over 265 retail locations that span the entire country. The example asks students to use the 6Ps to help decide whether Sleep Country Canada should sell a bed-in-the-box mattress sourced from China on its website and in its retail outlets in early 2017.

Using the 6Ps to Analyze Sleep Country Canada's Bed-in-a-Box Decision

Instructors should ask students to read Sleep Country Canada's 2016 Annual Report as preparation for answering the following case assignment questions:

1) Describe Sleep Country Canada's strategy in early 2017 using the 6Ps.
2) Recommend whether Sleep Country Canada should begin selling a bed-in-the-box offering that is produced in China on its website and in its stores in early 2017. Use the 6Ps (i.e. Performance = Purpose * Product * Process * People * Path) to describe your proposed strategy in a comprehensive, coherent and profitable fashion.
3) Justify your recommendation using the three tests to evaluate your new strategy.

Instructors can provide students with a diagram (see Figure 8.1) that describes the process to be used when answering the assigned case questions. The Sleep Country example provided in the chapter is a simple one, as the strategy alternative to analyze is provided to students – should Sleep Country Canada sell a bed-in-a-box mattress? If students are required to develop their own strategy alternatives for cases, they can be directed to use strategy formulation frameworks, such as brainstorming, Design Thinking (Liedtka & Kaplan, 2019), Blue Ocean Strategy (Kim & Mauborgne, 2005), or Core Adjacencies (Zook & Allen, 2003).

1. **Describe Sleep Country Canada's strategy in early 2017 using the 6Ps**
    Given that students cannot formulate effective strategies if they do not understand the organization's current strategy and how effective it has been, the first step in formulating alternative strategies is to describe and assess Sleep Country's position in early 2017 using the 6Ps. To generate insights to populate the 6Ps, students should be encouraged to do a thorough scan of Sleep Country's internal and external environments using strategy tools, such as the Five Forces, PESTEL, Value Chain, VRINE, and SWOT:
    - **Purpose**: Sleep Country is Canada's leading specialty retailer dedicated to sleep.
      Vision statement – A Better Sleep Starts Here.

Mission statement – A caring and rewarding work environment. Develop customers for life through unparalleled customer service and deliver on the promise of better sleep. Passionate industry-leading experts who continuously innovate and evolve profitable and sustainable business practices. Environmental leadership through recycling programs. Unwavering community and charity involvement.

● **Product**: Sleep Country sells exclusive lines of mattresses, bedding, pillows and bed frames at various price points. Sleep Country's customer value proposition is to provide an "unparalleled in-store experience with highly trained, friendly and knowledgeable sleep experts to match customers to the bedding solution that meets their sleep needs." (Sleep Country Canada, 2017). Sleep Country provides its customers with a 100-day price and comfort guarantee as well as offering third-party financing from Citibank for consumers who need financing. An additional benefit of having their own exclusive line of mattresses is that Sleep Country can offer price guarantees without worrying about honoring them, as Sleep Country is the only retailer that sells that exact mattress.

Sleep Country is the only specialty mattress retailer with stores located across Canada. It competes with other physical retailers of mattresses, such as Hudson's Bay, Leon's, The Brick and Costco as well as direct-to-consumer mattress retailers, such as Casper, Leesa and Tuft & Needle.

Sleep Country does not currently sell a bed-in-a-box mattress, rather it only sells mattresses from traditional mattress manufacturers. Attracted by high margins earned on mattresses, Sleep Country has been disrupted in recent years by a large number of online competitors offering a direct-to-consumer sale of bed-in-a-box mattresses. Sales of bed-in-a-box mattresses in Canada have grown from less than 1 percent in 2011 to over 6 percent in 2016 and are anticipated to rise to 15 percent by 2021. Sleep Country's online bed-in-a-box competitors typically do not have physical retail outlets; rather they attract customers through advertising, social media, customer testimonials and by offering free shipping and a 100-night return policy. These bed-in-a-box competitors advertise that they have one mattress that perfectly fits all sleepers and are typically priced at the lower end of what you would pay for a traditional mattress at Sleep Country. Bed-in-a-box mattresses target consumers, such as many of the millennial generation, who are comfortable buying products online, sight unseen.

Consumers typically replace their mattresses every eight to twelve years and as the size of houses increases along with the desire for better sleep, consumers are buying larger and higher quality mattresses. Mattress purchases are considered to be "blind," in the sense consumers do not know how well they will sleep on the mattress until they have slept on it for a period. Despite this, most customers prefer to view and try several different mattresses before buying. While consumers may perform some research online before entering a store to try out the mattresses, it is difficult to shop based on price as each mattress retailer sells its own exclusive line of mattresses made by the two largest mattress manufacturers, Serta Simmons and Tempur Sealy, as well as other mattress manufacturers (i.e. competitors sell the similar mattresses with different mattress names and slightly different mattress coverings). Given this, the potential for "showrooming" is low in the retail mattress industry.

- **Process**: Potential customers are enticed to visit Sleep Country's 265 physical stores through its heavy use of print and television advertising. Given its national scale, Sleep Country has the ability to advertise heavily, spending 5 percent of its revenues each year. After customers arrive at its stores, Sleep Country's sales staff first approach them to determine their sleep needs, and then match the customers' sleep needs with Sleep Country's exclusive line of mattresses, pillows, sheets and bed frames. Sleep Country provides free home delivery and recycles customers' old mattresses. Mattress manufacturers provide retailers with volume rebates, which means Sleep Country pays less per mattress than its competitors.

  The retail mattress industry is not capital-intensive. A typical Sleep Country store costs US$350,000 to set up and it only carries the inventory displayed on the floor. In fact, Sleep Country's JIT (just in time) inventory processes means it has negative working capital, as once a customer buys a mattress it receives the customer's payment within 2–3 days. Sleep Country then orders the mattress from the manufacturer and schedules delivery to the customer based on the manufacturer's delivery times. Sleep Country pays the mattress manufacturer 30–45 days later.

- **People**: Sleep Country's management team has a proven track record of success in the retail mattress industry, with an average of 20+ years relevant experience. Sleep Country has over 1,350 employees. All stores are corporate owned, enabling Sleep Country to develop its employees through extensive training and a strong culture of customer service. Sales employees are paid a base salary plus commission and their turnover is far below the industry average (16 percent for Sleep Country vs. 44 percent for the retail industry). The result is a consistent and superior in-store and home delivery customer experience.

- **Path**: Sleep Country started with four stores in 1994 and since then has grown organically by opening eight to twelve stores per year. It entered the Quebec market in 2006 with the purchase of five Dormez-vous? stores. The Dormez-vous? retail banner in Quebec has since grown organically to 53 stores. The company plans to launch its first eCommerce website in mid-2017.
- **Performance**: Sleep Country's revenues were US$403 million in 2016 (80 percent of Sleep Country's revenues are from the sales of traditional mattresses, while the remaining 20 percent are from the sale of sleep accessories, such as headboards and sheets). Revenues increased 15 percent over 2015, while industry growth was 1 percent. Sleep Country's operating profit was up 29.7 percent compared to 2015. Same store sales growth, a measure of revenue generated by existing Sleep Country outlets, increased 10 percent over 2015. Key performance indicators in the retail mattress industry include: Sleep Country is the #1 mattress retailer in Canada with a 25 percent market share. Sleep Country successfully converts over 60 percent of shoppers who visit its stores into mattress buyers. Reflecting the inability of customers to price shop and the difficulty of assessing mattress quality pre-purchase, Sleep Country earned margins on mattresses and accessories in excess of 30 percent.

2. **Recommend whether Sleep Country Canada should begin selling a bed-in-the-box offering that is produced in China on its website and in its stores in early 2017. Use the 6Ps (i.e. Performance = Purpose * Product * Process * People * Path) to describe your proposed strategy in a comprehensive, coherent and profitable fashion**

Students' recommended business strategies are commonly incomplete and/or not aligned. To address this common shortcoming, this step asks students to outline how their recommendation to add a bed-in-a-box mattress to Sleep Country's offerings affects its current strategy. Note: to avoid duplication, only the changes needed to implement the bed-in-a-box strategy are shown under each of the 6Ps below:

- **Purpose**: Adding the bed-in-a-box mattress to Sleep Country's stores does not require revising Sleep Country's current vision, mission and values.
- **Product**: Adding the bed-in-a-box mattress will involve making the following changes to Sleep Country's current product: The bed-in-a-box mattress extends Sleep Country's product line and increases its target market to include customers who are interested in buying latex foam mattresses that can be delivered to their door. The bed-in-a-box mattress should be priced a little lower than the established bed-in-a-box competitors, such as Casper, Leesa or Simba. In addition, Sleep Country will need to update its advertising flyers and TV ads to include the new product, and add the product to its website after it is established later in 2017.
- **Process**: Adding a bed-in-a-box mattress to its product line means Sleep Country will need to revise a number of its processes, including contracting with a reputable Chinese manufacturer and a logistics shipping company to transport the latex foam mattresses to Canada. Sleep Country will need to maintain a substantial inventory of bed-in-a-box mattresses in its distribution centers, given the long distance to the Chinese manufacturers. On the plus side, Sleep Country will enjoy lower customer delivery costs than its rivals as it can use its existing delivery infrastructure, whereas its rivals must use a third-party logistics provider, such as UPS or DHL, to deliver their bed-in-a-box mattresses to buyers.
- **People**: Adding a bed-in-a-box will entail training salespeople as to the benefits of a latex foam mattress relative to traditional spring mattresses so that they continue to match customers' sleep needs to the best mattress.
- **Path**: The introduction of the bed-in-a-box will require outlining the timing, the resources required, and who is responsible for each of the product, process and people initiatives listed above. For example, students should include these initiatives in their description of Sleep Country's path: locate a Chinese latex foam mattress manufacturer and arrange logistics, allocate space in its distribution centers to store bed-in-a-box mattresses, establish an eCommerce website and include the bed-in-a-box offering on the website, prepare new training materials for selling bed-in-a-box mattresses, train the sales staff, and update the marketing materials. An effective way to describe the Sleep Country's implementation Path is to use a Gantt chart that outlines the

following for each of the key initiatives: who is responsible for the initiative, the cost of the initiative, and its timing.

- **Performance**: Sleep Country should continue to assess its performance using total revenue, market share, operating margins by product, same store sales, and customer conversion rates. In addition, Sleep Country should set growth and sales targets for its new bed-in-a-box offering. For example, given that sales of bed-in-a-box mattresses are anticipated to increase to 15 percent of total mattress sales in Canada by 2022, Sleep Country should aim to have the same percentage of its mattress revenues by 2022.

3. **Justify your recommendation using the three tests to evaluate your new strategy**

   Students should be encouraged to test whether their business strategies are comprehensive, coherent and profitable before submitting them for grading.

Test 1: Is there external fit?

- Has the proposed strategy selected an attractive set of target customers and do these target customers see value in the proposed Product (i.e. customer value proposition)?
- *Yes, the new bed-in-a-box mattress targets consumers, such as millennials, who want a latex foam mattress that is easy to purchase at a lower cost than traditional spring mattresses. The size of the bed-in-a-box mattresses market is expected to increase to 15 percent of the total Canadian mattress market in the next five years.*
- Will the proposed Product (i.e. customer value proposition) win against rivals who are targeting the same set of customers?
- *Yes, it exploits Sleep Country's main advantage over its online rivals, its 265 stores across Canada. The advantage of Sleep Country's bed-in-a-box offering over its online rivals is that consumers will be able to try Sleep Country's bed-in-a-box mattress before deciding to buy one. If Sleep Country's bed-in-a-box offering is competitively priced relative to its online rivals, Sleep Country has a strong chance of enticing a significant amount of the consumers targeted to purchase it from Sleep Country.*
- Does the proposed strategy address future threats to the Product (e.g. new rivals, substitutes, regulations or new technologies)?
- *Yes, the strategy addresses the threat posed by the new rivals in the short term, however, it also may expose Sleep Country to risks in the longer term, which are discussed below under the point, "Can the proposed strategy be implemented at an acceptable risk?"*

Test 2: Is there internal fit between Product, Process, People and Purpose?

- Are the People and Processes aligned to efficiently deliver the firm's Product (i.e. its customer value proposition)?
- *Yes, the new strategy anticipates changes to the people by training the sales staff and changes to the processes required to efficiently source and sell the bed-in-a-box mattress from China.*
- Does the proposed strategy fit with the firm's Purpose?
- *Yes, there are a number of consumers who believe latex mattresses offer a good night's sleep.*

Test 3: Is the proposed strategy implementable?

- Does the firm have the people and other resources, such as cash, to execute the proposed strategy?
- *Yes, the firm has the necessary people and financial resources. Although Sleep Country's management team only has experience sourcing and selling traditional spring mattresses, the capabilities needed to successfully sell a bed-in-a-box mattress are very similar.*
- Can the proposed strategy be implemented at an acceptable level of risk?
- *There is a risk that offering bed-in-a-box mattresses may undermine Sleep Country's main competitive advantage, its physical locations. The bed-in-a-box is still a niche product, viewed by some with skepticism. If the leading specialty mattress retailer has a bed-in-a-box offering then it acts to legitimize the bed-in-a-box, which in the longer term may reduce Sleep Country's sales of traditional spring mattresses where it dominates. Having said that, the bed-in-a-box market is expected to grow to 15 percent of the US$1.6 billion Canadian mattress market in the next five years. An additional risk relates to inventory obsolescence. Due to the length of the supply chain, Sleep Country must hold significant amounts of bed-in-a-box mattresses in its inventory, which increases the working capital required, and leaves Sleep Country open to inventory obsolescence if its rivals introduce latex foam mattresses with more desirable attributes, such as mattresses that do not retain heat, are longer lasting, or are more environmentally friendly.*
- Will key stakeholders support the proposed strategy?
- *There is no reason to anticipate that stakeholders will not support this alternative.*
- Are the timing and resources needed to implement the initiatives outlined in the Path reasonable? Are any key initiatives missing?
- *The timing of the proposed initiatives and resources required appears reasonable. The list of key initiatives appears complete.*

Other Uses of 6Ps Strategy Framework

Aside from helping students to formulate comprehensive, coherent and profitable strategies, the 6Ps can also be employed by instructors in additional ways. It can help explain why two firms in the same industry may differ in performance. For example, instructors can use the 6Ps of Business Strategy to describe and then compare Amazon and Walmart's strategies. Given that the 6Ps includes all the elements necessary for success, the 6Ps can also be used to explain why a firm's strategy has failed to deliver the performance anticipated. For example, a firm with a great Product that is well-received by an amply-sized target market will not be successful if it cannot efficiently and reliably scale up to deliver the Product to its target customers (e.g. the inability of Tesla to produce enough units of its Model 3 to meet global market demand in 2018 and 2019). Similarly, if the firm's Product and Processes are great, but the firm lacks the proper People to complete the firm's Processes, its Performance will suffer. To have successful Performance firms need to effectively develop, align and execute each of their Product, Process, People, Path and Purpose.

The 6Ps overcomes a common critique of the resource-based view's VRINE framework as it provides a more holistic view of why some firms outperform other firms. The VRINE framework only focuses on a select, few elements that generate competitive advantage, rather than taking a systemic perspective of the factors that lead to competitive advantage (e.g. Porter, 1996). The resource-based view largely ignores the supporting activities that need to be present and aligned to generate value from the VRINE resource and capabilities (e.g. Priem & Butler, 2001; Sheehan & Foss, 2009, 2017). The 6Ps also addresses shortcomings with using the value chain framework to formulate strategy. While the value chain framework is excellent for evaluating and improving the organization's supply chain (i.e. Processes in the 6Ps framework), it is weak for evaluating and improving its human resources (i.e. People in the 6Ps framework), and its choice of value proposition and target market (i.e. Product in the 6Ps framework). The value chain framework also ignores the role of the firm's mission and vision (i.e. Purpose in the 6Ps framework) and the initiatives and timing of the initiatives required to implement the strategy (i.e. Path in the 6Ps framework).

CONCLUSION

The 6Ps of Business Strategy framework complements SWOT as it asks students to formulate and evaluate if the firm's internal elements, such as its product offering and its people, processes and purpose are aligned with elements in its external environment, such as its target market and consumer and technological trends. An advantage of the framework is that strategy implementation is not divorced from strategy formulation as students are asked to describe the Path (i.e. the initiatives and their timing) organizations need to follow to get their recommended strategy executed. Students note that they like the alliteration of the framework as all letters of the framework begin with the letter P, and that it encourages them to undertake systemic thinking by identifying the key elements and considering how they should fit together. While the strategic decision provided in the chapter to analyze was straightforward, the framework's strengths are clearest when the students are assigned longer and more complex strategy formulation teaching cases.

REFERENCES

Barney, J. (1991), 'Firm resources and sustained competitive advantage', *Journal of Management*, **17**, 99–120.

Bell, R.G., I. Filatotchev, R. Krause and M. Hitt (2018), 'Opportunities and challenges for advancing strategic management education', *Academy of Management Learning & Education*, **17**, 233–240.

Bell, R.G. and L. Rochford (2016), 'Rediscovering SWOT's integrative nature: A new understanding of an old framework', *The International Journal of Management Education*, **14**, 310–326.

Bloom, B.S. (1956), *Taxonomy of Educational Objectives, Handbook I: The Cognitive Domain*. New York: David McKay Co.

Bower, J.L. (2008), 'The teaching of strategy: From general manager to analyst and back again?', *Journal of Management Inquiry*, **17**, 269–275.

Carpenter, M.A. and W.G. Sanders (2009), *Strategic Management: A Dynamic Perspective Concepts and Cases*, 2nd ed., Upper Saddle River, NJ: Pearson Prentice Hall.

Grant, R.M. and C. Baden-Fuller (2018), 'How to develop strategic management competency: Reconsidering the learning goals and knowledge requirements of the core strategy course', *Academy of Management Learning & Education*, **17**, 322–338.

Gunn, R. and W. Williams (2007), 'Strategic tools: An empirical investigation into strategy in practice in the UK', *Strategic Change*, **16**, 201–216.

Hambrick, D.C. and J.W. Fredrikson (2005), 'Are you sure you have a strategy?', *Academy of Management Perspectives*, **19**(4), 51–62.

Helms, M.M. and J. Nixon (2010), 'Exploring SWOT analysis – where are we now?', *Journal of Strategy and Management*, **3**, 215–251.

Inamdar, S.N. and M. Roldan (2013), 'The MBA capstone course: Building theoretical, practical, applied, and reflective skills', *Journal of Management Education*, **37**, 747–770.

Kachra, A. and K. Schnietz (2008), 'The capstone strategy course: What might real integration look like?', *Journal of Management Education*, **32**, 476–508.

Kaplan, R.S. and D.P. Norton (1996), *The Balanced Scorecard: Translating Strategy into Action*. Boston: Harvard Business School Press.

Kim, W.C. and R. Mauborgne (2005), 'Blue Ocean Strategy: From theory to practice', *California Management Review*, **47**(3), 105–121.

Liedtka, J. and S. Kaplan (2019), 'How design thinking opens new frontiers for strategy development', *Strategy & Leadership*, **47**, 3–10.

Madsen, D. (2016), 'SWOT analysis: A management fashion perspective', *International Journal of Business Research*, **16**, 39–56.

Porter, M.E. (1980), *Competitive Strategy*. New York: The Free Press.

Porter, M.E. (1985), *Competitive Advantage*. New York: The Free Press.

Porter, M.E. (1996), 'What is strategy?', *Harvard Business Review*, **74**(6), 61–78.

Priem, R.L. (2018), 'Toward becoming a complete teacher of strategic management', *Academy of Management Learning & Education*, **17**, 374–388.

Priem, R.L. and J.E. Butler (2001), 'Is the resource-based view a useful perspective for strategic management research?', *Academy of Management Review*, **26**, 22–40.

Rumelt, R. (2011), *Good Strategy, Bad Strategy*. New York: Crown Publishing.

Sheehan, N.T. and N.J. Foss (2009), 'Exploring the roots of Porter's activity-based view', *Journal of Strategy and Management*, **2**, 240–260.

Sheehan, N.T. and N.J. Foss (2017), 'Using Porterian activity analysis to understand organizational capabilities', *Journal of General Management*, **42**(3), 41–51.

Sheehan, N.T. and R. Powers (2018), 'Setting and vetting strategy: Bridging the chasm between CEOs and boards', *Business Horizons*, **61**, 679–688.

Sleep Country Canada (2017), 'Investor relations: About us', accessed April 20, 2017 at https://www.sleepcountryir.ca/English/about-us/dormez-vous/default.aspx.

Valentin, E.K. (2001), 'SWOT analysis from a resource-based view', *Journal of Marketing Theory and Practice*, **9**, 54–69.

Valentin, E.K. (2005), 'Away with SWOT analysis: Use defensive/offensive evaluation instead', *Journal of Applied Business Research*, **21**(2), 91–105.

Waterman, R.H., T.J. Peters and J.R. Phillips (1980), 'Structure is not organization', *Business Horizons*, **23**(3), 14–26.

Wright, R.P., S.E. Paroutis and D.P. Blettner (2013), 'How useful are the strategic tools we teach in business schools?', *Journal of Management Studies*, **50**(1), 92–125.

Zook, C. and J. Allen (2003), 'Growth outside the core', *Harvard Business Review*, **81**(12), 66–75.

9. Teaching strategy by not teaching strategy

Robert P. Wright

THE BROADER CONTEXT IN WHICH WE TEACH STRATEGY

Two organizations are observed competing in a highly competitive market, yet why is it that one outperforms the other? This is the classic question in the study of strategy, strategizing and strategic management. To many, the practice and study of this important aspect of organizational life is filled with confusion, complexity and difficulty. Yet, is it *really* that difficult or is it blatantly obvious what successful companies do differently that sets them apart from the rest? At the core of all strategizing (and winning) lie some fundamental truths about why organizations (and key decision-makers) not only survive but thrive in good times and bad (Reeves et al., 2012).

Yet it is so easy to miss this message in the midst of the business landscapes we experience today. Managers have no choice but to continue to (re)interpret their current taken-for-granted assumptions of what works and what doesn't work to help (re)sustain their organization's success. As our world becomes more diversified, interconnected and exposed to the unanticipated, intended, unintended and the unexpected, we end up living in an age of paradox confronted with multiple tensions, demands and dualisms that we must work with, work through and work around (Schad et al., 2016; Wright, 2016a). For example, firms are expected to be both flexible and focused, big and small, learn and unlearn, aim for exploration and exploitation, have short-term goals and long-term plans, go global and act local, compete and cooperate, encourage change and yet foster stability, *inter alia.*

Nested throughout these seemingly opposing trade-offs are rigid polarities, false dichotomies, outdated assumptions, preconceived biases, complacency and the counterintuitive nature of success leading to failure due to one's inability to (un)learn during times of crisis (Nystrom and Starbuck, 1984; Wright and Mak, 2014). Indeed the context in which we teach our students strategic management is highly Volatile, Uncertain, Complex and Ambiguous (VUCA) (Schoemaker and Day, 2009). In essence, teaching strategy for a VUCA world has never been so unsettling (Levinthal and March, 1993); yet as I will discuss throughout this chapter, the fundamentals of how to strategize are surprisingly obvious: we look but we don't see; we hear, but we don't listen.

TEACHING STRATEGY WITHIN A BROKEN SYSTEM: TOO MUCH OF A GOOD THING

Strategy at my university is a compulsory core subject for all business majors, and is taught in the fourth and final year of the undergraduate degree program. It is also a popular elective for students from a range of other disciplines interested in the world of business. By the time I meet my students it is normally in their final semester and so there is a lot to do to ensure they are world-ready right before graduation. As educators, if we have done our jobs right, we have not only imparted important useful knowledge but also ensured we have gone beyond the subjects we teach as part of our drive for more whole-person development (Adler, 2016; Chia and Holt, 2008; Weick, 2007). This is where the real challenge lies and it is the big white elephant in the room that not many are willing to talk about.

As an institution of learning, knowledge generation and dissemination are imperative in helping move our field forward, receiving recognition in world rankings, increased government funding and extra resources. Yet too much attention on these key variables (as important as they are) may overlook the very people we are supposed to be grooming in better preparing them for a complicated world (Bennis and O'Toole, 2005; Greiner et al., 2003; Hambrick, 2007; Staw, 1981; Staw et al., 1981). Yet it is so easy to hit the target, but miss the whole point in ensuring our students are challenged, motivated and inspired to make a difference in the world.

To exacerbate matters further, I believe the system we work within has a tendency to "over-teach" our students with heavy reliance on one-way lecturing (death by PowerPoint – PPT), and too many assessments. This leaves very little time for questions, comments and sharing between students and between students and teacher. This sets off a vicious cycle focusing on *doing and memorizing* without much space for playfulness, emotional engagement and contemplation of why and what is being learned, and how such learning translates into different multiple real-world contexts (for example, through internship placements). There is of course clear evidence of exemplary best and next practices found in every institution (including my own) (Greiner et al., 2003; Weick, 2007).

Given this backdrop, it becomes clear as my teaching semester unfolds that my final year strategy students come ill-equipped and ill-prepared to learn and unlearn at the senior level. Because they have developed a "trained-incapacity" to simply rely on repeating what is stated in PPT slides and obediently listen to the professor/teacher in the front of the classroom, they dare not have the courage to express their opinions of what is placed before them (Poole and Van de Ven, 1989). They struggle to take ownership of what is rightfully already theirs (their right to learn and unlearn). This translates into poor persuaders who cannot see the importance of multiple ways of seeing because they find more comfort in "sameness" (what they are used to and the small circle of friends and habits they have developed over the first three years of their university education). Because "most" education systems have preached for results and not the process, students struggle with the importance of urgency (leaving most things to the last minute – becoming deadline chasers) and have a hard time working in teams (as paradoxical as this may sound because they have been working in groups since their first year). At the heart of all this, and because they have not been given the time and space for reflection (Schon, 1983; Wright, 2018b), my students enter the course with lack of confidence in their true potential. And if this is not enough of a challenge for any teacher, my students are not problem students – instead they are students with problems! Most of my students are coming from poor family backgrounds where their parents are cleaners, taxi-drivers, and blue-collar workers. They struggle to make ends meet. Some of my students have a parent or family member suffering from a terminal disease or have had a relative pass away; some experience domestic violence at home; parents going through a separation/divorce; bullying in the neighborhood and/or the student has health issues of their own, *inter alia*.

With all these challenges in mind, I firmly believe that it is not that our students are not interested in learning (strategy); it is that they are not taught HOW to learn and unlearn (Dewey, 1910; Wright, 2016c; Wright and Brown, 2014). I want to put meaning, curiosity, playfulness and the joys of learning back into my students' lives. The next section outlines the underlying philosophies that guide my approach to helping better prepare my students for a broken world (Wright, 2019). It has changed the lives of my students and it has changed me for the better in the process.

THE TEACHING PHILOSOPHIES THAT GUIDE MY PRACTICE

Helping Students Develop a "Complicated Understanding"

One of the greatest disservices we can do to our students is to over-simplify the world for them. If anything, we should be complicating matters in meaningful ways (rather than dumbing things down to the point that they don't need to "think") (Bartunek et al., 1983; Miller, 1993). Instead of only relying on linear step-by-step thinking and doing (just as we would lay things out in our course outlines and lecture PPT slides), we also need to complement this with more circular, oblique, multi-dimensional, holistic and counterintuitive thinking (Chia, 2013; Wright, 2016c).

When faced with highly complex unsolved problems, issues and challenges, research has shown that breakthrough ideas are generated when we practice more higher-order metacognition through integrative/paradoxical and Janusian thinking (Bosma et al., 2016; Martin, 2007). Specifically, we are forced to think in very different directions simultaneously (differentiation); yet to really see the picture holistically, we are encouraged to make connections between the ideas (integration) which in turn enables us to generate deeper broader insights about the phenomena of interest.

Teaching for Knowledge Transfer

I must say that most of my teaching career has been to teach a subject and ensure students understand what the core concepts and ideas are for them to pass the course. But somehow this does not sound right! It is only in the latter part of my career that I started to "*teach for knowledge transfer.*" Universities are very good at teaching our students "content" but not very good in how that content can be applied into different contexts (Mourshed et al., 2012). This changes the entire dynamics of what we do as educators when we teach. Making sure what we teach makes sense and that it can add value to organizations dealing with complex problems, issues and challenges is the real test of the impact we can make (Adler, 2016). Does our teaching (of strategy) have the power to change the way we think so that we can see things differently in order to see different things, and in this process, open up the alternatives (Kelly, 1955; Wright, 2016a)? This insight goes back to the fundamentals of our craft as scholars in the production of knowledge and the dissemination of that knowledge (Weick, 2002).

What we teach must be transferrable to real-world settings not just "after" student graduation but during their studies as well. Student work integrated education/placements are fertile ground to ensure we close the "knowing-doing" gap (Pfeffer and Sutton, 2000). It requires a continuous iterative and generative process between classroom learning and real-world situations and back again. Rather than just passing on the best research to our students, get them to test them out the moment they leave the classroom and into their internship/work experiences. The class discussions should go to the heart of our theories, models and concepts and to see which of our assumptions need revision or what new assumptions manifest (Wright, 2016b).

It is All About PROGRESS (Betterment)

Throughout the course of a semester, I unpack the complexities of this high-sounding elusive subject by literally taking my students back to primary school and what we learned then to exemplify how great companies and leaders strategize today. For example, at the end of the day, if you really don't have a good grasp of this subject, I would simply ask you to understand the word "*better*." Irrespective of all the wonderful well-articulated definitions you may see in textbooks, journal articles and in the public media (Nag et al., 2007), it is all about: How can we become a *better* organization? (Hedberg et al., 1976; Starbuck, 1983). How can we produce *better* products and services? How can I become a *better* leader, a *better* colleague, a *better* friend, a *better* son/daughter, a *better* husband/wife, a *better* me! In philosophical terms, it is all about "*being and becoming*" better (Chia, 2010; Priem, 2018).

Time and time again, companies, committees, leaders, and producers/suppliers (*inter alia*) are fixated on the routine of what they do and simply repeat what they do without thinking deeply about how they can do "*better*." Even as students, it is all about attending one class after another, one course after another, without really taking a step back to reflect on "how can I do *better* than before?" The essence of strategic management is about this, plain and simple.

If You Want to See the Future, Look for Places Where People are Having the Most Fun!

It seems so obvious, yet how often do we do it? When learners feel they are in a safe happy place, they become more open to learn (Ardley, 1967). In my classes, there are no right or wrong answers – only who has the *better* questions and who has the *better* answers! Given what I know about my students and the broader academic system in which they must function, I am not too fussed if they do not have time to prepare for their assigned weekly strategy debate topics. In fact, I still encourage them to come to class (and like my own piano teacher) tell them we are going to do "guided practice" together. The key is to simply come to class with an open mind, positive attitude to learn and be prepared to express your perspective. Of course for those students really wanting to learn and get a higher grade, they will come prepared (and this of course is encouraged at every point of the semester). With this in mind, students find the learning less stressful and engage more willingly with curiosity (and humour) to see who has something interesting and thought-provoking to share (Wright, 2013).

HOW I ORGANIZE AND RUN MY CLASSES

Beginning with the End in Mind – Every Class is a Job Interview!

What gets measured gets done in all great strategy and the same goes for a strategy class. To bring more reality and a sense of urgency to the learning, students sign off on a "learning contract" at the beginning of term. This one-page contract (see Figure 9.1) outlines the overall sentiments, expectations and the type of learning environment they will experience if they commit to the class. The emphasis is grounded on the importance of sharing, a positive learning environment, the backbone of the course (using a framework called FOCUSED) (Wright et al., 2011) and the expectation that the student will commit to continuous reflection so that s/he can demonstrate "*progress*" in the course. At the end of the day, it is not just about attending classes but the students must show in what specific way they are making *progress*. This changes the entire dynamics of how a course is taught and learned.

To further advocate the importance of progress (and more active learning), 30 percent of the course grade is allocated for "class *contributions*" (not class attendance). Here, all students are informed that "*every class is a job interview*" so come prepared to engage and discuss your points of view. This is not to say that students who are extroverts and/or can speak good English will be advantaged: far from it. The key is what you say and how you say it (not how much one says). I have given straight "A" to students who are quiet throughout the whole course, but because they have done their homework and come to class prepared (including online), they have been able to redirect conversations in ways that have taken our learning to a much higher level. Similar to the research and practice of strategic management, there is no one best way of doing and diversity of perspectives is encouraged.

Scaffolding Approach to Learning and Development

At the beginning of the course, I also carefully elaborate the expectations of the course by explaining what it will take to "win" using the assessment rubric (see Figure 9.2). We use this rubric for all aspects of assessment. The rubric also gives students deeper insights on how the course has been planned and what they are expected to achieve (as in any good

Robert's Strategic Management (SM) Class:
<u>Formal Learning Contract</u>

In order to nurture a whole new culture of learning that will further help elevate the good standing of PolyU business students, I fully support the need for our class to be more engaged, stimulating, thought-provoking, encouraging and based on sharing and team spirit. I support our class being video recorded (and uploaded onto our password-protect online platform) so we can reflect more deeply about our learning. In this endeavor, as a registered student in this class, I pledge that for every class I attend (physically and on-line), I will place a high priority in demonstrating ***PROGRESS*** each week. In this respect, I will be prepared to:

1. Bring a positive attitude to my learning experience
2. Share, discuss and engage in the true spirit of learning
3. Be a team-player and help other classmates
4. Discuss the success stories/ lessons learned from my WIE, Service Learning & competition experience (keeping in mind the Confidential Pledge I have signed with the organization(s))
5. Share my student exchange experience (where appropriate)
6. Share what I have learned from our flipped-class mini-online lectures and weekly handouts
7. Engage the above in class + our virtual SM Blackboard (BB) e-discussion board
8. Practice my persuasion, convincing and influencing skills by anchoring my points of view from authoritative sources. For example:
   Learning from current university course (based on theories, models, frameworks, approaches, discussions, skill-sets, attributes…); Academic research papers; Practitioner journals in your field (Harvard Business Review, McKinsey Quarterly…); Industry reports; Newspaper sources (The Economist, Financial Times…); New TV / radio reports (e.g.: BBC…); TED Talks; Inspiring mentor / supervisor / teacher; Life experience; and/or Training / university course(s) you attended in the past.
9. Practice & share my learning using the 14 pre-course whiteboard animations and the *"Stay FOCUSED"* philosophy which forms the backbone of this class
   F - Bring Fresh perspective
   O - Think, feel and act like an Owner / manager
   C - Show Connected-thinking
   U - Have a sense of Urgency
   S - Show team SPIRIT
   E - Always Engage
   D - Exercise Deliberate practice
10. <u>I also pledge to take time to reflect regularly about what we are doing each week</u>

Finally, I have thoroughly read our Course Outline, and the Assessment Rubric, including the two (2) important emails from our former Vice President (Academic Development) [VP (AD)] and fully understand the expectations, requirements and due dates of this course. If I am unclear about any of the expectations and requirements of the course, I will ensure to have them resolved with Robert before the end of the 2nd week of this semester. If I experience challenges throughout the course, I will make every effort to resolve them with Robert.

Student Name: _____ Student No.: _____ Student Signature.: _____ Date: _____
<u>**This Learning Contract is to be signed and UPLOADED to our BB within 2-8 days from your first class**</u>

Figure 9.1   Making expectations clear from week one of the course

The "Staying F.O.C.U.S.E.D." philosophy is a strategic thinking framework designed to help you better deal with UNSOLVED problems, issues and challenges. It has the power to help you open up ALTERNATIVES. By using this framework, you will learn *BETTER*, learn *FASTER* and learn *MORE* than you are used to.

Grade band descriptors

Unsatisfactory — F (below 40)	Shows complete lack of interest in subject matter; has no idea of fundamentals. Shows complete disregard to expectations.
"Less than satisfactory" — D	Struggles to understand basic concepts; Does not make good use of provided / available material.
To achieve a "C" or "C+" grade (Satisfactory) you need to: **describe** the key issues. This means you must:	Address the task as set and display a basic UNDERSTANDING of the **key concepts and assumptions** involved. Use the materials provided by the teacher in ways which are relevant/related/**relevate**. Display no major errors of understanding. Can persuade / convince / influence well at this level.
To achieve a "B" or "B+" (Credit) you need to do everything required for a "C" PLUS display good '**relational thinking**'. This requires:	Using a **variety** of authoritative **sources** (with correct **referencing**) to analyse, compare/contrast, and make connections between **competing ideas and assumptions** to provide alternative EXPLANATIONS (why) and **apply** them to a given phenomena of interest. Can persuade / convince / influence well at this level.
To achieve an 'A' or 'A+' (Distinction) you need to do everything required for a 'B' AND go beyond to '**extend ideas**'. This involves:	Seeing issues from **different angles** – allowing **originality** in challenging assumptions, theorising and hypothesising in counter-intuitive ways so that we can better ANTICIPATE possible alternatives. Can persuade / convince / influence well at this level.

Grade scale

F (below 40)	D (40–45)	D+ (46–49)	C (50–54)	C+ (55–59)	B (60–64)	B+ (65–69)	A (70–79)	A+ (80+)
1 – 2	3	4	5	6	7	8	9	10
			Collect Differentiation		Connect Integration		Create Insight	

FOCUSED dice descriptions

- **F** — "F" is the Yellow dice – it stands for a fresh perspective – bright and optimistic; creating new ways of thinking and new ways of doing.
- **O** — "O" is the Orange dice – it stands for *Think, Feel and Act like an Owner/Manager* – it's about taking ownership and doing it for real.
- **C** — "C" is the Blue dice – it stands for *Connected Thinking* - creating Blue Oceans when ideas (e)merge.
- **U** — "U" is the Red dice – it stands for a *Sense of Urgency* - taking action now with clear purpose and energy.
- **S** — "S" is the Purple dice – the psychology of this color means want and togetherness - it stands for *Team Spirit* - we can achieve much more when we do things together - it's a team-'sport'.
- **E** — "E" is the Green dice - it stands for *Engage* - spending more time in the garden to create a beautiful garden.
- **D** — "D" is the Indigo dice - the psychology of this color means introspection / looking deep into ourselves - it stands for *Deliberate Practice* - thinking more deeply about what we do and don't do.

187

© 14th Jan 2019, Robert Wright

Figure 9.2   FOCUSED assessment rubric grounded on Bloom's Solo Taxonomy, metacognitive, persuasion skills and theory-building strategizing). To the left are the seven core attributes (the FOCUSED framework) rated on a 1–10 scale (with highest 10 points scored toward the right of the rubric). At the top and bottom of the rubric, we provide a *scaffolding approach to their development*. Specifically, what is expected at each grade; coincidentally, this three-step process also aligns with how great theorizing is achieved in our own research endeavors (Christensen and Raynor, 2003; Weick, 2002). For example, to score a "C" grade you must demonstrate *better* UNDERSTANDING of the subject matter (can you describe what is happening?); to attain a "B" grade you must be able to *better* EXPLAIN (why certain practices, approaches work and why others do not). To score an "A" grade, you must be able to first demonstrate understanding, then explain, in order to *better* ANTICIPATE (what happens next; tell us something new, novel, question assumptions . . .). At the bottom of the rubric you see three categories that align with the awarding of the letter grades: collect (differentiation – get as many ideas about the topic as possible); connect (integration – looking for connections between the multitude of ideas); and create (insight – tell us something new). At each grade level, you will notice we also expect students to demonstrate their persuasion skills (as this is another core of how great strategy is crafted) (Yunis, 2018).

No More PPTs (Please): Make Room for Socratic Dialogue and Persuasion Skills

Great strategy is when we "do more with less," and so too is the way I conduct my "flipped" classes. From week one of the course students have access to all my flipped-class mini-video lectures on my teaching online platform, along with all the PPTs for the entire course including handouts I will distribute and my self-recorded videos explaining what is to be learned from each of them. You may wonder, if that is the case, and all the lectures and PPTs are done, then what do we do in class time for the rest of the semester?

All contact class time is to open up the discussion through Socratic Dialogues about each week's assigned debate topic. There is no lecturing and no PPTs. In fact, given the pressure and stress a lot of our students undergo these days, I am more flexible if students prepare their weekly topic or not. The absolute minimum requirement however, is to come to class with just "one" thing to share and be prepared to have a conversation about it. The discussion can be about anything so long as it has something to do with our course on strategy.

The underlying expectation, however, is to support your arguments grounded on authoritative sources coming from any one of the references

listed in the course outline from strategy and management academic journals, to *Harvard Business Review*, *The Economist*, BBC News, *McKinsey
Quarterly*, even TED Talks, *inter alia* (Rousseau and McCarthy, 2007).
Anticipating even if my students still don't have the time to read an article
or the newspaper (on current affairs), I demonstrate how easy it is to
prepare by showing them a 2 minutes 43 seconds video clip of Professor
Roger Martin explaining "what is strategy?" (*Harvard Business Review*,
2013). In these few minutes, I learned more about strategy than I have in
the 18 years I have been teaching the subject at my school! Again, because
students are thinking they are just "students," it prevents them from thinking of themselves as "owners" of their learning. What I am trying to do is
to help them find ways that will allow them to learn better, faster and more
than they are currently used to. Learning does not have to be long-winded
and taxing. It can be short, fun, impactful and profound. Of course, if we
can get students hooked on a neat idea, they will go deeper and learn for
themselves. The key is what baits are available for such purpose.

To stimulate more engaged and active learning, I also schedule one hour
distinguished strategy guest speaker sessions from industry (including
senior management of my own university) from week 7 of a 13 week
semester (five guest speakers in total per strategy class). Yet these are no
ordinary guest speaker sessions because there are no PPTs, no speeches
and no lectures. A student host and a back-up host are assigned to orchestrate and run the entire session with the guest speaker. The key is to open
up a discussion centering around four fundamental questions for every
guest speaker session:

1. What are the key challenges facing senior executives and board members when crafting winning strategies?
2. If strategy is so important, why is it that so many organizations don't
   do this right?
3. What makes issues "strategic"?
4. How can we learn to think more strategically in making significant
   contributions to the organization we work for?

Students are expected to support their ideas, questions, comments and
sharing grounded on the learning from the course using authoritative
sources. Such engagement with real executives allows students to test if
what we are learning in the classroom is relevant to the challenges facing
strategy as practiced. Beyond this, I encourage students they are not here
just to learn from the executives but to provide informed ideas (suggestions) in helping them open their own thinking to alternatives not yet
conceived . . .

Whether it is in front of our distinguished guest speakers and/or in our normal class discussions, I look for which students are making connections between different points of views expressed. I look for how a student demonstrates their persuasion skills; what story are they telling to make their case. All this makes for a highly energized and active learning intellectual environment: 40 students walk into a room and walk out with over 40 different ideas, every single class.

The Importance of the Physical Class Setting

Before every class starts, all students are requested to help (re)arrange the room so that the tables and chairs are facing inwards as in auditorium style (to replicate the Harvard-style classroom). Every student has a paper name tent (which has reminders of the foundation of the course printed at the back, facing them). Every class is video recorded (with consent, as per learning contract) and for purposes of review and development not just for the student but for me as the teacher as well. The set-up uses a simple home video camera on a stand with one student volunteering for the first half of class to zoom-in/out and pan around the room to capture the essence of the discussions. After a short break another student volunteers. All volunteers are also treated equally as participants and are required to engage in Socratic Dialogue. Within two days of the class, I upload the recording onto our password protected teaching Blackboard online platform for students' own reflection/reflexion.

The Power of a Lesson Plan

Like all strategy, we need a plan; and teaching a strategy course is no exception. Yet how often do we hear our colleagues talk about this? We all know it makes good sense to have a plan, yet how many of us actually do it for a strategy class? After 30 years in the job, I must say I still do (see Figure 9.3). Lesson plans have helped me significantly in planning what it is I must achieve by the end of each lesson. They help me structure my thoughts, my learning outcomes, how I will start and end the class and what research papers, resources and teaching approaches I will need to effectively achieve the outcomes. Yet, I will admit that I don't always follow the plan (and rightfully so). Things happen along the way, just as in real strategy implementation and when things don't go to plan, we review, reframe, improvise and adapt along the way. This in and of itself, is strategy: we learn it by teaching it too.

LESSON PLAN - Teaching for Knowledge Transfer

Class Date/

Session Title:

Learning Objectives - By the end of this class, students will be able to:
* *
* *
* *

My reflections _at the end of this class:_
1
2
3
4

My self appraisal score out of 100 points: _____ %

FLOW OF THE SESSION

Timing (mins)	Opening Remarks: What Story Will You Tell?	Teaching Method	Resources Needed	Key References
	(Summary of Key Points from Previous Session / Q&A)			
	*			
	*			
	Main Topics to be Covered in this Session			
	How Will You End the Session with Key Takeaways?			
	*			
	*			
	*			
	Total mins			

© Robert Wright 15th January, 2019

Figure 9.3   Lesson plan is my strategic plan for each lesson!

191

It Has "Nothing" to do With Strategy, Yet it Has "Everything" to do With Strategy

One of the ways I widen my students' perspective-taking is to bring in everyday examples they are familiar with and show them how they can teach us a great deal about what strategy, strategizing and strategic management is all about. Take the example of "color-mixer" – an activity we performed when we were in primary school where we mix one color with another to get a totally different color. Needless to say this has absolutely nothing to do with how companies craft great strategy; or does it? Here I am really teaching students the power of merging opposing ideas to create something breath-taking. This is also very similar to an oxymoron (where you combine two very different words to create something new); or combining two very opposing ideas (like "less" and "more" to create the concept of "do more with less") (Chia, 2013; Martin, 2007).

The use of metaphors also has a very powerful effect in the teaching of strategy because metaphors make the *unfamiliar familiar* (Heracleous and Jacobs, 2011). Within the first four weeks of term I always ask students to upload a picture (any picture) and provide a short explanation of why that picture best represents strategy to them. I call it "strategy-in-pictures." The effect to the learning is profound. Another similar concept I use a lot is to ask students to *"relevate": make the irrelevant relevant* (or joining dots when dots don't normally join) (Chia, 2013). A good case in point is our local train company. Here is a train company that does not think it is a train company (and that in and of itself is a compelling insight). Here the train company is also doing "underground shopping malls." It also builds residential properties above its stations and also manages these properties. Moreover it generates money by using its empty wall spaces for advertising. And given its many years of experience operating a train business, it is also into consultancy. The point here is that normal train companies only think train; yet the example I provide shows that *"when we see things differently, we see different things"* and there lies the insight in the theory and practice of strategy.

We also learned about "joining dots" when we were little. Yet, what would happen, instead of joining dots 7 to 8 to 9, we join with dot number 78 then to 56, 22 and back down to 10? We would get a totally different picture. The core of great strategizing is how we "re-connect" the dots. I would then provide a wealth of examples throughout the course using examples outside company strategy to show how great songs, great sports people, great leaders and great civilizations show the same pattern which leads to greatness. The secret can be found in positive "*Re*-words." This is because such words open us to other ways of seeing: re-invent, re-construct, re-imagine, re-define, re-interpret, re-examine, re-frame. I often give students a rhetorical maths problem to solve: what is 5+5? Then I deliberately re-frame this problem and ask "what are any two numbers equal to ten?" Suddenly a whole plethora of possibilities opens up (Kelly, 1955; Wright, 2016a).

Our Routine Class Learning is "Consistently Inconsistent"

Another powerful approach to learning strategy in the way I design the course is that I give students a more agile understanding of the whole concept of "routines" (Parmigiani and Howard-Grenville, 2011). Routines are important for a well-functioning organization. They advocate the same thing being performed; sometimes they become so repetitive that it becomes boring and the mental effort needed to perform them significantly reduces. On the other hand, and similar to the metaphor of an MMA (mixed martial arts) fighter, the everyday practice and training is consistently inconsistent: it has to be – given the dynamics and ever-changing nature of the combat fighting, one has to be on constant high alert and in a state of readiness. And so too is every class discussion. Although we do have a set and linear list of topics to be covered for each week, once the class starts we become MMA fighters – and the discussions and arguments can come from any direction. Training students this way, also makes them more agile (mentally, emotionally and behaviorally).

A PEDAGOGICAL FRAMEWORK THAT TEACHES US TO FISH

To help my students better learn to (un)learn, I have been successfully using a framework I invented 10 years ago called, "staying FOCUSED" (Wright, 2018c; Wright et al., 2011). The philosophy of FOCUSED was grounded on an extensive faculty-wide survey with just one burning question: *"What is one thing our students need to do, and if they did that one thing, it will take their learning to a whole new level?"* Over 400+ responses culminated in seven (7) themes much sought after in the real world:

F – Bring **FRESH perspective**
O –Think, feel and act like an **OWNER/manager**
C – Show **CONNECTED-thinking**
U – Have a **sense of URGENCY**
S – Show **team SPIRIT**
E – Always **ENGAGE**
D – Exercise **DELIBERATE** practice

To operationalize the philosophy I later used the aid of seven dice, printing the most representative and thought-provoking questions, prompts and statements from survey data onto the six sides of each color-coded dice. This serendipitously brought in the element of playfulness and a novel heightened sense of anticipation and curiosity into the learning process as students roll the dice (Ardley, 1967). Figure 9.4 provides a good overview of the meaning and the psychology of color behind each dice, and what questions, prompts and statements are associated with each core competency of the seven FOCUSED dice framework.

The framework can be used individually and/or within project groups. First, students are given a strategic problem, issue or challenge to solve. This can be either a major semester long project or an assigned class exercise/case study to discuss (F.O.C.U.S.E.D., n.d.). For example: *Your business school is facing a rising number of complaints by employers about students' inability to contribute/add-value during student internship placements. If you were the Dean, what would you do?*

Students think about the problem and then roll all seven dice. They then pick up one dice at a time, reading out aloud the side of the dice facing up (for example from the "D" dice: *"what are we NOT doing that we should be doing?"*); think about it for a moment then open up a discussion. It does not matter if you start this process in sequence from the "F" dice to the "D" dice, or you randomly start with any dice. In fact, depending on the situation, you may pick up a particular dice first, say the red dice, because we are in a "sense of urgency" (one item states: "look for examples") (who is dealing with a similar problem really well?); or you may start off with the "E" dice because you want to be more engaged with the problem and read out "don't be afraid to experiment," and so on. Whichever is the case, the key is to use all seven dice to help you get a peripheral vision about the problem you are currently dealing with. At any point, you may stop and roll the dice again and see what item(s) on the dice stimulates and redirects the conversation.

After testing this framework with students and managers over an extended period of time, I discovered that when we deal with complex unsolved problems, issues and challenges, there is a *need* to look at things from multiple perspectives, holistic thinking, using both left and right brains simultaneously, developing a complicated understanding through both differentiation and integration to transcend a situation and gain a better peripheral vision (Wright et al., 2013). Specifically, there is a *need* to bring a fresh perspective (tell us something new/novel); there is a *need* to think, feel and act *"as if"* you are the owner/manager (taking ownership of your problems) (Vaihinger, 2009); there is a *need* to connect ideas and different points of view together; there is a *need* for a sense of urgency (it's all about now with purpose); there

The seven (7) key elements of the "Staying F.O.C.U.S.E.D." framework represent core competencies needed when dealing with complex unsolved problems, issues and challenges	Each group of six (6) prompts, questions and statements encapsulates and triangulate a core theme for each category of the F.O.C.U.S.E.D. framework.	Each three dimensional dice represents a core theme of the F.O.C.U.S.E.D. framework
F "F" is the Yellow dice – it stands for *Bring a Fresh Perspective* – bright and optimistic; creating new ways of thinking and new ways of doing	1. Who are our new customers / competitors? 2. How does this advance what we already know, don't know and need to know? 3. When we see things differently, we see different things. 4. What would happen if you did the opposite? 5. Think value co-creation. 6. Redefine / reinterpret / reconstruct / reframe / rethink.	
O "O" is the Orange dice – it stands for *Think, Feel and Act like an Owner/Manager* – it's about taking ownership and doing it for real	7. Understand the context (situation, time, history, relations…). 8. What are the current taken-for-granted assumptions? (and question your assumptions). 9. Visualize your goals. 10. Talk to more people in and outside your field for feedback. 11. Anticipate the future (what if…). 12. Think like your competitor.	
C "C" is the Blue dice – it stands for *Show Connected-thinking* – creating Blue Oceans when ideas (e)merge	13. What are the current conversations in the field? 14. Either / Or logic versus And / Both logic. 15. Every expert knows there are alternative explanations for a given phenomenon of interest. 16. Think multi-discipline, multi-level, multi-method, multi-time, multi-space. 17. What is in the foreground and background? 18. Best ideas come from outside of your field.	
U "U" is the Red dice – it stands for *Have a Sense of Urgency* – taking action now with clear purpose and energy	19. Set agenda and timelines (prioritize / write it down). 20. Say more with less. 21. Begin with the end in mind. 22. Sometimes we need to let go… 23. Look for examples. 24. What if tomorrow never comes?	
S "S" is the Purple dice – the psychology of this color means warm and togetherness – it stands for *Show Team Spirit* – we can achieve much more when we do things together – it's a team-sport!	25. If you want to go fast, go alone; if you want to go far, go together. 26. Respect each other's strengths and weaknesses. 27. Each of us has something meaningful to contribute. 28. Imagine you are in a S.W.A.T. (Special Weapons and Tactics) team. 29. Who has the most expertise on the issue? 30. Spend more time together to know ourselves.	
E "E" is the Green dice – it stands for *Always Engage* – spending more time in the garden to create a beautiful garden	31. It's all about the gardening. 32. Look for similarities and differences / sameness and otherness / and their inter-relationships. 33. You have to believe you can. 34. What story will you tell? 35. Be positive. 36. Don't be afraid to experiment.	
D "D" is the Indigo dice – the psychology of this color means introspection / looking deep into ourselves – it stands for *Exercise Deliberate Practice* – thinking more deeply about what we do and don't do	37. Are we measuring the right things? 38. What are the critical success factors? (What does success look like?) 39. What are we doing now that we should not be doing? 40. If you want to change the result, you need to change the process. 41. What are we NOT doing that we should be doing? 42. Take a quiet moment to stay calm, pause and reflect.	

Note: A free pre-prototype app is available – search for "*focused dice*." For detailed descriptions of each item printed on the seven dice, please refer to this link: https://qrgo. page.link/jcj8F.

Figure 9.4 FOCUSED framework designed to help you better deal with your unstructured problems, issues and challenges

is a *need* for team spirit (especially when solving big problems require us to work together. It's a team-sport); there is a *need* to engage with our problems (spending more time with them to get a deeper sense of them); and there is a *need* to take a step back to reflect on what it is we are doing and not doing in regards to the challenge we are facing.

By helping students and managers structure highly unstructured problems, issues and challenges, the framework guides the users' thinking, feeling and acting. Because of its pluralistic nature and the importance of looking at different and distinct things simultaneously, the framework is designed to help you learn better, learn faster and learn more than you are currently used to (Wright, 2017). The framework is not just about problem-solving but also about problem-*setting*. It is not just a thinking tool, but thinking, feeling and acting (Kelly, 1955). And it is not just a creativity tool, but a tool designed to open you to otherness: other forms of reasoning, other forms of logic, other forms of explanations and to other ways of knowing. This in turn, will help you open up the alternatives to your unsolved problems, issues and challenges.

CONCLUSION

The real world is indeed complicated! It is filled with the complex problems of our times. A complicated world requires complicated thinking in students. This kind of thinking allows students to develop a deeper understanding of a contradictory, unanticipated, fast-paced, dynamic and constantly redefined world of competing demands. While traditional approaches to teaching and learning strategy still have their advantages, we require complementary approaches that help our students learn better, learn faster and learn more than they are used to. Bringing our students closer to the real world's unsolved problems/issues/challenges inside real organizations and getting them to reflect more deeply about the "knowing-doing" gap through the "FOCUSED" framework, has the power to inject a sense of urgency, excitement and meaning back into their learning and better prepare them for a complicated world (Adler, 2016; Wright, 2018a; Wright, 2018b).

Today, what started as a simple teaching pedagogy to help those left behind (my students) is now being used by students from multiple disciplines, professors, researchers and senior executives of listed and private companies to help them open up the alternatives to their complex unsolved problems, issues and challenges. The FOCUSED framework forms the backbone of how I teach strategy (by not teaching strategy). Given the approach that I use in teaching strategy, many of my students at the beginning of term think there is *madness in my methods*. It is only when they reach the end of term that they truly appreciate that there is a *method in the madness*; and this is the true deception of strategy revealed.

REFERENCES

Adler, P.S. (2016). 2015 Presidential Address: Our Teaching Mission. *Academy of Management Review*, 41(2), pp. 185–195.

Ardley, G. (1967). The Role of Play in the Philosophy of Plato. *Philosophy*, 42(161), pp. 226–244.

Bartunek, J.M., Gordon, J.R. and Wathersby, R.P. (1983). Developing "Complicated" Understanding in Administrators. *Academy of Management Review*, 8(2), pp. 273–284.

Bennis, W. and O'Toole, J.O. (2005). How Business Schools Lost Their Way. *Harvard Business Review*, 83(5), pp. 98–104.

Bosma, B., Chia, R. and Fouweather, I. (2016). Radical Learning Through Semantic Transformation: Capitalizing on Novelty. *Management Learning*, 47(1), pp. 14–27.

Chia, R. (2010). Shifting Paradigms Through "Letting Go": On Allowing Oneself to Become a Management Education Scholar. In C. Wankel and B. DeFillippi (eds.), *Being and Becoming a Management Education Scholar*. Series: Research in management education and development. Charlotte, NC: Information Age Publishing, pp. 11–41.

Chia, R. (2013). In Praise of Strategic Indirection: An Essay on the Efficacy of Oblique Ways of Responding. *M@n@gement*, 16(5), pp. 667–679.

Chia, R. and Holt, R. (2008). The Nature of Knowledge in Business Schools. *Academy of Management Learning & Education*, 7(4), pp. 471–486.

Christensen, C.M. and Raynor, M.E. (2003). Why Hard-Nosed Executives Should Care about Management Theory. *Harvard Business Review*, 81(9), pp. 66–75.

Dewey, J. (1910). *How We Think*. Boston: D.C. Health & Co. Publishers.

F.O.C.U.S.E.D. (n.d.). Staying F.O.C.U.S.E.D. Learn Better, Learn Faster, Learn More Than You Are Used To. https://www.focused-polyu.com/ (accessed November 29, 2019).

Greiner, L.E., Bhambri, A. and Cummings, T.G. (2003). Searching for a Strategy to Teach Strategy. *Academy of Management Learning & Education*, 2(4), pp. 402–420.

Hambrick, D.C. (2007). The Field of Management's Devotion to Theory: Too Much of a Good Thing? *Academy of Management Journal*, 50(6), pp. 1346–1352.

Harvard Business Review. (2013). *Roger Martin: The Two Choices to Make in Strategy*. HBR video, January 29. https://hbr.org/video/2228473588001/the-two-choices-to-make-in-strategy (accessed December 15, 2019).

Hedberg, B., Nystrom, P. and Starbuck, W. (1976). Camping on Seesaws: Prescriptions for a Self-Designing Organization. *Administrative Science Quarterly*, 21(1), pp. 41–65.

Heracleous, L. and Jacobs, C. (2011). *Crafting Strategy: Embodied Metaphors in Practice*. Cambridge: Cambridge University Press.

Kelly, G.A. (1955). *The Psychology of Personal Constructs: A Theory of Personality*. London: Routledge.

Levinthal, D.A. and March, J.G. (1993). The Myopia of Learning. *Strategic Management Journal*, 14(S2), pp. 95–112.

Martin, R. (2007). How Successful Leaders Think. *Harvard Business Review*, 85(6), pp. 60–67.

Miller, D. (1993). The Architecture of Simplicity. *Academy of Management Review*, 18(1), pp. 116–138.

Mourshed, M., Farrell, D. and Barton, D. (2012). Education to Employment: Designing a System that Works. *McKinsey Centre for Government: McKinsey & Co.* https://www.mckinsey.com/industries/social-sector/our-insights/educa tion-to-employment-designing-a-system-that-works (accessed October 27, 2019).

Nag, R., Hambrick, D.C. and Chen, M-J. (2007). What is Strategic Management, Really? Inductive Derivation of a Consensus Definition of the Field. *Strategic Management Journal*, 28(9), pp. 935–955.

Nystrom, P.C., and Starbuck, W.H. (1984). To Avoid Organizational Crises, Unlearn. *Organizational Dynamics*, 12(4), pp. 53–65.

Parmigiani, A. and Howard-Grenville, J. (2011). Routines Revisited Exploring the Capabilities and Practice Perspectives. *Academy of Management Annals*, 5(1), pp. 413–453.

Pfeffer, J. and Sutton, R.I. (2000). *The Knowing–Doing Gap: How Smart Companies Turn Knowledge into Action*. Boston, MA: Harvard Business School Press.

Poole, M.S. and Van de Ven, A.H. (1989). Using Paradox to Build Management and Organization Theories. *Academy of Management Review*, 14(4), pp. 562–578.

Priem, R.L. (2018). Toward Becoming a Complete Teacher of Strategic Management. *Academy of Management Learning & Education*, 17(3), pp. 374–388.

Reeves, M., Love, C. and Tillmanns, P. (2012). Your Strategy Needs a Strategy. *Harvard Business Review*, 90(9), pp. 76–83.

Rousseau, D.M. and McCarthy, S. (2007). Educating Managers from an Evidence-Based Perspective. *Academy of Management Learning & Education*, 6(1), pp. 84–101.

Schad, J., Lewis, M.W., Raisch, S. and Smith, W.K. (2016). Paradox Research in Management Science: Looking Back to Move Forward. *Academy of Management Annals*, 10(1), pp. 5–64.

Schoemaker, P. and Day, G. (2009). How to Make Sense of Weak Signals. *MIT Sloan Management Review*, 50(3), pp. 81–89.

Schon, D.A. (1983). *The Reflective Practitioner: How Professionals Think in Action*. London: Routledge.

Starbuck, W. (1983). Organizations as Action Generators. *American Sociological Review*, 48(1), pp. 91–102.

Staw, B.M. (1981). The Escalation of Commitment to a Course of Action. *Academy of Management Review*, 16(4), pp. 577–587.

Staw, B.M., Sandelands, L.E. and Dutton, J.E. (1981). Threat-Rigidity Effects in Organizational Behavior: A Multilevel Analysis. *Administrative Science Quarterly*, 26(4), pp. 501–524.

Vaihinger, H. (2009). *The Philosophy of "As If": A System of the Theoretical, Practical and Religious Fictions of Mankind*. Translated by C.K. Ogden,

Mansfield Center: CT Martino Publishing (Original English work published 1924).

Weick, K.E. (2002). Puzzles in Organizational Learning: An Exercise in Disciplined Imagination. *British Journal of Management*, 13, pp. S7–S15.

Weick, K.E. (2007). Drop Your Tools: On Reconfiguring Management Education. *Journal of Management Education*, 31(1), pp. 5–16.

Wright, R.P. (2013). Bringing Teaching and Research Together Through a "F.O.C.U.S.E.D. Dice" Game. *Proposal presented to the inaugural AOM Teaching Conference of the American Academy of Management*, Orlando, USA, August.

Wright, R.P. (2016a). Organizational Paradoxes: When Opposites Cease to be Opposites. In D. Winter and N. Reed (eds.), *Wiley-Blackwell Handbook of Personal Construct Psychology*. London: Wiley-Blackwell, pp. 306–319.

Wright, R.P. (2016b). Insights: "Staying F.O.C.U.S.E.D." and Make a Real Impact to Your Work Integrated Education!. *Career Connect*, September issue #2. Office of Careers and Placements (CAPS), Centre Student Advancement and Resources, The Hong Kong Polytechnic University.

Wright, R.P. (2016c). A Strategic Thinking Framework to Help "Complicate" Our Students' Learning. *Paper Presentation to the Strategic Management Society*, Berlin, Germany. September.

Wright, R.P. (2017). Re-examining What we "Anticipate" in a Constructed World. In R. Galavan, K. Sund and G. Hodgkinson (eds.), *Methodological Challenges and Advances in Managerial and Organizational Cognition – New Horizons in Managerial and Organizational Cognition*. London: Emerald Publishing, pp. 219–240.

Wright, R.P. (2018a). Strategy Students' Cognition of Opening up Alternatives to Complex Challenges. *Paper Presented to the Strategic Management Society*, Paris, France. September.

Wright, R.P. (2018b). Using Reflective/Reflexive Practice to Stay F.O.C.U.S.E.D. in a Complicated World. *Paper Presented to the West East Institute WEI International Academic Conference*, Harvard Faculty Club, Boston, USA, August.

Wright, R.P. (2018c). Learning to (Un)learn by Staying F.O.C.U.S.E.D. *Faculty of Business Magazine*, The Hong Kong Polytechnic University. December Issue, pp. 26–27.

Wright, R.P. (2019). When Leaders Better Anticipate the Unknown. *Faculty of Business Magazine*, The Hong Kong Polytechnic University. June Issue, pp. 4–5 (feature article).

Wright, R.P. and Brown, K.G. (2014). *Educating Tomorrow's Thought-leaders: Distinguished Scholars Answer a Burning Question*. https://qrgo.page.link/LX9AY (accessed January 30, 2016).

Wright, R.P., Hung, P., Lau, P. and Lo, V. (2011). Staying F.O.C.U.S.E.D. in a Complicated World. *Official Newsletter of the Department of Management & Marketing*, Faculty of Business, The Hong Kong Polytechnic University. July Issue, pp. 11–12.

Wright, R.P. and Mak, W.M. (2014). Using Oppositional Analysis Grounded in Personal Construct Theory to Elicit Strategic Tensions. Philadelphia, PA: *Academy of Management Conference Proceedings*.

Wright, R.P., Paroutis, S.E. and Blettner, D.P. (2013). How Useful Are the Strategy Tools We Teach in Business Schools? *Journal of Management Studies*, 50(1), pp. 92–125.

Yunis, H. (ed.) (2018). *Aristotle: The Art of Rhetoric*. Oxford world's classics. Translated from Ancient Greek by R. Waterfield. Oxford: Oxford University Press.

PART III

Teaching strategic management for particular groups of learners and teaching settings

10. Strategic management in online and hybrid courses

David R. King and Aiden E. Sizemore

Teaching is personal, and there is not a single solution for how to teach strategic management, or other subjects. This chapter builds on the authors' experience with online courses. The author team combines an instructor experienced with teaching strategy at all levels and methods of delivery with an expert in instructional support, including course design within learning management systems at all levels and across multiple disciplines. Online delivery of courses presents unique challenges. For example, actively engaging students with online content represents a common challenge in teaching online and in hybrid courses (e.g. Green et al., 2018). Before going further, we define three different types of courses:

- *Traditional:* A class taught face-to-face in a classroom in a lecture and discussion format that may have online content. In strategy courses, case studies or simulations are often used to demonstrate ideas (Jennings, 1996; Kachra & Schnietz, 2008; Wolfe, 1997; Zantow et al., 2005).
- *Hybrid:* A class that has part of the content online, but it also still meets face-to-face. For these courses, the classroom is often "flipped," or the lecture component is put online and time in class focuses on the application of concepts that students have already reviewed. The intent is to use class time for higher value activity, but it depends on adequate student preparation.
- *Online:* A class where all content and deliverables are within an online learning management system where summarizing and applying concepts can occur synchronously or asynchronously. Synchronous-based courses provide specific times that students log into an online course environment for interaction with content and activities, and asynchronous-based courses rely on the student to pace themselves on content and activities. While there are pros and cons to each mode of delivery, asynchronous provides greater flexibility for students' schedules.

Moving forward, we briefly cover reasons why online teaching is important (section 10.1), what differences teaching online means for instructors, and differences across levels of instruction and type of institution. Following this background, we develop sections on different considerations for an online course (section 10.2), syllabus development (section 10.3), exercises and cases (section 10.4), discussion questions (section 10.5), and grading (section 10.6) for online courses. We then conclude (section 10.7) with encouragement that the covered ideas can help address the challenges of teaching online and with recognition that the need to teach online is not going to go away.

10.1 ONLINE TEACHING ENVIRONMENT

Hybrid and online courses shift in the locus for instructor preparation and student responsibility. For both students and instructors, online classes demand more preparation (Hewling, 2005). For instructors, the increased online content drives greater preparation before a semester starts to create and structure content in a learning management system. It begins with having base content prepared and available to students for initial review, and then augmenting it with options for student feedback and contact. For example, instructors can hold synchronous webinar sessions or virtual office hours. Class size also plays a role, as the larger the enrollment in an online course, the bigger the challenge is to clarify concepts for students that typically require additional, personalized attention to grasp course concepts. This opens up the risk that some students may fall behind, or the need to develop a course's organization and instructions to account for the lowest common denominator.

Taking steps to improve online teaching is relevant for two reasons. First, improving online teaching is important, as content delivery moves into digital format even for corporate training (Adamy, 2018). In college education, this manifests with the increased use of learning management systems (e.g. *Blackboard, Canvas, Sakai*, etc.), and flipping classrooms to present material outside the classroom and focus on applying information in the classroom (Toqeer, 2013). Second, evidence on general teaching effectiveness suggests that the impact of the top 10 percent of instructors on students is three times greater than the bottom 10 percent of instructors (*Economist*, 2016). In other words, small improvements by instructors in online and hybrid courses can have significant impacts on student outcomes across different levels of instruction (e.g. doctoral, graduate, or undergraduate).

- Doctoral seminars do not typically lend themselves to the online environment, but it may derive value from hybrid models. However, discussion of readings in seminars may represent a precursor to "flipped" classrooms. Further, doctoral courses generally require some synchronous dialogue, due to a greater focus on theoretical relationships, research methodology, and summarizing differences across theoretical perspectives.
- At the Master's level, applying concepts using case studies has been successful in stimulating discussion of theory, relationships between concepts, and structuring logical arguments. This can be achieved with active engagement in the discussion by the instructor to increase student participation (see also section 10.5) and developing a student's ideas through peer interaction. For example, Master's students tend to have more work experience that leads to greater engagement.
- The biggest difference in teaching strategy is between Master's and undergraduate levels, and the focus of this chapter is largely on undergraduate strategic management courses. The reason for a focus on teaching undergraduate strategy online is that it represents a greater challenge.

The author team has experience across different institutions, including private and public universities and across international borders. The type of student at different institutions varied with greater student engagement expected at private institutions, but a primary consideration has been the size of the course. In this chapter, a small enrollment consists of 75 or fewer students and a large enrollment consists of over 75 students. This demarcation comes from personal experience. At private educational institutions, class sizes are typically smaller to allow for more qualitative assignments and personalized feedback from an instructor. For example, written student case assignments or essay questions are easier to implement for courses with smaller enrollment. For qualitative assignments and feedback, differences between whether a class is face-to-face or partially or fully online are minimal. This is because student work on qualitative assignments occurs outside of class, and instructors evaluate and create associated feedback outside the classroom. In assessing student written work, hybrid and online courses have an advantage in that learning management systems often have the capability to automatically detect plagiarism, as well as check for grammar. For larger course enrollment, the ability to provide meaningful feedback to students on qualitative assignments confronts limits. One method around this limit is to assign students to groups, or to rotate assignments across enrolled students so that approximately one-third complete a case assignment. However, the ability to manage qualitative assignments diminishes beyond 75 students.

While more tied to culture at a particular institution (versus the type of institution), the extent that students prepare can vary widely. For locations where students are less prepared, teaching hybrid and online courses has a greater challenge. In further exploring this subject, the primary frame of reference for this chapter is public institutions with larger undergraduate course enrollments and greater diversity in student preparation. Again, this likely reflects a more challenging environment for teaching hybrid and online courses that are developed next. We also focus primarily on asynchronous online courses. However, synchronous elements to provide specific engagement opportunities between instructors and students are possible, and synchronous lectures are more similar to traditional instruction.

10.2   DEVELOPING AN ONLINE COURSE

For an instructor, the main challenge presented by a hybrid or online courses is the need to create and host content in advance of the course starting, as well as designing a rhythm for student engagement. In creating a rhythm for a course, we encourage summarizing foundational knowledge and heuristics (e.g. Porter's 5-forces) before showing how it applies to organizations (e.g. case study). Alternating material covered between presenting concepts and showing their application, can be effective in an online course. Once the content of a course is developed, it is easy to replicate it to subsequent offerings. Still, be cautious in making changes during a term. For example, while it is "easier" to make changes in a learning management system, it is "harder" to implement the changes during the semester. In other words, communicating changes to students in an online course and having them adjust to new expectations has increased difficulty. For changes, multiple methods of communication are needed. Even then, 20 percent of students may "miss" that there was a change, leading to the need for individual adjustments on top of the initial change. Overall, these considerations place more importance on the initial design of the course to develop the syllabus and grading. The following subsections discuss online teaching challenges with solutions (see Table 10.1). Syllabus development is covered in section 10.3, and grading in section 10.6.

Table 10.1   Online teaching challenges and solutions

Challenges	Solution
1. Technology	• University staff • Tutorials • Online search
2. Text	• Integrated electronic text • Flexibility in required text
3. Hosting lectures	• Virtual meeting • Voice over PowerPoint • Video lectures
4. Engaging students	• Weekly assignments/quizzes • Weekly messages to students
5. Applying concepts	• Video lecture with case example • Discussion boards • Online submission of assignments • Strategy simulations
6. Student cheating	• Alternating assignments across semesters • Plagiarism detection • Randomizing exam questions • Limiting the time available for completing an exam

10.2.1   Learning Management Systems

The initial hurdle in transitioning from a traditional to a hybrid or online course can be gaining familiarity with available technology. Many instructors will have limited experience with online courses before developing one. Some of the initial work is pre-defined. For example, your college or university will have selected a learning management system (e.g. *Blackboard, Canvas, Sakai*, etc.). While the functionality of the different systems varies, they offer similar capabilities for uploading files, creating discussion boards/threads (see also section 10.5), student submission of assignments, and online quizzes or exams. Learning management systems also include calendars that remind students of events, and they provide an ability to: (1) make "announcements" and/or message students in a course, (2) detect plagiarism, and (3) track student grades and activity in a course. The cost of gaining familiarity with a learning management system provides benefits for an instructor, and it is worth integrating a learning management system into traditional courses.

While online teaching may be new to you, there will be others where you are located that are familiar with the associated technology who can help. For example, your university likely has a teaching center or instructional technology staff that can be of assistance. Most learning management systems also come with tutorials. While they vary in quality, internet searches will identify how to complete basic functions with text descriptions or online videos. Additionally, learning management systems often have a community where you can actively post ideas or questions you have about not only the system's functionality. Typically, individuals participating in these communities are highly engaged instructors or instructional technology professionals that teach or design online courses or instructional materials.

10.2.2 Selecting and Integrating a Text

The selection of a text is more complicated for hybrid and online courses. In a traditional course, the instructor identifies the text and students have different options for accessing it. By integrating an electronic text into hybrid and online courses, students have fewer options. Integrating a text with a learning management system offers advantages in assigning readings, and it provides instructors the ability to insert highlighting of important material or quiz questions as part of the reading. Additionally, book representatives and publishers can help with setting up a course and integrating an electronic text. However, the primary disadvantage is that the text really becomes a required expense for students taking the course. For strategy texts, existing titles cost around $100 for access to an electronic text for one semester. This is significantly higher than the cost of a used textbook, and it does not provide students with a lasting reference. Another solution is to avoid tightly integrating an electronic text with the learning management system, retaining student choice for how to purchase a textbook, or using an open source textbook (e.g. *Open Textbooks*, *FlatWorld*, etc.). However, stress to students that a text is important in providing a common baseline for terminology and concepts covered, and that students retain primary responsibility for gaining familiarity to course concepts.

10.2.3 Hosting Content

An additional challenge relates to instructors considering how to host lectures within a learning management system. One option is to hold synchronous sessions, such as a virtual class where students and an instructor log into a meeting platform at the same time for an instructor to provide a lecture or answer questions. This option is less realistic for larger course enrollments as there are inevitable conflicts that require recording the sessions to be available to students that miss the session or for later student review. Recordings of a virtual class can also be of lower quality (sound and video) and tend to be longer than necessary, and these limitations reduce student engagement. Another option is to provide content asynchronously by "recording" lectures and posting the associated files within a learning management system.

One option available to nearly everyone will be to record "voice over PowerPoint" lectures. In this situation, an instructor simply takes what are likely existing slides and with a microphone records their "lecture" over the slides. The resulting files are generally very large, but once uploaded they can be "played" by students. Overall, the advantage of simply using existing slides has several disadvantages, including: (1) using existing slides fails to adapt how material is presented, (2) the resulting files are large and can have problems with uploading and playing, and (3) most students will not be able to listen to what are typically long lectures in this format. A workaround is to break up longer lectures into smaller parts; however, this method of delivery (voice over PowerPoint) remains less engaging than video. For example, students routinely comment that they prefer to see the lecturer when watching educational content. This also provides remedial benefits in how students approach instructors when communicating in a non-traditional environment. Students now associate the course with a physical person, and they are more likely to maintain a professional demeanor.

While not available to everyone based on available software and infrastructure, screen capture video on laptops can enable an instructor to appear in a window with slides or notes on the same screen. Brief videos from a smartphone can also provide status updates. Some universities will also have professional recording studios and video editing services available. Still, online lectures need to be brief. Part of the success of TED Talks is limiting talks to specific ideas that are covered in less than 18 minutes (Gallo, 2014); however, research suggests the "optimal" length of video is less than six minutes (Emporia State University, 2018). We also recommend posting PowerPoint files of lecture slides for students to facilitate studying and note taking. In summary, the more time and higher technology level used to convey content by an instructor in as little time as possible, the better the outcomes.

10.2.4   Engaging Students

A perennial challenge involves how to engage students in a course. This is harder for an online course, as the responsibility for being prepared and meeting course deadlines for assignments and exams rests with students. This frequently means that students only engage with online material when they are required. As a result, exams and other assignment milestones drive a spike in student activity that can be ineffective for learning. The solution is to create a rhythm for an online course where students have an incentive to engage with material each week, while maintaining a regular pace to help students retain information. If an electronic text is integrated within the learning management system, then readings can be assigned and quizzes either integrated with the reading or separately assigned in the publisher's platform for the text. Quizzes on assigned readings can also be created in the learning management system. The latter approach allows students to purchase or access a text in multiple ways (i.e. used text), to test additional readings (i.e. electronic handouts or articles), and to develop test questions on lectures however they are delivered. Additionally, setting up discussion forums for frequently asked questions (FAQs) or content clarification can be beneficial to providing opportunities for students to engage with the instructor and each other to provide peer-to-peer learning opportunities. A final recommendation for engagement is to compose weekly messages for students to provide responses to common questions or preview of an upcoming week/module.

10.2.5   Applying Course Concepts

A challenge in translating theory and methodology online is making the content relatable to students, including engaging students to applying course concepts (Grant & Baden-Fuller, 2018). One option is to use case studies of organizations that students are familiar with to develop a better understanding of complex concepts. For example, students often have a consumer focus and struggle with understanding who the customer is for non-consumer focused organizations. However, cases can be more difficult to present online. The application of a specific strategic analysis tool, such as Porter's 5-forces or SWOT (Wright et al., 2013), in online classes, can be done with a video lecture to summarize a concept and another video lecture to apply that concept to a specific company. This allows the separation of concepts with their application and enables the viewing of shorter video lectures by students. It also provides opportunities for real-world application of theory to augment student understanding. Other options for applying concepts online include: (1) case assignments (see section 10.4), (2) discussion boards (see section 10.5), or (3) simulations (e.g. *Business Strategy Game*, *CAPSIM*, etc.). Simulations can be effective in demonstrating the complexity and interconnectedness of business decisions (Finland, 2018). While considering effectiveness, it is important to vet the simulation to ensure it offers sufficient robustness to meet learning objectives. For example, simulations that lack variation in "answers" risk student cheating that limits any learning benefit.

10.2.6 Student Cheating

With less interaction and development of a relationship between instructors and students, cheating in online classes is more prevalent. When it comes to graded work (i.e. quizzes, exams, assignments), it creates a concern that students may not provide the required effort for the grades achieved or retain an understanding of course content. The primary solution is for assignments to vary each semester or for assignments to be highly personalized to discuss student experiences with respect to a topic. For longer assignments, having multiple turn-ins can provide feedback and help students avoiding starting work on a large assignment at the last minute that is associated with greater temptation to cheat. Most learning management systems come with tools for plagiarism detection (e.g. *Turnitin*). There are also separate and free options, such as *Grammarly*, that are available to provide limited reporting on plagiarism.

Still, there is simply greater availability of information for online courses, resulting in less control over content. Once content is available online students have the opportunity to download it and share it. For example, *Quizlet* is a platform where students can share information about a course, including exam questions. Additionally, students can create private groups to share information on *Facebook* and other social media platforms. Specifically, one student can take a quiz or exam, and then take photos of the questions or from memory post them online for others. This drives the need to randomize questions from a larger test bank and to implement controls, such as test proctoring. For example, *Examity* provides online test proctoring. If proctoring is not possible, then the time available for students to take an exam should be limited, as time pressure can help cause students to complete an exam without resorting to outside resources. Instructors can also create their own exam questions and not rely on test banks provided with a text. Simply, you have to assume that standardized test banks from publishers are available to students online. For additional content created for students by the instructor, an immediate advantage is that the material will not be widely available online. It also offsets the disadvantages of an electronic text, because students can keep instructor developed handouts as a lasting reference.

A final suggestion to round out the learning experience for students is to provide plenty of opportunities for practice. Research has shown that students who feel they do not have adequate preparation through regular practice is one of the drivers of cheating behaviors (Jordan, 2001; West et al., 2004). Building confidence to mitigate this risk is relatively simple by providing many opportunities to practice applying course objectives and theory through assignments that demonstrate the type of questions they will receive and the style that instructors present the material in exam format.

10.3   SYLLABUS DEVELOPMENT

The prior summary of challenges with delivering instruction on strategy online highlights the need for upfront planning. Begin familiarizing yourself with the tools available to develop your course including any templates or required content for your institution. The learning management system used will also have a format for organizing information. To the extent possible, streamline your course's appearance to students and organize it into weekly modules. While streamlining, consider the points of access for any given content that students may need during the semester. It is key to minimize the number of ways that students get to information, so that the organization and delivery of the content is direct and deliberate. This also will assist in the administrative questions that students will present when asking for clarification on where content or aspects of the course are located. After determining the text and content to cover, the next consideration is how to assess student performance.

Assessing student performance begins with knowing your audience or considering the size of the course and level of instruction. For smaller course enrollments and graduate level instruction, more qualitative assignments and assessments can be included. However, qualitative assignments become more difficult for larger courses and lower levels of instruction where student performance on conceptual assignments can vary widely, and it comes with challenges in communicating expectations to students. Invariably, this means a greater reliance on multiple choice exams and auto-graded deliverables. While they are more difficult to write, it is worth the effort to use questions that are more application oriented or that go beyond factual knowledge to test conceptual and procedural knowledge (Simkin & Kuechler, 2005). Still, it is useful to mix in short written assignments using discussion boards to help engage students prior to exams. The combined effect of balancing multiple exams with quizzes and short written assignments is two-fold. First, it keeps a course present in the minds and activities of students to aid engagement of students with material and a course. Second, it lowers the impact of any one exam on a student's grade. The course syllabus needs to show how assigned work factors into student grades, and this is often part of "grade books" that are part of learning management systems.

Carefully consider the weighting of the elements that comprise the course grade. Student interactions with online material requires repetition and practice to absorb the content. With respect to exams, it is necessary to cover less material (fewer chapters) on an exam in an online course, and to provide quizzes to help prepare students for exams. Overall, this means offering more exams and quizzes throughout the term than you might in a traditional class setting. When developing exam content, balance questions across all levels of difficulty and location (i.e. video lecture or reading). Again, learning management systems can assist with grouping and randomizing questions on different topics. Additionally, there need to be quizzes to drive student preparation before exam dates to avoid counterproductive cramming for an exam at the last minute. Again, quizzes also serve as a way to give the students familiarity with the different type of questions that they will see on exams. By providing opportunities to practice applying course objectives and theory, students develop mastery of material. For example, quizzes within a learning management system can be set up to provide feedback to students automatically upon completion. Additionally, most learning management systems support general feedback on questions (i.e. correct or not) with options to add feedback for each answer selection available. This provides an increased opportunity to personalize learning for students while guiding them to retain course objectives and theory.

Another consideration for syllabus development involves instructor policies. A recommended policy is not allowing late work. If late work is allowed, then an instructor risks creating what are essentially multiple versions of a course that complicates managing students and meeting milestones, such as grade submission. Allowing late assignments is also not fair to the students that are able to submit their work in a timely fashion. A way to reinforce a "no late" policy is to have an early assignment with low points, so students realize a "no late" policy will be enforced before a large assignment is due. Simply, students will test whether a "no late" policy will be enforced, and this allows you to enter a zero for a small assignment and deflect complaints with the need to submit the next assignment on time. In a weekly email, an instructor can also remind students of the upcoming assignment and that there is a "no late" policy. Cover your policy toward late work and other issues (e.g. discussion etiquette) in an "introduction" video with student acceptance indicated through a pass/fail assignment to acknowledge the policies.

After considering how to start a course, it is also worth considering how to end or wrap up a course. Strategic management is typically a capstone course, or students often take it during the semester when they will graduate. This contributes to a suggestion to avoid the use of a final exam, when students have legitimate competing demands. Instead, it is important to design a meaningful assignment or experience at the end of a term. The size of course enrollment will often drive the selection between two options: (1) a multi-stage case study, or (2) short written assignments.

For smaller enrollments, a *multi-stage case study* works best with individual students. With a multi-stage case assignment, students turn-in written assignments that build upon each other from an initial summary of an organization, adding an analysis of its external environment, outlining how a firm matches its external environment, and concluding with recommendations. How these different parts are separated to build on each other can be varied, but multiple turn-ins of assignments decrease the amount of material reviewed each time (at the expense of looking at it more frequently) and it can ensure the assignment keeps the attention of students with a rhythm established between a turn-in due and provided feedback.

For larger classes, *short written assignments* are a viable option. For example, three paragraph assignments can be quickly graded and remain meaningful. In an "admired leader" assignment instructors can ask students to identify a person and cover three topics: (1) background on them and some of their accomplishments, (2) a look beyond a person's accomplishments to identify "capabilities" contributing to their success, and (3) how the person impacted a student's life. The assignment can be written on anyone (i.e. alive/dead, nonfictional/fictional) and it involves a positive experience for students and an instructor. For example, students often write about family members that allows students to share the assignment with the person. The assignment is also useful in that it drives reflection of how a student wants to act and it can allow reinforcing material on strategic leadership, vision, and organizational culture and values. It is also an assignment where students generally perform well, or it is a nice parting gift for students to complete and an instructor to read.

10.4 EXERCISES AND CASE ANALYSIS

Experiential learning can result in better student outcomes (King & Jennings, 2004), and two methods of actively involving students with strategic management concepts is through exercises and case analysis. For hybrid classes, in-class exercises can be an effective means to engage students and quickly demonstrate concepts. A good resource of ideas for class exercises is the Carpenter Strategy Toolbox (https://carpenterstrategytool box.com/tag/experiential-exercise/), and reviewing what others have done can still spark ideas on how to adapt exercises online.

Integration of exercises and cases into online courses depends on enrollment. For smaller courses, a useful and popular assignment is to have a multi-stage strategic analysis of a company that a student selects and is instructor approved. This can be a relevant and meaningful assignment that shows how to apply ideas with staged feedback to improve analysis and give students a better understanding of a firm or industry where they may want to work before graduation. Another option that can work with both small and large classes is to provide a common experience by showing a short video clip. Short video clips can also be shown inside an instructor's video lecture to allow "real-time" commentary similar to a traditional class to highlight concepts demonstrated. For example, the department of motor vehicles scene in the Disney movie *Zootopia* can help to demonstrate differences in culture in relation to tempo, or speed that an organization operates. TED Talks also provide a good source of short, engaging videos that can convey complex topics well. You can also assign external videos viewed and have the material assessed in a weekly quiz or by having students post their thoughts or reactions in discussion boards.

Case analysis is a common way that strategic management concepts are demonstrated (Kachra & Schnietz, 2008). However, adapting case analysis to hybrid or online formats is not the same. In the case of hybrid courses, content occurs online and case discussion or other application of concepts becomes the primary focus of course meetings. In other words, case analysis does not have to be different for hybrid courses. However, case analysis has to be adapted for online courses. The same level of interaction is not possible, but two methods can be effective.

First, students can submit written assignments either individually or in groups. However, depending on the number of students enrolled, group work with online classes presents additional challenges of coordination among students. If utilizing groups, determine what tools can aid in student communication, and some learning management systems have built-in tools (i.e. group homepages). However, there are also publicly available technology options to facilitate collaboration (i.e. Skype, Google Drive, etc.) While groups can enable refining a student's understanding of material through communication with peers, using groups also lowers the grading workload for an instructor. Still, there really is no substitute for individualized feedback on assignments. Additionally, not all students contribute to group assignments equally, so integrate peer evaluations into grades for group work. One method is to have a set amount of points that a student has to assign to other members of a group (not themselves). Another consideration is the need for the instructor to summarize important concepts for students, so high- and low-performing groups have an equal opportunity to learn by summarizing ideas in an email or a video after students have submitted a case assignment. If you do decide to use written assignments in larger enrollment courses, you can also flip providing feedback with peer review tools within most learning management systems. If electing this method, provide a rubric to guide the student's feedback. Additionally, you will want to consider how to assign peer reviews (i.e. randomization).

Second, an instructor can provide a video lecture that summarizes key ideas from a case. A drawback is that this is less interactive and individualized. Still, selection of a familiar company can develop how information beyond obvious aspects of a company enables an improved understanding. Overall, try to create experiences in an online class to help students engage with course material. Another option of using discussion questions is covered next.

10.5   DISCUSSION QUESTIONS

Discussion boards are essentially short answer questions where students post a reply that is visible to other students. Learning management systems provide a variety of settings to assist students in creating original content based on what they have learned over the course, provide feedback on student understanding of material, and give instructors control on how students interact. While a common method for increasing engagement, having students reply to discussion posts can become unwieldy to manage as the number of students and responses grows, and this increases the challenge for assessing them. Generally, for larger course enrollments, requiring threaded discussions where students respond to other posts can become overwhelming. *PackBack* offers an AI tool for managing discussion posts, and it can facilitate the use of discussion boards in large classes. In smaller course enrollments, instructors can generally manage threaded discussions. The key to a robust discussion in this format is active engagement in the discussion by the instructor to increase student participation, so students interact with their peers. Another consideration for discussions is that some information requested may not be appropriate for public posting due to a variety of reasons. When this is the case, assign short written assignments that are only visible to an instructor.

The primary advantage of discussion questions is that they facilitate students' connecting course content to their personal or work experience (Johnson, 2013). As a result, discussion threads can contain a lot of useful material that demonstrates course ideas that are relevant to students. Here the role of an instructor in an online discussion is similar to facilitating discussion in a traditional classroom. Initially, an instructor needs to show they are present or "listening" to give students space to offer ideas. As student responses begin to fill in and students begin to respond to each other's posts, instructor comments can shape the discussion through comparison and contrast and providing context. For example, an instructor needs to summarize core concepts or ideas to relate the discussion back to course content.

After understanding that the role of an instructor in online discussions is similar to traditional classes, clearly define the role of students in an online discussion. Outline the requirements for student participation and the requirements for student responses to discussion questions. For example, student posts need to reflect a conversation. In other words, a student should avoid commenting on similar student posts or all at the same time. The length of posts also needs to avoid being either too long or too short. Begin with a prompt that requires a paragraph (few sentences) for each question prompt. It is also worthwhile to emphasize the need for proper grammar and spelling and keeping the tone cordial. It may help to recommend that students first write their responses in a word processor that can check for spelling and grammar before posting responses, and then deduct points from students that post responses with grammatical issues. Again, a tool provided by the firm *PackBack* can facilitate managing student discussions.

Next, there is a greater need to consider how to design discussion prompts and their frequency. First, the questions need to be open ended. In addition to an answer, students need to be challenged to explain why they think the way that they do. This can come from external references to course material or their personal experience. By basing answers in experience, students can better understand that more than one answer exists and the circumstances where one answer may be better than another. It can be useful for students to make recommendations or to consider how they would approach a similar experience differently after reading the material or other student posts. Second, as discussion questions are developed, consider the timing or frequency of discussion posts. We recommend only having one discussion post each week, to provide time for students to complete and respond to postings.

10.6   GRADING

Grading online has important differences and considerations. The most obvious difference is that in a traditional class an instructor can better communicate expectations through explanation and from answering student questions that everyone in a class can "hear." While an email or an announcement can answer common questions, an instructor cannot rely on students seeing information sent out to clarify information in the syllabus. As a result, edit assignment descriptions and possibly ask a colleague to proofread them. Where possible, provide "sample" assignments of what is expected. Additionally, we recommend providing a rubric for written assignments to students in advance, and these can be integrated with assignments in learning management systems. Further, it is important to mix assessment methods across different weeks. For example, quizzes are better for testing factual knowledge and confirm student familiarity with concepts that can be better developed and demonstrated with discussion posts, or other short written assignments.

Having a rubric can also ease grading by providing a template for comments and more structure to assignment grading. Further, some learning management systems enable linking a rubric with an assignment to facilitate grading of student work. Using a rubric offers multiple advantages, including: helping to communicate expectations, providing structured feedback, making grading easier, faster, and consistent, and reducing perceptions of subjectivity that can lead to student complaints (Boettcher & Conrad, 2016). Additionally, if you have the opportunity to have a teaching assistant or online mentor that can assist with grading, then rubrics help to ensure objective and consistent student feedback.

If threaded discussions are used, there is also a challenge in how to assess student contributions. Reviewing student comments can be time consuming and raise questions on how to grade them. One approach is to divide responses into categories (e.g. acceptable/not acceptable; exemplary/ proficient/marginal), and then focus on providing feedback to students that are below expectations to signal what is expected. The simple way to facilitate this is again with rubrics. Threaded discussions also raise potential concerns of appropriate discussion and comments or etiquette for proper discourse, and this needs to be covered in the course syllabus. It can be worthwhile to also provide criteria under the rubric, so that there are clear expectations and consequences if students do not adhere to standards. For example, it may be necessary to pre-identify penalties for lapses in etiquette or professional behavior online.

10.7 CONCLUSION

The need to offer more material and courses online is here to stay, and greater familiarity with different types of instruction can ensure instructor skills remain relevant. Further, incorporating a learning management system or aspects of an online class to a traditional class can offer benefits. This can also make the move to a hybrid or online course easier, as an instructor will already be familiar with some of the technology and functionality available, such as online assignment submission. Learning management system tools are important to enhancing the experience of both students and an instructor in online classes. For hybrid classes, there is an opportunity to take the best of both traditional and online courses by maximizing the value gained in class time. This can enable making material normally covered in class available to students asynchronously where they can interact with content multiple times. For online classes, additional modification from traditional instruction and unique challenges may arise, but information covered in this chapter can make it manageable. While instructors may face compromises in workload, assignments, and student engagement for teaching online, preparation, as well as available learning management systems, can address associated challenges and concerns.

REFERENCES

Adamy, J. (2018). Ready, set, strive – Gen Z is coming – battle-scarred, they are sober, driven by money and socially awkward: A 1930s throwback. *Wall Street Journal*: September 7, p. A1.

Boettcher, J. and Conrad, R. (2016). *The Online Teaching Survival Guide: Simple and Practical Pedagogical Tips*. Hoboken, NJ: John Wiley & Sons.

Economist. (2016). How to make a good teacher. June 11, p. 13.

Emporia State University. (2018). Video length in online courses: What the research says. https://emporiastate.blogspot.com/2018/04/video-length-in-online-courses-what.html?_ga=2.244617409.531735919.1547603754-1726451368.1547603754 (accessed February 22, 2019).

Finland, C. (2018). 6 effective business simulation games teaching strategies. https://www.cesim.com/blog/6-effective-business-simulation-games-teaching-strategies (accessed February 22, 2019).

Gallo, C. (2014). The science behind TED's 18-minute rule. LinkedIn. https://www.linkedin.com/pulse/20140313205730-5711504-the-science-behind-ted-s-18-minute-rule (accessed February 22, 2019).

Grant, R. and Baden-Fuller, C. (2018). How to develop strategic management competency: Reconsidering the learning goals and knowledge requirements of the core strategy course. *Academy of Management Learning & Education*, 17(3), pp. 322–338.

Green, R., Whitburn, L., Zacharias, A., Byrne, G. and Hughes, D. (2018). The relationship between student engagement with online content and achievement in a blended learning anatomy course. *Anatomical Science Education*, 11(5), pp. 471–477.

Hewling, A. (2005). Understanding culture in the virtual classroom: Students expectations of an education environment, and what they experienced once online. In *E-Learn: World Conference on E-Learning in Corporate, Government, Healthcare, and Higher Education* (pp. 2593–2595). Association for the Advancement of Computing in Education (AACE).

Jennings, D. (1996). Strategic management and the case method. *Journal of Management Development*, 15(9), pp. 4–12.

Johnson, A. (2013). *Excellent Online Teaching: Effective Strategies for A Successful Semester Online*. Cambridge: Aaron Johnson.

Jordan, A. (2001). College student cheating: The role of motivation, perceived norms, attitudes, and knowledge of institutional policy. *Ethics & Behavior*, 11(3), pp. 233–247.

Kachra, A. and Schnietz, K. (2008). The capstone strategy course: What might real integration look like? *Journal of Management Education*, 32(4), pp. 476–508.

King, D. and Jennings, W. (2004). The impact of augmenting traditional instruction with technology-based experiential exercise. *Journal of Financial Education*, pp. 9–25.

Simkin, M. and Kuechler, W. (2005). Multiple-choice tests and student understanding: What is the connection? *Decision Sciences Journal of Innovative Education*, 3(1), pp. 73–98.

Toqeer, R. (2013). Flipped classroom concept application to Management and Leadership course for maximizing the learning opportunities. *Business & Management Review*, 3(4), pp. 137–144.

West, T., Ravenscroft, S. and Shrader, C. (2004). Cheating and moral judgment in the college classroom: A natural experiment. *Journal of Business Ethics*, 54(2), pp. 173–183.

Wolfe, J. (1997). The effectiveness of business games in strategic management course work. *Simulation & Gaming*, 28(4), pp. 360–376.

Wright, R., Paroutis, S. and Blettner, D. (2013). How useful are the strategic tools we teach in business schools? *Journal of Management Studies*, 50(1), pp. 92–125.

Zantow, K., Knowlton, D. and Sharp, D. (2005). More than fun and games: Reconsidering the virtues of strategic management simulations. *Academy of Management Learning & Education*, 4(4), pp. 451–458.

11. Teaching strategic management for media students

Geoffrey Graybeal

11.1 TEACHING CHALLENGES AND SOLUTIONS

When I was in graduate school at the University of Georgia, I was part of a handful of students from the Grady College of Journalism and Mass Communication who walked up the hill to the Terry College of Business to take courses alongside business students. Business students earning a Master's in business administration had established teams that worked together throughout all of their courses. So, the students from the communication school had to form our own teams rather than integrate with the set business teams. I distinctly remember in one marketing management course, we worked on a rebranding project for Caribou Coffee. In a separate project, we were able to choose our own subject matter so we selected a project around a prominent regional newspaper chain. Focusing on the marketing and management of a media company was familiar terrain for us after all. Examining a retail store was completely different, and unfamiliar, territory at first.

As communication students taking a business course we were outsiders learning new and different materials from our communications-centric education. That experience stuck with me over the years and not only do I look back on it fondly, but try to be mindful of the differences as an educator on the other side of the classroom equation. I taught management and entrepreneurship courses in a media and communication school for years, before teaching in a business college as I do now.

For the majority of media students, management is typically an afterthought. In a diverse college with students exploring careers in broadcast and print journalism, public relations, advertising, marketing, visual communication, creative industries, entertainment, film, music, publishing, speech communication or other subject areas the excitement to study management of these industries may be small to moderate.

Thus, when teaching strategic management for media students, educators are faced with many of the same challenges of teaching any course on management, economics or entrepreneurship to media students. An entire subdiscipline of academic scholarship dedicated to media management, economics and entrepreneurship exists in part for this reason. Recognizing that the management of media, strategic or otherwise, may differ from the management of consumer products, for instance is the first challenge. This was the case during my graduate education. The managerial challenges we faced in the newspaper project, where the paper's journalistic mission and government watchdog role may have conflicted with the profit motive, differed from that of the project aimed at getting new consumers to buy cappuccinos and lattes at retail coffee shops.

While the business side of media industries and management matters may be of little familiarity or interest to media students, the opposite issue can be found in teaching media to business students. Business and management students are likely to have no or little prior knowledge about media and may have no interest in the industry.

Such students could be guided to a discussion of how the underlying economics of media products differ from those of other types of consumer products and how that should affect the product development and strategic management of media companies (Hollifield, 2008; Priest, 1994). Curriculum should reflect some of these fundamental differences, with foundational efforts established early in the course. Works published in journals such as the *Journal of Media Economics, International Journal on Media Management*, and *Journal of Media Business Studies* are excellent resources for seminal works on some of these differences, as well as scholarship on strategic management in media areas.

The first challenge when teaching strategic management to media students is to recognize that *doing* strategic management in media may differ from strategic management in other disciplines, with the solution being to turn to extant literature in this subdiscipline that examines the unique nature and characteristics of media products (Mierzjewska & Hollifield, 2006).

Another challenge in teaching strategic management to media students may lie in the differences across media products. Media is a nebulous term that encompasses many distinct industries, with unique considerations among them. For example, the strategic management of a news operation such as a print newspaper would differ drastically from that of an entertainment company like a film studio. Case studies and industry-level analysis and discussion are a solution to this issue as students are introduced to the various histories, operations, business models, principal companies, managers and management of radio, television, music, film, gaming, newspapers, magazines, and book publishing among others. Such examination can help students discern industry leaders and their strategies and operations, identify emergent competitors and trends, notice key elements such as distribution channels and role of geography, and regulation historically and in present. Media industries have been marked in modern times by not only consolidation across sectors but by digitization and technological disruption, which leads to the next point.

The rapidly changing nature of both media and media education is a third, and perhaps most vital, challenge of teaching strategic management to media students. The first two challenges address the need to install foundational knowledge of media fields and the scholarly discipline of media management, economics and entrepreneurship that has emerged in recent decades.

In a 2015 study examining the state of media management education, Förster and Rohn identified interdisciplinarity, internationality, and innovations and dynamics as modern challenges to teaching media management (Förster & Rohn, 2015). These challenges result from transformations to the media landscape driven by technology, globalization and changing audiences. Media markets are characterized by multicasting, multiple distribution outlets, digitization, changed media value chains, new revenue alternatives and the three big C's of convergence, consolidation and conglomerates (Chan-Olmsted, 2006a). These rapid shifts in both the nature of media and media education pose a particular challenge in teaching strategic management of media companies and products.

Netflix makes for an interesting case study that highlights these shifts, and how the underlying business model and strategic landscape has changed and continues to change. The Harvard Business School has a useful case study that looks at Netflix's use of mail order subscription discs to disrupt Blockbuster and other similar physical movie rental stores. Netflix, in short-lived fashion, attempted to split its business operations into two separate businesses, Netflix and Qwikster. Netflix then led the charge into online streaming of content as younger audiences moved away from traditional cable and broadcast appointment television viewing. All of these efforts centered around Netflix as a distributor of media content. Then Netflix marked a third major shift in strategic direction as rather than merely distributing content created from other companies Netflix invested heavily in creating its own exclusive original content. Thus, Netflix became a content creator in addition to a content distributor.

Content creators responded by getting into the content distribution game, as Disney became the most high-profile direct Netflix competitor with the launch of its Disney Plus streaming service. Disney's $71.3 billion purchase of the film and TV assets held by 21st Century Fox in 2019 also highlights the "three big Cs" of converging conglomerates consolidating through mergers and acquisitions.

Of course, Netflix's content availability also differs from country to country depending on available media rights and varying regulations. Netflix, largely regarded as a tech company, going head to head with traditional media companies is also indicative of many of these sweeping changes as so-called tech companies continue to offer media services and create or distribute media, while media companies pursue technology-based distribution platforms.

To recap, there are at least three major unique teaching challenges when it comes to teaching strategic management for media students. I will offer a brief synopsis of the challenge and a short summary of proposed solutions to overcoming these challenges.

Challenge 1: Managing media, strategic or otherwise, may differ from the management of consumer products or other industries.

Solution: Turn to extant literature and existing research and resources from the field of media management, economics and entrepreneurship and related disciplines (such as media industries, journalism studies, creative industries, media entrepreneurship, entrepreneurial journalism) to introduce students to the unique characteristics of media and information and why the field exists independent from management, economics and entrepreneurship.

Challenge 2: Media is a nebulous term that encompasses many distinct industries, with unique considerations among them.

Solution: Lessons can be centered around various media industries as historically and traditionally defined. You and your students can examine strategic management issues by industry.

Challenge 3: Media and media education is rapidly changing.

Solution: Have readings, assignments and discussions that pertain to the changing nature of media. Case studies, in particular, are helpful to address this as are relevant examples from the news to remain current. Netflix, for example, is one such company that offers insights into many of the issues of the changing nature of media and media education.

11.2   SYLLABUS DEVELOPMENT

In developing a course on strategic management for media students, you will want to consider textbook and assigned readings, course format and method of instruction, course size, learning objectives and desired educational outcomes, projects and assignments and of course, the students taking the course when developing the syllabus. While published research centered on the managerial and economic aspects of media industries can be identified as early as the 1940s in the United States, in more recent

decades a discipline focused on media management, economics and entrepreneurship has developed into its own growing field with the establishment
of organizations, journals and university programs dedicated to its study.
The establishment of three journals in subsequent decades, the *Journal of
Media Economics* in 1988, the *International Journal on Media Management*
in 1999 and the *Journal of Media Business Studies* in 2004, helped solidify
a group of scholars known for their groundwork in the field. In the area of
media management, this meant drawing from the generally-agreed upon
schools of management: the classical school, the behavioral school and the
modern school of management with strategic management falling under the
modern approach that considers both the micro and macro forces impacting the organization in order to improve productivity. Media management
scholars have produced books, textbooks and other forms of scholarship
in addition to the aforementioned journals that helped pave the way for
disciplinary legitimacy, and proliferation. Some suggested resources:

11.2.1   Textbook and Assigned Readings

Lucy Küng's *Strategic Management in the Media: From Theory to Practice*
(2008) and the 2017 second edition are comprehensive source materials
for teaching strategic management in the media, precisely as the title of
the book conveys. This textbook is highly recommended as a cornerstone
to build and develop a course around. The second edition offers several
case studies that are more timely and relevant, which illustrates the teaching challenge of the changing nature of media mentioned earlier in the
chapter. While having solid research that underlies the book as Küng is an
exceptional scholar in our field, the book is relatively easy for students to
read, and an enjoyable text. The Küng books are foundational, as they do
a nice job describing sectors of the media along function and content type,
with examples probing broadcasting (radio and television), print (newspapers, magazines, journals and books) and motion picture and recording
industries and explore trends in the strategic environment and convergence
and its causes. The books have chapters on creativity and innovation and
leadership among other subjects. The second edition has more current
examples with cases from Buzzfeed, Netflix and Vice, among others. Given
the rapid rate of change in media and media education, one of the challenges is finding texts that remain current and relevant. This book holds up
relatively well over time, or at least has done so to date.

Media Management: A Casebook Approach (5th edition, 2016), by
Hollifield et al., uses media-based cases to address issues of diversity, group
cultures, market-driven journalism, and training among other topics. I've
used this book and found the media-based cases particularly worthwhile

for teaching a media management course. In fact, I used the extended case assignments in lieu of an applied group project, and the deliverables for the fictional company held up as well as the deliverables for a real-world client.

Albarran's *The Media Economy* (2010) and Doyle's *Understanding Media Economics* (2013) are useful for examining industry. The Albarran book analyzes the media industries and their activities from macro to micro levels. It examines how media industries function across different levels of society (global, national, household and individual), and looks at key forces (technology, globalization, regulation and social aspects) evolving and influencing the media industries. A course pack of additional assigned readings could be constructed from the two editions of the *Handbook of Media Management and Economics* (2006), edited by Albarran et al. and the *International Journal on Media Management, Journal of Media Economics* and *Journal of Media Business Studies*, and other studies.

Chan-Olmsted has published an extensive amount of research on strategic management in media and I would highly recommend finding studies or materials from her when teaching a course on strategic management for media students. Her chapter on "Issues in Strategic Management" in the first edition of the *Handbook of Media Management and Economics* (Chan-Olmsted, 2006b) is recommended as source material for students in your course, as is the "Strategic Management" chapter (authored by Nabyla Daidj) in the second edition of the text (Daidj, 2018).

The *Handbook of Media Management and Economics* is a comprehensive textbook, and includes chapters on strategic management that may be useful for a course on strategic management for media students. The most recent volume of the *Handbook of Media Management and Economics* (2nd edition) is an entirely new book that picks up where the first volume left off, not merely an updated version of the text. The second edition (edited by Alan A. Albarran, Bozena I. Mierzejewska and Jaemin Jung), pulls from the three journals mentioned above, synthesizing and updating the latest research since publication of the first edition in 2006.

In addition to these suggested textbooks and assigned reading materials, Table 11.1 provides details of other resources recommended to help with course construction, syllabus development and course source materials:

These organizations focus their efforts primarily on media management, which is why they come highly recommended as references and source material when teaching strategic management for media students, however, other broader management organizations are also recommended. The Academy of Management, for example, has a Strategic Management division and a slew of relevant and applicable programming at its annual conference. Other great instructional resources and source material outside the media management, economics and entrepreneurship subfield include

Table 11.1 Organizations related to media management, economics and entrepreneurship

Organization	Website	History	Mission	Resources
Association for Education in Journalism and Mass Communication (AEJMC) Media Management, Economics and Entrepreneurship (MMEE) division.	https://mmedivision. wordpress.com	Current bylaws adopted 2006	Committed to a global perspective and focus, with internationality a core goal. Members come from media & communication as well as business schools.	Teaching resources section on website that includes a syllabus exchange and other materials. Previous winners of the Robert Picard Award for Books and Monographs listed as well.
European Media Management Association	https://www.media-management.eu	Founded in 2003	International not-for-profit academic organization to support growth in media management research, scholarship and practice throughout Europe and around the world.	The group hosts an annual conference in a European city with research focusing on media management, and a bi-annual summer school for graduate students. Conference papers could prove a source for course materials as does their flagship journal the *Journal of Media Business Studies*.
World Media Economics and Management Conference	http://www.wmemc. org	Established in 1994 by Dr. Robert Picard who acted as	A biennial conference of media business scholars. Previous conferences have been held in South	Archives of some previous conference websites are available online, and conference proceedings

Organization	URL	Origin	Description	Resources
		conference chair until 2018	Africa, New York, Brazil, Greece, Columbia, Portugal, China, Canada, the United Kingdom, Finland, Spain, Switzerland, and Sweden.	have been published in the past. There may be research studies you discover that are appropriate to include as course material when teaching strategic management to media students.
International Media Management Academic Association (IMMAA)	https://immaa.org	Spearheaded by Dr. Paulo Faustino, a current initiative formally begun in 2012; origins trace back to 2004 when then-Medill Dean John Lavine (Northwestern University) started the International Media Management Academic Forum.	A global association of academics researching critical issues of media management with a goal of improving practice and understanding of media markets and institutions for the benefit of media managers and students who will be the media managers of the future. Previous conferences have been held in the United States, Portugal, Russia, Germany, South Korea, Brazil and Qatar.	*The Journal of Creative Industries and Cultural Studies* is affiliated with IMMAA, as are a number of books which may be of use. *The Business of Media: Change and Challenges* (Herrero & Wildman, 2015), and *Looking to the Future of Modern Media Management* (Scholz & Eseinbeis, 2008) are among the highlighted books offered.

the extensive collection of *Harvard Business Review* case studies which has many cases suited for strategic management in media.

Of course, the appropriateness and suitability of the material should be considered based on the academic level of the course (undergraduate, graduate, etc.) and the instructional delivery method (face-to-face, online, blended, etc.) and format (lecture hall, seminar, lab, lecture–lab combo, etc.) Many of the media management, economics and entrepreneurship texts discussed thus far are primarily suited for upper level undergraduate students, or graduate students in a Master's or doctoral program. When I have taught strategic management to media students it has usually been in either a capstone undergraduate course with primarily graduating seniors or a Master's level course. I have taught strategic management through a series of asynchronous online modules to students earning a Master's degree through an entirely online program in strategic communication and innovation. I have also taught an elective media management course to a group of American and German students simultaneously taking the course together as part of a study abroad (for the Americans) program. I would advise you to read the promotional materials of texts you are considering in terms of what the publisher and authors recommend for suitability for class level. Table 11.2 offers some of the ways I have used and encountered the materials referenced above.

Table 11.2   Teaching material for media management, economics and entrepreneurship instruction

Material	Levels used	Format
Küng text	Undergraduate (upper level); Graduate	Face-to-face; Online asynchronous
Hollifield et al. text	Graduate (Master's)	Online asynchronous
Albarran text	Undergraduate (upper level)	Face-to-face
Handbook of Media Management and Economics (1st edition)	Graduate (Master's and Ph.D.)	Face-to-face; seminar style courses
Coursepacks using journal material	Primarily graduate (Master's and Ph.D.)	Face-to-face (seminar style courses); online asynchronous modules
Case studies	Master's graduate level Upper level undergraduate*	Works best in face-to-face classroom setting**

Notes:
*Common instructional method in business schools.
**Interactive and multimedia cases are suitable for online courses.

11.3 METHODS

Following a traditional management school's lead in use of teaching cases, the case study is a useful method of instruction in teaching strategic management for media students as well. Case instruction is chiefly designed to be conducted in a face-to-face classroom setting, where students read the materials before coming to class and prepare for the discussion. Candidly, I tried using traditional Harvard Business School cases in the online course I taught and it did not work very well at all. The in-class case discussion is not easily replicated in an online environment as discussion boards and online forums do not offer nearly the same level of engagement. Now, I was required to teach in an asynchronous manner, as students accessed the material at their own leisure and time frame within the deadlines of the module. Perhaps, in a synchronous environment, a case discussion would work just as well when all students are able to be online at the same time, contributing to an online chat room or forum, for example. But the delays in timing and most students waiting until the end to contribute to a discussion thread in an asynchronous manner did not have the desired effect.

Rather, the use of multimedia cases was more relevant, applicable and effective in an online setting and in this case an asynchronous manner. I used a few Harvard "multimedia" case studies that incorporated video, audio, and multimedia presentations instead of traditional text-based assigned "readings." The deliverables changed as well, as students were asked to submit multimedia presentations and reports.

A group project is one commonly used assignment. Student teams are formed early on and the same teams work on group project(s) throughout the semester. When I used the Hollifield et al. book, student teams were assigned two major group projects. One was an extended case study project that came directly from the textbook. The second project was an experiential one with a real-world client. This course was the online version. Module assignments accounted for 40 percent of the class grade, while the HBR case study discussions accounted for the remaining 20 percent. My current college recommends having group work account for no more than 30 percent of a student's grade, largely to eliminate the "free rider" problem of a student doing little group work and earning a stellar grade based on the efforts of his or her peers. In the online course, the modules accounted for the crux of the course. Group projects are generally recommended in a strategic management course as teamwork and leadership are important competencies to develop and teach.

Whenever I assign a group project, I usually build in a peer assessment that can alter the grades based on an individual's contribution to the group project. For example, if the student's peers rated the student below an 80,

5 points off the group grade would be deducted for the individual student grade.

When assigning a group project, the team formation plays an important role. I've assigned teams, allowed students to choose and form their own teams, allowed some choice within assigned constraints, assigned by project role and used other sorting mechanisms. I typically require students to take the free personality test assessment available at 16personalities.com, and then ask students to assess the personality assessment. The personality type is one method that can be used to sort teams so you wind up with students with complementary strengths, rather than a team of similar personalities. Although there are costs associated with the program, the CATME tool is another excellent program that offers a team builder function and a peer assessment option. In other iterations of courses I have taught, a research project took the place of the group project. This was conducted in assigned pairs, and involved a traditional research paper.

Overall, I recommend using a mix of instructional methodologies, ranging from cases to simulations or applied activities, regardless of the course delivery mechanism. Experiential education may also be appropriate for strategic management for media students. A real-world client-based approach works if you're capable of finding media clients who need assistance on projects and are willing to employ the student help. More specific examples of assignments, cases and activities will be discussed later in the chapter.

11.4   ASSIGNMENTS

This section provides some detailed examples of assignments that can be used for the methods just described.

11.4.1   Sample Assignment (Group Project)

One consideration for teaching strategic management to media students is to employ a client-based approach whereby the students work throughout the semester on a project for a client in the "real world." My students have conducted research and developed a strategic marketing plan for U.S.-based media companies, media startups, and a local "mom and pop" business owner/operator with a venture in the food service industry.

Similar to how public relations, advertising and marketing classes work on "campaigns" for clients, students can be given a brief from the client that outlines deliverables desired and objectives for what their needs are and what they're trying to accomplish. Multiple teams can work on the same client in the course or you could have different teams take on different clients in the semester. You can tailor the assignment to the needs of the client.

Here is a sample assignment from a client-based group project. The clients differed from semester to semester. The chapters mentioned in this assignment come from the Hollifield et al. textbook referenced above. Having students craft a Strategic Marketing Plan for a media company makes for a comprehensive semester-long term project that culminates in a final deliverable offering a demonstration and comprehension of strategic management material covered throughout the course.

Strategic Marketing Plan:
Your group will develop a Strategic Marketing Plan for your assigned Media Product that should include the following three elements:

1. **Target audience(s).** Identify, quantify, and describe in detail at least one primary and secondary target audience or target market for your assigned product. Describe the number in the target audience, its demographics, psychographics, and other characteristics in detail. Explain how and why the content focus will appeal to your primary and secondary audiences. Review Chapters 5 and 7 before answering this question.
2. **Market analysis.** See details below.

Funding. Identify and describe in concise detail a minimum of three categories of funding sources (e.g. advertisers, foundations, etc., depending on whether you propose a nonprofit or for-profit site) and five examples of each category (e.g. at least five major advertisers who might buy ads on the site). In other words, consider the following questions. How should funding be raised for the site? What types of funding should be targeted? Why? What type of funding sources should be developed? Then select a minimum of three categories of funding sources, and identify and describe at least five examples of potential donors, sponsors or advertisers, and so on, for each category. Explain in detail why these are good potential funding sources and why these potential advertisers or donors are good prospects. In addition, discuss the negative consequences or downside of using each type of potential donor you recommend. Identify what managerial or organizational resources may be needed to manage each different type of funding source. Review Chapter 8 before answering this question.

Market Analysis

Define Your Market
Market strategies are the result of a meticulous market analysis. A market analysis forces the entrepreneur to become familiar with all aspects of the market so that the target market can be defined and the company can be positioned in order to garner its share of sales. A market analysis also enables the entrepreneur to establish pricing, distribution and promotional strategies that will allow the

company to become profitable within a competitive environment. In addition, it provides an indication of the growth potential within the industry, and this will allow you to develop your own estimates for the future of your business.

Begin your market analysis by defining the market in terms of size, structure, growth prospects, trends and sales potential.

The total aggregate sales of your competitors will provide you with a fairly accurate estimate of the total potential market. Once the size of the market has been determined, the next step is to define the target market. The target market narrows down the total market by concentrating on segmentation factors that will determine the total addressable market – the total number of users within the sphere of the business's influence. The segmentation factors can be geographic, customer attributes or product-oriented.

For instance, if the distribution of your product is confined to a specific geographic area, then you want to further define the target market to reflect the number of users or sales of that product within that geographic segment.

Once the target market has been detailed, it needs to be further defined to determine the total feasible market. This can be done in several ways, but most professional planners will delineate the feasible market by concentrating on product segmentation factors that may produce gaps within the market. In the case of a microbrewery that plans to brew a premium lager beer, the total feasible market could be defined by determining how many drinkers of premium pilsner beers there are in the target market.

It's important to understand that the total feasible market is the portion of the market that can be captured provided every condition within the environment is perfect and there is very little competition. In most industries this is simply not the case. There are other factors that will affect the share of the feasible market a business can reasonably obtain. These factors are usually tied to the structure of the industry, the impact of competition, strategies for market penetration and continued growth, and the amount of capital the business is willing to spend in order to increase its market share.

Defining the market is but one step in your analysis. With the information you've gained through market research, you need to develop strategies that will allow you to fulfill your objectives.

Positioning Your Business

When discussing market strategy, it's inevitable that positioning will be brought up. A company's positioning strategy is affected by a number of variables that are closely tied to the motivations and requirements of target customers within as well as the actions of primary competitors.

Before a product can be positioned, you need to answer several strategic questions such as:

- How are your competitors positioning themselves?
- What specific attributes does your product have that your competitors don't?
- What customer needs does your product fulfill?

Once you've answered your strategic questions based on **research of the market**, you can then begin to develop your positioning strategy and illustrate that in your

your plan. A positioning statement for a business plan doesn't have to be long or elaborate. It should merely point out exactly how you want your product perceived by both customers and the competition.

Pricing
How you price your product is important because it will have a direct effect on the success of your business.

Distribution
Distribution includes the entire process of moving the product from the factory to the end user. The type of distribution network you choose will depend upon the industry and the size of the market. A good way to make your decision is to analyze your competitors to determine the channels they are using, then decide whether to use the same type of channel or an alternative that may provide you with a strategic advantage.

Promotion Plan
With a distribution strategy formed, you must develop a promotion plan. The promotion strategy in its most basic form is the controlled distribution of communication designed to sell your product or service. In order to accomplish this, the promotion strategy encompasses every marketing tool utilized in the communication effort.

Smaller assignments

Not all assignments need to be semester-long in-depth and group assignments. I've assigned students "mini cases" of companies or organizations to research and either turn in and/or report back to the class the findings, typically examining aspects relevant to strategic management. For example, in a course module on media companies who implemented cooperative working spaces, accelerators, incubators and other intrapreneurial activities, students were tasked with an examination and analysis of the resources allocated to the project, in line with the resource based-view of strategic management. The resource-based view (RBV) of strategic management infers that an organization holds a unique set of resources that provide it with a unique set of strategic advantages to set itself apart from other organizations (Hitt et al., 2001; Peteraf, 1993; Wernerfelt, 1984). RBV is primarily concerned with the diverse resources an organization has that give it a competitive advantage over other organizations. In order for an organization to gain a competitive advantage, it must exhibit four performance characteristics – value, rareness, non-substitutability, and inimitability. For this particular assignment, students look at full time equivalents, physical space and financial resources as well as startup and entrepreneurial resources allocated in terms of funding, space and other.

11.5 DISCUSSION QUESTIONS

This section introduces some "themes" worth class discussion including suggested discussion frames:

1) Role of strategic decision making based on the environment a firm is operating in

   When a firm enacts a strategic decision-making process, it has historically been designed to obtain a sustained competitive advantage. This would often occur through organizational managers conceiving and utilizing strategies and resources unique to the firm. Scholars in the past two decades, however, have called into question the notion of a sustained competitive advantage, particularly in unstable environments. Strategy now takes place in a "hypercompetitive" (D'Aveni, 1994) and "high velocity" (Eisenhardt, 1989) environment, which scholars contend has altered the strategic decision making process (Eisenhardt, 2002).

   Competitive advantages can be disrupted by rivals or new entrants with superior knowledge about the market and/or technological, socioeconomic or cultural shifts that uncover new market opportunities that threaten a current advantage (Sambamurthy et al., 2003).

   A "high velocity environment," is characterized by rapid, discontinuous change in demand, competitors, technology, and regulation. Firms in such an environment can take a "wait and see" approach or "me too" decision strategies, which may also result in failure in a high velocity environment because competitive windows change and opportunities close (Bourgeois & Eisenhardt, 1988). Thus, strategy can be either a piecemeal (adaptively in small chunks) or comprehensive (large, purposeful chunks) approach. Major decisions are characterized as entering a new product market, altering the firm's established identity, betting the firm on a totally new product, or going public. A high velocity environment places a premium on high quality, fast, innovative decisions (Bourgeois & Eisenhardt, 1988).

   Media industries have certainly experienced high-velocity hypercompetitive environments. Students can identify various media industries and discuss the state of that industry's environment and whether any evidence exists of management approaches differing.

2) Strategic management in media industries in general

   Media scholars have found evidence that many media managers have reduced the strategic management process to one of trial and error (Dimmick, 2003; Hollifield et al., 2004; Roehrich, 1984). Media firms have such limited experience making strategic decisions (Picard, 2004) and have struggled with addressing the rapid pace of change to the point that the viability of their strategies has been questioned (Van Kranenberg, 2006). A class discussion can occur as to why media managers seemingly struggle with strategic management compared to other (non-media) industries.

3) Role of innovation in managing media companies
    While the strategic management literature addresses unstable managerial environments, a separate stream within the management literature addresses how these "disruptive" markets develop, often in the face of technological advances. Emerging technologies are scientific innovations that disrupt existing markets, products and models (Day & Schoemaker, 2004). This disruptiveness aspect is a defining feature of emerging technologies, because the change is often large-scale, radical and sweeping. The adjective "disruptive" became a catchphrase during the first Internet era in large part due to the popularity of Clayton Christensen's theory of incumbent failure when faced with what he first termed "disruptive technology" and later renamed "disruptive innovation" (Bower & Christensen, 1995; Christensen & Bower, 1996; Christensen & Overdorf, 2000; Christensen et al., 2002; Küng, 2008).

    Students can discuss innovation within the media industry and whether products have been disruptive or incremental.

11.6   CONCLUSION

I've had students and classmates go on to management roles at media and technology companies as well as non-media companies in the years since they left the classroom. One of the joys of teaching is the ability to stay connected with former students, friends and professional acquaintances to not only follow their career progression but because it often can lead to a cyclical effect in the classroom. Students will point to how what we did in class aids them in their managerial roles in industry. A fond reflection on assignments past indicates how the lessons learned remain current and relevant when applied outside of academia. At the same time, these graduates of the program can indicate current trends and ways of doing business that as an instructor you can incorporate or share in your teaching today. Many will often be willing to come back to their alma mater, or as a favor to you, share their knowledge with students in the form of guest speaking, lectures, and mentoring. Many provide internships or opportunities for current students as well. You also gain the added benefit of having informed voices within the management of these companies and industries studied that can share inside knowledge beyond what can be gleaned from textbook or book assignments.

I've been fortunate to be able to share wisdom from managers at Twitter, WarnerMedia, the National Football League, ESPN, Google, Facebook, Home Depot, Coca-Cola, just to name a few. Others have founded entrepreneurial ventures at either a local/regional level or that have grown and scaled internationally. Others meanwhile have worked at various agencies, or as independent creatives working on client-based consulting projects. Each role provides differing managerial challenges and opportunities that provide case lessons that can be applied to the curriculum I develop and teach each semester. Just as my own education influences my pedagogy and teaching today.

REFERENCES

Albarran, A.B. (2010). *The Media Economy*. New York: Routledge.

Albarran, A.B., Chan-Olmsted, S.M. & Wirth, M.O. (Eds.) (2006). *Handbook of Media Management and Economics*. Mahwah, NJ: Lawrence Erlbaum.

Albarran, A.B., Mierzejewska, B. & Jung, J. (Eds.) (2018). *Handbook of media management and economics* (2nd edition). New York: Routledge.

Bourgeois, L.J. III & Eisenhardt, K.M. (1988). Strategic decision processes in high velocity environments: Four cases in the microcomputer industry. *Management Science*, 34(7), 816–835.

Bower, J.L. & Christensen, C.M. (1995). Disruptive technologies: Catching the wave. *Harvard Business Review*, 43–53.

Chan-Olmsted, S.M. (2006a). *Competitive Strategy for Media Firms: Strategic and Brand Management in Changing Media Markets*. Mahwah, NJ: Lawrence Erlbaum.

Chan-Olmstead, S.M. (2006b). Issues in strategic management. In Albarran, A.B, Chan-Olmsted, S.M. & Wirth, M.O. (Eds.) *Handbook of Media Management and Economics* (pp. 161–180). Mahwah, NJ: Lawrence Erlbaum.

Christensen, C.M. & Bower, J.L. (1996). Customer power, strategic investment, and the failure of leading firms. *Strategic Management Journal*, 17(3), 197–218.

Christensen, C.M. & Overdorf, M. (2000). Meeting the challenge of disruptive change. *Harvard Business Review*, 78 (2), 66–75.

Christensen, C.M., Verlinden, M. & Westerman, G. (2002). Disruption, disintegration and the dissipation of differentiability. *Industrial and Corporate Change*, 11(5), 955–993.

D'Aveni, R.A. (1994). *Hypercompetition: Managing the Dynamics of Strategic Maneuvering*. New York: Free Press.

Daidji, N. (2018). Strategic management. In Albarran, A.B., Mierzejewska, B. & Jung, J. (Eds.) *Handbook of Media Management and Economics* (2nd edition) (pp. 111–129). New York: Routledge.

Day, G.S. & Schoemaker, P.J. (2004). *Wharton on Managing Emerging Technologies.* Hoboken, NJ: John Wiley & Sons.

Dimmick, J.W. (2003). *Media Competition and Coexistence: The Theory of the Niche.* Mahwah, NJ: Lawrence Erlbaum.

Doyle, G. (2013). *Understanding Media Economics.* London: Sage.

Eisenhardt, K.M. (1989). Making fast strategic decisions in high-velocity environments. *Academy of Management Journal*, 32(3), 543–576.

Eisenhardt, K.M. (2002). Has strategy changed? *Sloan Management Review*, 43 (2), 88–91.

Förster, K. & Rohn, U. (2015). Media management education: Key themes, pedagogies, and challenges. *Journalism & Mass Communication Educator*. https://journals.sagepub.com/doi/abs/10.1177/1077695815593983.

Herrero, M. & Wildman, S. (2015). *The Business of Media: Change and Challenges.* Porto: Media XXI.

Hitt, M.A., Ireland, R.D. & Hoskisson, R.E. (2001). *Strategic management: competitiveness and globalization, Volume 1.* Sydney: South-Western College Publishing.

Hollifield, C.A. (2008). Invisible on the frontlines of the media revolution. *International Journal on Media Management*, 10, 179–183.

Hollifield, C.A., Wicks, J.L., Sylvie, G. & Lowrey, W. (2016). *Media Management: A Casebook Approach* (5th edition). New York, NY: Routledge.

Hollifield, C.A., Vlad, T. & Becker, L.B. (2004). Market, organizational, and strategic factors affecting media entrepreneurs in emerging economies. In Picard, R. (Ed.), *Strategic Responses to Media Market Changes* (JIBS Research Reports No. 2004–2, pp. 133–153). Jönköping, Sweden: Jönköping International Business School, Media Management and Transformation Centre.

Küng, L. (2008). *Strategic Management in the Media: From Theory to Practice.* Los Angeles: Sage.

Küng, L. (2017). *Strategic Management in the Media: From Theory to Practice* (2nd edition). London: Sage.

Mierzjewska, B.I. & Hollifield, C.A. (2006). Theoretical approaches in media management research. In Albarran, A.B., Chan-Olmsted, S.M. & Wirth, M.O. (Eds.), *Handbook of Media Management and Economics* (pp. 37–66). Mahwah, NJ: Lawrence Erlbaum.

Peteraf, M.A. (1993). The cornerstones of competitive advantage: A resource-based view. *Strategic Management Journal*, 14 (3), 179–191.

Picard, R.G. (2004). Environmental and market changes driving strategic planning in media firms. In Picard, R. (Ed.), *Strategic Responses to Media Market Changes.* (JIBS Research Reports No. 2004–2, pp. 65–82). Jönköping, Sweden: Jönköping International Business School, Media Management and Transformation Centre.

Priest, C. (1994). The character of information: Characteristics and properties of information related to issues concerning intellectual property. Center for Information, Technology, and Society. http://www.eff.org/Groups/CITS/Reports/cits_nii_framework_ota.report. Last accessed July 13, 2012.

Roehrich, R. (1984). The relationship between technological and business innovation. *Journal of Business Strategy*, 5, 60–72.

Sambamurthy, V., Bharadwaj, A. & Grover, V. (2003). Reconceptualizing the role of information technology in contemporary firms. *MIS Quarterly*, 27(2), 237–263.

Scholz, C. & Eseinbeis, U. (2008). *Looking to the Future of Modern Media Management.* Porto: Media XXI.

Van Kranenburg, H.L. (2006). Strategic options for the newspaper publishing companies. In Grossmark, P.E. (Ed.), *Advances in Communications and Media Research*, Volume 3 (pp. 85–97). Hauppauge, NY: NovaScience Publishers.

Wernerfelt, B. (1984). A resource-based view of the firm. *Strategic Management Journal*, 5(2), 171–180.

12. Teaching strategy work to business students

Rita Järventie-Thesleff and Janne Tienari

12.1 THE RELEVANCE DEBATE AND THE SHADOW OF POSITIVISM

For at least the past two decades business schools and their teaching practices have come under persistent criticism (Pfeffer & Fong, 2002; Ghoshal, 2005; Kachra & Schnietz, 2008; Rousseau, 2012; Wright et al., 2013). Such criticism has been intensified by questioning the relationship between business education and the crude misconduct of some large corporations and by considering whether the recent financial crisis could have been avoided had business education been different. However, most of the criticism still revolves around the relevance debate (Pfeffer & Fong, 2002); are business schools failing to realize their primary purpose, which is to "produce" professional managers? (Rousseau, 2012). This leads to three key questions. First, does current teaching help future managers make better and more ethical business decisions and equip them for a complex world? Second, what is the relationship between the business school curriculum and the skills and knowledge needed for success? Third, what is the impact of research on management practice and is management research capable of producing knowledge that can improve the performance of future managers?

There are doubts about the quality of business education. Recently, the relevance debate has picked up steam due to the disruptive environment and unparalleled uncertainty characteristic of "wicked problems." As Clegg et al. (2013, p. 1247) put it, "we live in 'wicked times', marked by problems beyond simple description, beyond single discipline solutions that call for responses as yet unknown, or perhaps underexplored." These authors contend that the legitimacy of business schools is at stake and that we should be able to prepare students more effectively for the ethical problems they will confront and also to enhance the strategic capabilities needed for understanding and shaping organizational practices amidst numerous and often interrelated global crises.

What exactly is wrong with current business education in general and strategic management education in particular? The prevalent teaching seems to be based on positivism and "causal or functional modes of explanation" (Ghoshal, 2005, p. 79), where managerial decision-making is simplified and based on quantitative analytical techniques (Porter & McKibbin, 1988; Kachra & Schnietz, 2008). These techniques often imply that by following a specific set of procedures, managers can somehow expect to produce predictable results. Traditional strategy courses seem to overemphasize such analyses and by so doing develop future managers who believe that there is a single, right answer to all business problems and that by using certain methods great outcomes can be achieved (Kachra & Schnietz, 2008; Clegg et al., 2013). However, there has been persistent criticism that both the teaching methods and the learning experiences of students are too far removed from the actual context of doing business and strategy (Mintzberg, 1996). Further, both business practitioners and media ask whether strategy teaching focuses solely on strategic planning and whether students should also be taught the art and craft of getting things done (Heskett, 2003). We argue that an approach to strategy that discards the dichotomy between planning and implementation and looks instead at strategy as something that people in organizations do, that is strategy work, can be used to teach strategic management in the contemporary world.

This new approach to strategy research is called "strategy-as-practice." It is gaining ground and focuses on what strategists actually do when they strategize (Ezzamel & Willmott, 2004). The principal idea is to concentrate on strategy as a social practice and to study how strategy practitioners act and interact. Development of the strategy-as-practice approach was fueled by complaints about overemphasis on macro-level strategy research, the pursuit of causally related variables, and neglect of human beings (Jarzabkowksi et al., 2007). According to the practice-based view, strategy is not only a property of an organization, something that an organization has, but also something that the organization does (Jarzabkowski et al., 2007; Johnson et al., 2007). However, materials on how to apply strategy-as-practice to teaching are still relatively sparse. Jarzabkowski and Whittington (2008a, 2008b) called for a closer connection between academic theory and management practice and proposed further integration of the strategy-as-practice perspective with strategy teaching. In a similar vein, Paroutis et al. (2013) argued that the practice-based approach to strategy could and should inform the teaching of educators and that it could help students understand how strategy is done in organizations and how it can be done even better.

12.2 CONSTRUCTIVISM AND A PRACTICE-BASED APPROACH

We concur with strategy-as-practice scholars about the need to incorporate the practice approach into contemporary strategy teaching. In their book, *Practicing Strategy: Text and Cases* (2013) Paroutis et al. encourage increased appreciation of the micro-level aspects of strategy making and execution. They argue that such appreciation can benefit both business and education. Shedding light on the micro-level aspects of strategy-making and execution can help managers (and other practitioners) make sense of the strengths and weaknesses of these processes. In the context of teaching, the authors call for closer links with the sociology of practice and argue that strategy-as-practice research can re-orient strategy teaching toward the practitioner as a complex, socially-embedded, and reflective being. Paroutis et al. (2013) introduce an array of interesting questions that are covered by strategy-as-practice scholars, and they stress how highlighting different aspects of the "doing" of strategy can be of interest to business students. These include how and where strategy work is done; the role of various organizational actors as strategists; and how common tools and techniques for strategizing are developed and used in practice.

Jarzabkowski and Whittington (2008a, 2008b) sought to open a dialogue between two opposing views of strategy teaching: the theoretical and the practically informed. These apparently opposing views consist of strategy teaching based on economic theory (Grant, 2008), which has been criticized for focusing excessively on the strategist as a simple agent for profit maximization, and practically informed teaching (Bower, 2008), which has been said to run the risk of lapsing into cognitive recipes based on little more than folk wisdom and anecdotes. Jarzabkowski and Whittington (2008a, 2008b) conclude by stating that strategy-as-practice rejects the choice between theory and practice and call for more practice-based research that could inform strategy teaching.

These insights provide valuable input for our endeavor to dig deeper into how incorporating the strategy-as-practice approach into teaching strategic management – or, as we prefer to call it, strategy work – could benefit business students. We therefore advocate a shift from a positivistic approach to a more constructivist teaching philosophy. Traditional strategy teaching has to a large extent been based on a positivistic worldview. It has focused on transferring knowledge and centered on mastering concepts, techniques, and tools. Nevertheless, the ever-changing global economy of the twenty-first century places increasing demands on future managers, and teaching should equip business students with skills and competences that go beyond mere cognitive knowledge and technical skills.

In constructivist and holistic learning philosophy, knowledge is constantly reflected on and altered through new insights and learning occurs when students become actively involved in the process of constructing meaning and knowledge. Cunliffe's (2002) work is an example of this. She suggests that management learning should be reframed as a "reflexive dialogical practice" and believes that learning takes place when people reflexively engage in internal and external dialogue in an attempt to make sense of their experiences (p. 36). Cunliffe contends that "the issue of reflexivity is central to critical management studies because it draws on postmodern and social constructionist suppositions to highlight the inconsistent and problematic nature of explanation – that we construct the very accounts we think describe the world" (p. 38). In order to understand what she means by reflexive dialogical practice it is important to understand the difference between reflection and reflexivity. A mirror reflects an image, and as a thought process, reflection is concerned with simplifying experience. Reflexivity means complexifying thinking or experience by exposing contradictions, doubts, dilemmas, and possibilities (Cunliffe, 2002). It is reflection on reflection.

To apply the strategy-as-practice approach to business school teaching, we suggest that educators build on a constructivist teaching and learning philosophy and incorporate reflexive dialogical practice into their teaching methods. Sandberg and Tsoukas (2011, p. 339) argue that the theory–practice gap within management and organization studies can be narrowed by adopting an ontological–epistemological framework that they call "practical rationality." Research and teaching drawing on this framework can shed light on how organizational practices are constituted and enacted by strategy practitioners.

12.3 STRATEGIC THINKING AND STRATEGY TOOLS

The practice approach to strategy is often presented by introducing three different, yet interlinked lenses through which strategy and strategizing can be studied and taught. These lenses consist of strategy praxis, practitioners, and practices (Jarzabkowski et al., 2007; Whittington, 2006). Jarzabkowski and Whittington (2008b, p. 282) introduce them as follows:

> Praxis refers to the work that comprises strategy: the flow of activities such as meeting, talking, calculating, form filling, and presenting in which strategy is constituted. Strategy practitioners are those people who do the work of strategy, which goes beyond senior managers to include managers at multiple levels of the firm as well as influential external actors, such as consultants, analysts,

and regulators. Strategy practices are the social, symbolic, and material tools through which strategy work is done.

The scope of strategy practices is sometimes broadened by urging researchers to go beyond actual visible activities and to explore "not only what is done, but what is not done, that what is not practiced, that what is not said, using external stakeholders' articulations as signs of what might be but is not" (Carter et al., 2008, p. 94).

12.3.1 Strategic Thinking

We argue for a practice-based, constructivist approach to teaching strategic management. Research that draws on the framework of praxis, practitioners, and practices helps capture the "doing" of strategy in organizations and is thus well equipped to prepare students for their future manager roles. However, we suggest that to capitalize fully on the practice approach and analyze and build on the micro-level aspects of strategy, students need to develop their strategic thinking capabilities (Hamel & Prahalad, 1989; Mintzberg, 1994; Liedtka, 1998; Santalainen, 2006). This is especially important in teaching students with little prior knowledge of strategy and limited work experience. Liedtka (1998, p. 120) joins the critics of the traditional strategic planning approach by arguing that "the traditional processes have choked initiative and favoured incremental over substantive change. They have emphasized analytics and extrapolation rather than creativity and invention." Instead, managers and organizations should foster strategic thinking. Both Mintzberg (1994) and Liedtka (1998) distinguish between strategic planning and strategic thinking. According to Mintzberg (1994), strategic planning is an analytical process aimed at programming already identified strategies. Its outcome is a plan. Strategic thinking is a synthesizing process, utilizing intuition and creativity; its outcome is "an integrated perspective of the enterprise" (p. 108). Liedtka (1998) contends that managers frequently focus their attention on dealing with day-to-day crisis situations and having certain strategic processes in place can help assure that they also attend to strategic issues.

For educational purposes, it is essential to define strategic thinking in more detail. According to Liedtka (1998, pp. 122–124), strategic thinking is characterized by a systems perspective, a focus on intent, intelligent opportunism, and thinking in time, that is, operating from a temporal perspective. It also is driven by hypotheses. First, strategic thinkers need a systems perspective based on an understanding of both the external and internal context of the organization; they should be able to discern the interdependencies between different contexts, to understand the relationships between corporate, business-level, and functional strategies and to connect this understanding to the choices they make on a daily basis. Second, strategic thinking is intent-driven. According to Hamel and Prahalad (1989), strategic intent conveys a sense of direction, discovery, and destiny. Strategic thinking is driven by the shaping and reshaping of intent. Third, strategic thinking must accommodate intelligent opportunism; strategic thinkers should not only further the intended strategy but also be prepared for the emergence of new strategies. Fourth, thinking in time, that is, adopting a temporal perspective, leads practitioners to ask what the organization must keep from its past, lose from its past, and create in the present to reach the envisioned future. Fifth and finally, strategic thinking is an hypothesis-driven process that should accommodate both creativity and analysis.

12.3.2   Strategy Tools

In addition to strategic thinking, discussing strategy tools is important in teaching strategic management. We take distance to positivistic, "causal or functional modes of explanation" (Ghoshal, 2005, p. 79), where managerial decision-making is simplified and based on quantitatively analytical tools and techniques (Porter & McKibbin, 1988; Kachra & Schnietz, 2008). Instead of considering strategy tools as miraculous instruments for prediction and control, we view them as knowledge artefacts and heuristic devices that can guide and inform managers and develop their strategic thinking and practice (Jarzabkowski & Wilson, 2006). Strategy tools can help managers structure their thinking, recognize the distinct features of the problem at hand, and inform their judgment (Rousseau, 2012). In the spirit of the strategy-as-practice approach, we encourage educators to include strategy tools in the teaching of strategic management in ways that highlight how these tools can perform different functions. In addition to information generation and providing structure for the analysis of complex issues, they can encourage dialogue and exchange of ideas between and within managerial levels in the organization (Wright et al., 2013). However, strategy tools are never a substitute for strategic thinking. They are merely one element of strategy work.

12.4   THEMES FOR A COURSE SYLLABUS

Next, we introduce a set of themes to be included in a syllabus for teaching strategy work to business students. In our view, a course on strategy work should: (a) sensitize students to the practice-based view of strategy; (b) improve their strategic thinking capabilities; and (c) equip them with the skills and knowledge needed to act as responsible and ethical strategic managers today and in the future.

12.4.1 History of Strategy and Strategic Management

In order to support the development of strategic thinking on the part of students, the course can commence by discussing strategy as a trans-historical concept (Carter, 2013). Students should become familiar with the historical development of strategy and strategic management in order to become sensitized to the societal, political, and historical context within which various theories, frameworks and tools were developed. The "theory" of strategy is based on a long historical tradition, especially in the context of politics and warfare, both of which emphasize the importance of winning (Rumelt et al., 1994; Clegg et al., 2017). However, "accounts of how to wage warfare and exercise statecraft in ancient times are not always sound strategic guides to the twenty-first century world of modern organizations" (Clegg et al., 2017, p. 3). Students must also become familiar with the most popular conceptions of strategy and the context within which they were developed. For example, the following frameworks and tools can be covered (Kachra & Schnietz, 2008): Michael Porter's Five Forces Model and Generic Strategies; the SWOT matrix; Value Chains; Boston Consulting Group (BCG) Matrix; McKinsey 7S Framework; Balanced Scorecard; Strategy Clock; Strategic Group Maps; Strategic Factor Analysis Summary (SFAS); and Blue Ocean Four Action Framework.

12.4.2 Strategy Language and Discourse

After covering the historical development of the field, strategy as discourse and commonplace activity should be explained and discussed. This perspective develops students' strategic thinking skills and is useful in opening up the practice-perspective on strategy. Discussing strategy as discourse helps students in seeing the relationship between corporate, business-level, and functional strategies and understand their connection to the personal, everyday choices of individual managers. Strategy has become highly institutionalized as a practice across organizations and it provides a language through which organizations can be understood and managed (Carter, 2013, p. 1047). Focusing on strategy as a discourse and being aware of how language is used by different actors enables students to realize how the use of different frameworks, tools, and techniques masks power relations in and beyond organizations (Carter, 2013, p. 1048). Knights and Morgan (1991, p. 251) introduced the discursive perspective to the study of corporate strategy. They drew on the ideas and concepts of Michel Foucault and suggested that corporate strategy can be seen as a discourse with its own specific conditions of possibility.

Students must learn to appreciate the importance of the different strategy languages, which represent the multiplicity of approaches present in an organization. This is explained by Kachra and Schnietz (2008, p. 480): "managers who primarily see business issues through the prism of accounting will resolve issues differently than managers who take a more pluralistic approach. Similarly, managers who can conceptualize at an overall corporate level will make different recommendations than managers who have difficulty thinking past the business unit level." If students are to develop a practice-approach to strategy and the ability to think strategically, they need skills in recognizing the variety of strategy languages and acting upon them.

12.4.3   Dynamics of the Business Environment

The world will never be the same as it was. Organizations and strategy practitioners operate under conditions of unparalleled uncertainty that alter the way people live, work, and relate to each other. The utility of traditional long-range planning has long since disappeared (Clegg et al., 2013); future managers will need a different approach to strategy and strategizing as it is becoming more and more difficult to predict the future. There is a lot of hype about the speed and complexity of the contemporary global economy. Some call it hypercompetition – rapid escalation of competition where businesses and industries vanish overnight and others pop up in new forms elsewhere. Industry boundaries become blurred and competitive advantages become unsustainable. Standards and rules are in flux. Just when you have learned to cope, the odds are that you will be forced to rethink the foundations of your strategy. Hence, it is useful to include a discussion on megatrends and key dynamics in the contemporary global economy and to contemplate together how they are going to influence what is likely to happen and what the bigger picture of the world might look like in the future.

Strategic foresight is a concept that captures the forward-looking nature of strategy work. According to Marcus (2009), it is the practice of envisioning potential futures and engaging people in figuring out ways to impact the most preferred future. Some people prefer to talk about scenarios and scenario planning, but it is not the label that matters. The term "megatrend," first coined by Naisbitt (1982), has become an important part of the vocabulary of strategic foresight. Megatrends are forces in societal development that are likely to have a significant effect on the future in all areas of life. Identifying megatrends in the operating environment and working out what they mean for business should be an integral part of any exercise in strategic foresight. This type of discussion will help future managers learn to think strategically over time. Tienari and Meriläinen (2009) offer an example of a framework of intertwining dynamics that can be used as the basis for such discussion. Their framework consists of technology (and technologization), finance (and financialization), culture (and multiculturalism), media (and mediatization), and environment (and ecologization).

12.4.4 Strategic Change

Strategic thinking is intent-driven and strategic intent motivates organizational members in doing strategy (Liedtka, 1998). Traditional strategy courses tend to begin by focusing on strategy formulation and address implementation only at the end of the course (Kachra & Schnietz, 2008, p. 478). Strategy formulation and a hierarchical expression of strategic statements are, of course, still common activities in many organizations. Companies use "mission" statements to describe why they exist, "values" to express what the company believes in and how they intend to behave, and "visions" for stating what they want to be (Collis and Rukstad, 2008). It is crucial to understand that strategy making is always context-dependent and varies from one company to another. Some companies rely on a planning approach, others on a more emergent one.

In order to sensitize students to different approaches of doing and conceptualizing strategy, Henry Mintzberg's work is useful. According to Mintzberg (1987), there are five different ways of conceiving strategy. He calls them the "Five Ps." Strategy can refer to a plan, ploy, pattern, position, or perspective. Although this is obvious when pointed out, we too often assume the existence of a shared definition when we talk strategy with others. Talking about strategy as if it were a plan is perhaps the most traditional and common way. Strategy takes the form of a carefully crafted set of steps that a firm intends to follow in the pursuit of success. Viewing strategy as a ploy, in turn, refers to specific moves designed to outwit or trick competitors. Pattern refers to the degree of consistency in a firm's strategic actions, while position means a firm's place in the industry relative to its competitors. Finally, strategy can be understood as a perspective; how decision-makers interpret the competitive landscape around them. A single management team may represent very different ideas about what strategy is all about. In other words, there are likely to be different ways of thinking and talking about strategy represented by the "Five Ps" and based on different assumptions.

The practice-based approach to strategy shuns the dichotomy between the planning (or formulation) and implementation and emphasizes the continuous doing of strategy. Consequently, we need to know how to incorporate strategic thinking in today's planning process (Liedtka, 1998, p. 121). Understanding how to manage continuous change supports students' capabilities to think strategically. Strategic change is defined as a change in the direction and scope of an organization over the long term (Johnson et al., 2005). Nevertheless, there is no all-embracing, widely accepted single theory of change or changing. In line with the discussion about deliberate and emergent strategies, Mintzberg and Westley (1992) argue that change can be conceived as deductive or inductive. Deductive change proceeds from thought to action, whereas inductive change is more tangible and proceeds from the concrete to the conceptual in an emergent fashion. Revolutionary change, also referred to as radical and discontinuous, involves doing something fundamentally different to what you have done before. Lewin's (1947) three-stage process of change – "unfreeze–change–refreeze" – remains a popular model for understanding organizational change processes. Kotter's (1996) ideas follow Lewin by viewing change as a series of steps over time. Evolutionary change, also referred to as incremental or continuous, means doing slightly more or less of what the organization already does.

Tsoukas and Chia (2002, p. 579) are proponents of a less intentional way of conceptualizing change, believing that "change in organizations occurs without necessarily intentional managerial action as a result of individuals trying to accommodate new experiences and realize new possibilities." This view is based upon the belief that change is inherent in human action, which changes continuously in the organizational context. We argue that understanding both the deliberate and the emergent aspects of change will improve the ability of students to both think strategically and eventually contribute to the creation of ambidextrous practices in their organizations. Ambidexterity allows organizations to continuously explore new ways of doing business while exploiting existing capabilities (March, 1991; O'Reilly & Tushman, 2008). Exploitation is about efficiency, increasing productivity, control, certainty, and variance reduction. Exploration, by contrast, is about search, discovery, autonomy, innovation, and embracing variation.

12.4.5 Participation in Strategy Work

An understanding of company-internal issues such as resources, capabilities, and culture is at the heart of the strategy-as-practice perspective and directs attention to the micro-level social activities, processes, and practices that characterize organizational strategy and strategizing (Johnson et al.,

2003; Golsorkhi et al., 2015). For example, Mantere and Vaara (2008) offered a new understanding of the problems of participation in strategy work. On the basis of their research in a range of companies they came up with particular images for making sense of the challenges faced in realizing strategy. The dark side of strategy is filled with talk and practices that hinder participation. This is exemplified by the first image, which Mantere and Vaara call mystification. In some companies, strategy is discussed as if it were a secret art reserved for the chosen few; those who know better than others and who have earned the right to be involved in the process. When the time comes for the others to enjoy the fruits of the strategists' labor – in other words, when strategy is "communicated" to them – it is no wonder that little happens. Strategy remains detached from the everyday realities of the organization. It remains a mystery.

Technologization in strategy work, in turn, is about frameworks and tools taking over (Mantere & Vaara, 2008). In some companies, tools and techniques – plans, scorecards, and the like – hinder and obstruct strategy work. A lot of irrelevant and unproductive effort goes into figuring out and fulfilling the requirements of specific tools, for example, coming up with figures to a scorecard. Strategy work becomes an ordeal filled with confusion and agony, while the real issues remain untouched. Strategy can also come across as punishment. In some companies, strategy work is all about disciplining others with regulations and requirements. Ignorant and ungrateful recipients of change need to be put in their place and punished with strategy. It is no wonder they do not feel like participating. In contrast, according to Mantere and Vaara (2008), the brighter side of strategy work is all about making it concrete and filling it with meaning. Strategy work feels right when it is an essential part of everyday life in the organization.

To summarize, what we offer to students is a map of the changing strategy landscape; a synthesis of what strategy and being a strategist are about today. Understanding strategy is not about having all the bits and pieces of information at your disposal, because that is never possible. The idea is to generate enough knowledge to make sound judgments and, most importantly, to act.

12.5 TEACHING METHODS AND EXAMPLES OF COURSE FORMATS

In addition to the constructivist teaching philosophy, the practice-based approach to strategy, and the themes suggested in the syllabus, the chosen teaching methods are of the utmost importance for developing students' strategic thinking and their ability to reflect critically on strategy work and its social environment. The dominant pedagogy in our field is a mixture of lectures and generally available cases, often using the latter as illustrations of management theory and behavior (Kachra & Schnietz, 2008). We do not believe that this is sufficient to equip students with the skills and knowledge future managers need. Our complementary teaching methods include panel discussions and guest speakers from business and industry (Hamilton et al., 2000) who offer "real cases" for students to work on (Grant, 2008).

We apply student-centered learning methods in our courses. This is based on constructivist learning theory, which emphasizes the critical role of the learner in constructing meaning from new information and prior experience. Student-centered learning emphasizes each student's interests, abilities, and learning styles, making the teacher a facilitator of learning for individuals and groups. Our lectures are always interactive, and they include classroom exercises where students participate in activities that let them work directly with research or corporate materials. We often incorporate a form of "flipped learning" in our courses; students are introduced to learning materials before class and classroom time is then used to deepen understandings through discussions with peers and guests and through problem-solving activities facilitated by teachers. One of the core objectives of the flipped approach is to activate students, to engage them in collaborative activities and in peer and problem-based learning. The role of the teacher shifts toward that of a facilitator and coach who empowers students to take control of their own learning. Active use of technology platforms enriches the flipped learning process and promotes skills that are essential for twenty-first-century learning and management practice.

There are different ways in which strategy courses for business students can be organized in practice. In the following, we offer two examples based on our own experiences. The first example describes the strategy course taught by the first author. It focuses on strategizing and strategic change in a global context. The second example is a strategy course by the second author, organized in a different business school. The main theme in this course varies from year to year, and recently it centered on people and technology in strategy work.

12.5.1 Course Example 1

The course adopts a practice-based view on strategy and aims at supporting students in the development of strategic thinking. It combines theory-focused sessions, company visits, student-centered exercises, and presentations. It takes an interactive, student-oriented approach to teaching with multiple real cases presented by guests from industry and management consulting companies and discussed with them.

Students should acquire the following from the course:

1. An understanding of the link between micro and macro level views of strategy.
2. An understanding of "orthodox" strategy processes and the most common strategy tools.
3. An understanding of the variety of approaches to strategy work in a turbulent environment.
4. Practical insights into strategy work through discussions with guests from companies.
5. Experience in strategy work, i.e. by working in teams to solve real cases.

Students are assessed on the basis of four assignments: strategy learning platform and reflection (individual assignment, 20 percent of course grade), real-life company case (team assignment, 40 percent), reflective journal (individual assignment, 30 percent), and active participation (lectures, discussions, 10 percent). The idea of the reflective journal is to map changes in students' thinking concerning strategy, strategizing, and change.

This course consists of eight three-hour classroom sessions. For each session the students are asked to read 2–3 articles (specified in the syllabus). The course schedule and format is as follows:

Session 1: Introduction

- The learning objectives, the course overview together with the course deliverables are introduced.
- Based on pre-readings, strategy as a cultural, organizational and political phenomenon is introduced. Strategy as a commonplace activity and master concept of contemporary times is discussed.

Session 2: The origins of contemporary business strategy

- Prior to the session, the students do an online assignment using a self-guided tool for individual and independent learning. The tool introduces a planning approach to strategy and strategizing that separates planning from implementation. The students are asked to compare this approach with Henry Mintzberg's views on emergent strategy. During the class different approaches are discussed.
- The historical development of strategic management and the most common strategy tools are also introduced.

Session 3: Strategy-as-practice approach

- The origins and basic ideas of the practice-based view on strategy are introduced and discussed on the basis of pre-readings.
- A representative of a multinational company introduces their "everyday" strategy work. The key messages consist of describing how everyone does strategy, how strategizing is messy and organic, and how strategy is evolution rather than revolution. The students do a role-play related to strategic change.

Session 4: Strategic change and changing

- Different aspects of strategic change (continuous, incremental, and radical change) are introduced and discussed. After a thought-provoking video on continuous change, the class is divided into two and pros and cons of different change philosophies are debated. Different ways to support organizational and individual ambidexterity are also discussed.
- Leading and accelerating change are illustrated and discussed with a company representative from a multinational company.

Session 5: Culture and organizational identities

- Does culture eat strategy for breakfast? Based on pre-readings, the relationship between strategy, culture, and organizational identity is discussed.
- Students analyze the organizational identities of the companies represented by visitors to the course and work on a mini-case related to a deliberate organizational identity change initiative.

Session 6: Strategy, resources and capabilities

- The basic idea of the resource-based view of the company is introduced and discussed.
- In the current business environment, organizations need digital capabilities to be able to transform their customer experiences, operational processes, and business models (Westerman et al., 2012). A representative of a multinational technology company introduces and discusses both the challenges and opportunities of digitalization.

Session 7: Going global

- Based on both pre-readings and a video, various perspectives on globalization are discussed. The topics of ethics and sustainability are highlighted. A controversial case against child labor is discussed.
- A company representative introduces and discusses both leadership and long-term success in a large multinational company.

Session 8: Case presentations

- Student teams present their solutions to the real-life company case in the presence of company representatives who comment actively on the feasibility of students' proposals.
- The course is closed by discussing the key take-aways and learnings.

12.5.2   Course Example 2

This course is about strategy work in organizations. Building upon an understanding of strategy as something that people in organizations do (the strategy-as-practice approach), the course offers a theoretically grounded and practically relevant overview of key questions in achieving strategic change. The course sessions address questions related to implementation, communication, and participation involving humans and non-humans such as artificial intelligence. The sessions highlight how cultures impact strategy work in organizations. The course offers up-to-date knowledge on strategy work and the strategy-as-practice approach, shows how to use it to analyze the daily business of companies and other organizations, and elucidates how to apply it as a frame for strategic decision-making.

Students should learn from the course to:

1. Recognize how corporate professionals approach strategic change, how they define current challenges and opportunities in the business environment, and what it means to be a manager involved in strategic change processes.
2. Develop a substantiated view of change in the contemporary global economy through extant theory, real-case examples, group work, and personal reflection.
3. Scrutinize notions of strategic management with the strategy-as-practice approach.

In this course, students are assessed on the basis of four tasks: two short papers (individual assignments, 2 x 15 percent of the course grade), essay (individual assignment, 40 percent), and a case study (team work, 30 percent).

The course operates on a Moodle platform, which enables real-time interaction with students. Student assignments are assessed and graded immediately after each deadline; as the course progresses, this provides opportunities for discussion in the classroom sessions of what students have learned.

This course consists of six three-hour classroom sessions. The schedule and format are as follows:

Session 1: Introduction

- Introductions and overview of course.
- Analytical framework underlying the course: Strategy as practice.
- Instructions for short paper 1 (individual assignment, reflective diary): Strategy and me (13.5 h scheduled work). Format: text. Deadline: one week after the last course session.

Session 2: Strategy and external advice

- Guest session with a partner and strategy consultant from a global consultancy.
- In the volatile and fast-moving global economy, concepts such as service design hold great promise in extending understandings of strategy work. The idea is to understand client behavior and to use this understanding in mapping and developing the elements needed to deliver a better service experience. Visualization is an integral part of service design. When a service is portrayed visually, it is possible to make explicit those elements that cannot be articulated in words and figures and to envisage new solutions for a better service experience. Students have an opportunity to practice visualization in this session and in case study 1. Our guest consultants offer one of their recent client cases for students to work on. Students take on the role of management consultants in analyzing a real case and in presenting their findings and suggestions.
- Instructions for case study 1 (individual assignment, in collaboration with the global consultancy): Consulting strategy (36 h scheduled work). Thematic options (choose one): (1) international growth or (2) sustainability and branding. Format: consultant-type slide deck. Deadline: two days before session 5.

Session 3: Panel discussion on strategy, technology, and people

- This session is based on a panel discussion with a corporate executive and a digital transformation trainee as panelists. The following question is addressed: Technology is changing our lives fast – how about strategy?

- This session sensitizes students to technology and people in strategy work. The relevance of big data is first discussed (McAfee & Brynjolfsson, 2012): purchasing information, location data from mobile phones, readings from censors, clicks on websites, and stuff going through social media. Finding patterns in client behavior and figuring out what they mean for business today and tomorrow is discussed. However, technology in strategy work today is much more than big data. The session discusses how artificial intelligence (AI) and machine learning impact how humans and non-humans engage in strategy work. At the same time, our established understandings of who the strategists are in organizations are made explicit and challenged. One of the panelists is a young, technology-savvy digital transformation trainee in the company who demonstrates what it means to do strategy work in digital environments today.
- Instructions for short paper 2: Strategy, people, and technology (individual assignment, 13.5 h scheduled work). Format: text. Deadline: one day before session 4.

Session 4: Corporate videos as part of strategy work

- Guest session with head of communications for a company in turmoil: Strategy, change, and videos as tools.
- This session offers students opportunities to see how new means of communications such as online videos (vlogs) change the way strategy work is carried out in organizations. It also shows how corporate strategy work is opened up for key stakeholders such as clients. Giving the client a chance to get under the skin of the company can make the difference that is needed in order to stand above the competition.
- Instructions for case study 2: Case company in change (team case study, 27 h scheduled work). Format: online video + executive summary text (max 2 pages). Deadline: two days before session 6.

Session 5: Debriefing case study 1

- Guest session with a partner and strategy consultant from a global consultancy.

Session 6: Team videos and take-aways from course

- Case study 2 student team videos: Case company in change.
- Course summary and key take-aways.

12.6 CONCLUDING REMARKS

In this chapter, we have offered examples of what it means to teach strategic management – or, as we call it, strategy work – to business students. Taking the volatile and uncertain operating environment of the contemporary global economy as a point of departure, we have argued for an approach based on strategy-as-practice as an alternative to teaching traditional positivistic techniques of strategic inquiry. Based on our own teaching experiences we have offered concrete suggestions about teaching philosophy and learning outcomes. We have also proposed a set of themes to be included in the course curriculum, and discussed the various pedagogical methods needed to synthesize research and business practice. Hence we have argued that there is a strong case for rethinking strategic management education in business schools. We offer the following as key take-aways from this chapter:

1. Approach strategy as something that people do together.
2. Encourage students to develop their capabilities in strategic thinking.
3. Encourage students to develop their capabilities in recognizing and understanding different languages of strategy.
4. Engage business practitioners (corporate executives and managers, more junior practitioners, and management consultants) to share their insights and interact with students.
5. Encourage students and business practitioners to learn from each other in envisioning strategy work now and in the future.

REFERENCES

Bower, J.L. (2008), 'The Teaching of Strategy, From General Manager to Analyst and Back Again?', *Journal of Management Inquiry*, **17** (4), 269–275.
Carter, C. (2013), 'The Age of Strategy: Strategy, Organizations and Society', *Business History*, **55** (7), 1046–1057.
Carter, C., S. Clegg and M. Kornberger (2008), 'Strategy as Practice?' *Strategic Organization*, **6** (1), 83–99.
Clegg, S., W. Jarvis and T. Pitsis (2013), 'Making Strategy Matter: Social Theory, Knowledge Interests and Business Education', *Business History*, **55** (7), 1247–1264.

Clegg, S., J. Schweitzer, A. Whittle and C. Pitelis (2017), *Strategy: Theory and Practice, Introduction*. London: Sage Publications.

Collis, D. and M. Rukstad (2008), 'Can You Say What Your Strategy Is?', *Harvard Business Review*, **April**, 82–90.

Cunliffe, A. (2002), 'Reflexive Dialogical Practice in Management Learning', *Management Learning*, **33** (1), 35–61.

Ezzamel, M. and H. Willmott (2004), 'Rethinking Strategy: Contemporary Perspectives and Debates', *European Management Review*, **1** (1), 43–48.

Ghoshal, S. (2005), 'Bad Management Theories are Destroying Good Management Practices', *Academy of Management Learning & Education*, **4** (1), 75–91.

Golsorkhi, D., L. Rouleau, D. Seidl and E. Vaara (2015), *Cambridge Handbook of Strategy as Practice*. Cambridge: Cambridge University Press.

Grant, R. (2008), 'Why Strategy Teaching Should Be Theory Based', *Journal of Management Inquiry*, **17** (4), 276–281.

Hamel, G. and C. Prahalad, C. (1989), 'Strategic Intent', *Harvard Business Review*, **May/June**, 63–78.

Hamilton, D., D. McFarland and D. Mirchandani (2000), 'A Decision Model for Integration Across the Business Curriculum in the 21st Century', *Journal of Management Education*, **24** (1), 102–126.

Heskett, J. (2003), 'Can Business Schools Teach the Craft of Getting Things Done?', *Harvard Business School, Working Knowledge*. https://hbswk.hbs.edu/item/can-busi ness-schools-teach-the-craft-of-getting-things-done (accessed February 29, 2020).

Jarzabkowski, P., J. Balogun and D. Seidl (2007), 'Strategizing: The Challenges of a Practice Perspective', *Human Relations*, **60** (1), 5–27.

Jarzabkowski, P. and R. Whittington (2008a), 'Directions for a Troubled Discipline', *Journal of Management Inquiry*, **17** (4), 266–268.

Jarzabkowski, P. and R. Whittington, (2008b), 'A Strategy-as-Practice Approach to Strategy Research and Education,' *Journal of Management Inquiry*, **17** (4), 282–286.

Jarzabkowski, P. and D. Wilson (2006), 'Actionable Strategy Knowledge: A Practice Perspective', *European Management Journal*, **24** (5), 348–367.

Johnson, G., A. Langley, L. Melin and R. Whittington (2007), *Strategy as Practice, Research Directions and Resources*. Cambridge: Cambridge University Press.

Johnson, G., L. Melin and R. Whittington (2003), 'Guest Editors' Introduction: Micro Strategy and Strategizing: Towards an Activity-Based View', *Journal of Management Studies*, **4** (1), 3–22.

Johnson, G., K. Scholes and R. Whittington (2005), *Exploring Corporate Strategy, Text and Cases*. Harlow: Financial Times Prentice Hall (7th edition).

Kachra, A. and K. Schnietz (2008), 'The Capstone Strategy Course: What Might Real Integration Look Like?', *Journal of Management Education*, **32** (4), 476–508.

Knights, D. and G. Morgan (1991), 'Corporate Strategy, Organizations, and Subjectivity: A Critique', *Organisation Studies*, **12** (2), 251–273.

Kotter, J. (1996), *Leading Change*. Brighton, MA: Harvard Business Review Press.

Lewin, K. (1947) 'Frontiers in Group Dynamics: Concept, Method and Reality in Social Science; Equilibrium and Social Change', *Human Relations*, **1**(1), 5–41.

Liedtka, J. (1998), 'Can Strategic Thinking be Taught?', *Long Range Planning*, **31** (1), 120–129.

Mantere, S. and E. Vaara (2008), 'On the Problem of Participation in Strategy: A Critical Discursive Perspective', *Organization Science*, **19** (2), 341–358.

March, J. (1991), 'Exploration and Exploitation in Organizational Learning', *Organization Science*, **2** (1), 71–87.

Marcus, A. (2009), *Strategic Foresight. A New Look at Scenarios*. New York: Palgrave Macmillan.

McAfee, A. and E. Brynjolfsson (2012), 'Big Data: The Management Revolution', *Harvard Business Review*, **October**, 59–68.

Mintzberg, H. (1987), 'The Strategy Concept 1: Five Ps For Strategy', *California Management Review*, **30** (1), 11–24.

Mintzberg, H. (1994), 'The Fall and Rise of Strategic Planning', *Harvard Business Review*, **January–February**, 107–114.

Mintzberg, H. (1996), 'Ten Ideas Designed to Rile Everyone Who Cares About Management', *Harvard Business Review*, **July–August**, 61–68.

Mintzberg, H. and F. Westley (1992), 'Cycles of Organizational Change', *Strategic Management Journal*, **13**, (S2), 39–59.

Naisbitt, J. (1982), *Megatrends. Ten New Directions Transforming Our Lives*. New York: Warner Books.

O'Reilly, C. and M. Tushman (2008), 'Ambidexterity as a Dynamic Capability: Resolving the Innovator's Dilemma', *Research in Organizational Behaviour*, **28**, 185–206.

Paroutis, S., D. Angwin and L. Heracleous (2013), *Practicing Strategy: Text and Cases*. London: Sage Publications.

Pfeffer, J. and C. Fong (2002), 'The End of Business Schools? Less Success than Meets the Eye', *Academy of Management Learning & Education*, **1**, 78–85.

Porter, L. and L-E. McKibbin (1988), *Management Education and Development: Drift or Thrust into the 21st Century*. New York: McGraw-Hill.

Rousseau, D. (2012), 'Designing a Better Business School: Channeling Herbert Simon, Addressing the Critics, and Developing Actionable Knowledge for Professionalizing Managers', *Journal of Management Studies*, **49** (3), 600–618.

Rumelt, R., D. Schendel and D. Teece (1994), *Fundamental Issues in Strategy*. Brighton, MA: Harvard Business School Press.

Sandberg, J. and H. Tsoukas (2011), 'Grasping the Logic of Practice: Theorizing Through Practical Rationality', *Academy of Management Review*, **36** (2), 338–360.

Santalainen, T. (2006), *Strategic Thinking*. Helsinki: Talentum Oyj.

Tienari, J. and S. Meriläinen (2009), *Johtaminen ja organisointi globaalissa taloudessa*. Helsinki: WSOYPro. [Management and organizing in the global economy.]

Tsoukas, H. and R. Chia (2002), 'On Organizational Becoming: Rethinking Organizational Change', *Organization Science*, **13** (5), 567–582.

Westerman, G., D. Bonnet and A. McAfee (2012), 'The Digital Capabilities Your Company Needs', Cambridge, MA: MIT Sloan Management Review.

Whittington, R. (2006), 'Completing the Practice Turn in Strategy Research', *Organization Studies*, **27** (5), 613–634.

Wright, R., S. Paroutis and D. Blettner (2013), 'How Useful Are the Strategic Tools We Teach in Business Schools?', *The Journal of Management Studies*, **50** (1), 92–125.

13. Teaching strategic management for executives

Dianne Tyers and John Bourke

13.1 INTRODUCTION

Teaching strategic management in executive education magnifies two challenges facing anyone teaching any subject matter – what to teach and how best to teach it. The reason for this amplification is the characteristics of executive learners. As adult learners, executives bring much more to the strategic management classroom than a typical student: life and work experience, in-depth knowledge, and clear ideas about how they want to learn. Effective strategic management executive education then, starts with understanding executives.

If our executive education courses are to be fit-for-purpose and effective in these times of rapid change, they must move beyond merely teaching about strategy to helping executives learn how to be strategic. The majority of strategic management assumes strategy creation and implementation are separate. We hold that this conceptualization of strategic management is counterproductive – it over-emphasizes the importance of analysis and overlooks execution. It also assumes that strategy formation and strategy implementation are separate, sequential activities while in reality they tend to be intertwined (Mintzberg et al., 2003). While theory and tools are useful as a starting point in strategic management, they cannot be the end point, particularly for executives tasked with implementation. What exactly to teach in strategic management for executives, therefore, needs to include knowledge of theory and tools for both analysis and application including strategy formulation and implementation.

A variety of approaches is used to teach strategic management (Jennings, 2002). However, strategic management education still tends to rely heavily on lectures, readings, and case studies. This combination is supposed to expose students to new information and to foster the development of their critical thinking (McDade, 1995). However, these traditional approaches have been subject to much criticism. For example, case studies – long a core pedagogical approach used in teaching strategic management – have been criticized for having the instructor dominate classroom interaction and for undermining double-loop learning (Argyris, 1980). They are also contextualized in a time and place, making them susceptible to overgeneralization (and, some would argue, any generalization is overgeneralization) and they are difficult to teach well (Shulman, 1992). While case studies may have a place in our strategic management executive education, our classroom practice needs to include a much wider range of approaches and corresponding activities to enable executives to learn to be strategic, not to just learn strategic management theory.

13.2   EXECUTIVES AS LEARNERS

Although executives can be seen as students, the characteristics associated with the construct – inferior, subordinate, lacking in knowledge and life experience, in need of guidance – do not apply. Rather than being "students", executives are professionals, experts and experienced practitioners, who, while having things to learn from us and their peers, also have things to teach us and their peers. This framing of executives as having multiple roles in our classes is not trivial. How we perceive executives influences, at least on a sub-conscious level, how we behave when interacting with them, the relationships we build with them and ultimately, how successful we are in enabling their strategic management learning.

Executives are adult learners and as such they are independent and self-directed, with extensive life and work experience, and knowledge. They have been successful in their careers to date, and thus they are confident and assertive. They have established values, beliefs and opinions and usually have some degree of self-awareness. They have ideas about how they like to learn, based on previous education experiences, and want to play an active role in their learning (Collins, 1998; Fenwick et al., 2006).

Not all of the characteristics of executives enable their success in our strategic management classes. Their past successes may lead them to believe that they already know what they need to know about strategic management. Some of what they have previously learned may need to be un-learned. They may be excessively proud or aggressive. They may compete for talking time to appear smart, pressuring others in the class to remain silent. They may believe that academics or executives from other sectors lack the understanding of the contextual specifics of their industry and organization necessary to help them. In short, executives as adult learners can be a difficult audience if we make suboptimal choices about what to help them learn and how to help them learn it (Collins, 1998; Fenwick et al., 2006).

Until now, we have spoken about executive learners as if they are all the same; they are not. Executives, like all adult learners, are diverse in background, experience, age, personality, organizational role and sector. They are equally diverse in their knowledge, application and perspectives on strategic management. Finally, their beliefs about learning, the internal barriers to learning they have constructed, and their purposes for taking our executive education courses all vary. There will be executives in our classes who want to be there and are eager to learn; there may also be executives who are there because they're required to be by their organizations or to complete mandatory professional development. The former group are intrinsically motivated to learn and focused on the learning process. They know why they are studying and what they want to get out of the classes. The latter group, less so. It is our responsibility to help all of them push through any motivational barriers they have constructed for themselves (Knowles, 1981).

Regardless of the above variation, there is one way that the executives are all the same. They are our customers. Executive education is a substantial financial and time investment, either by the executives themselves or by their organizations. Executives expect to be treated as customers and will demand all of the rights of customers – to have their voices heard and their needs and expectations met. Executive education is a lucrative but highly competitive education space. Customers can and will take their education dollars elsewhere if we deliver a substandard education experience.

The characteristics discussed make executives distinctly different from the learners we traditionally teach and so we need to adjust how we perceive and enact our relationship with them. If we try to engage with our executives in "teacher mode" we will unintentionally create interpersonal friction and tension, leading to unsatisfactory results in our course delivery and their learning. Executives are not open to being taught in the traditional understanding of the word, so anything we do to "teach" them will be ineffective or even counter-productive.

Instead of visualizing ourselves as imparting our impressive knowledge and wisdom to eager, receptive and adoring minds, there are a number of more appropriate ways to conceptualize our interactions with executives. We can consider ourselves to be facilitators who nurture their learning. We can be helpers or enablers as they construct their own knowledge. To be more poetic, we can picture ourselves as gardeners cultivating their learning. Regardless of the metaphors we use, this mind-shift that requires us to step back from a teacher-centered, all-knowing role in our executive classes, is fundamental to our success or failure teaching strategic management to executives.

13.3   EXECUTIVE EDUCATION COURSES

In addition to the variation we encounter with executives in our classes, we also have to manage variation in the executive education courses we are assigned. We may have customized or standardized courses, shorter or longer courses, and courses with homogeneous or heterogeneous class compositions. Each of these variations in course characteristics requires us to be flexible, adaptable, creative and agile.

13.3.1   Standardized versus Customized

Our executive education courses can be standardized, customized or a hybrid variation falling between the two. Courses toward the standardization end of this continuum have elements that don't change regardless of who the learners are and who is delivering the course. With courses that have standardized elements, our unique contribution in delivering the course is our personal approach, our communication style, the experiences we have to share and the emphasis we put on different topics. In these courses we can have executives complete a checklist at the beginning of the course to indicate which course content is most relevant to them, and then emphasize that content accordingly.

In courses toward the customization end of the continuum, we can put our personal touch on the course in many more ways through our choice of rationale, objectives, content, approach and activities, materials, and assessments. We base our choices on a needs analysis completed as part of the course design process, which will be discussed in more detail below.

13.3.2   Shorter versus Longer

Our executive education courses vary in length. We may be assigned a one-day seminar or a week-long course or we may be assigned a course that spans an academic term in a program that takes more than a year to complete. With shorter courses, we have fewer, very targeted objectives and limited content to cover. We also have less time to make an impact with the executives. First impressions matter. We have to be disciplined as we deliver the course to stay on track. We have very little time for tangents.

With longer courses, we have more objectives and can cover more content in more depth. We have more time to build deeper relationships with the executives and gain their respect and trust. We also have more time to share our personal experiences and to have the executives share theirs. We can take more tangents based on their interests.

13.3.3 Homogeneous versus Heterogeneous

Even though, as discussed above, there is extensive variation among executives individually, we may have a course in which the class composition is either homogeneous or heterogeneous. In homogenous classes there are clear commonalities among the executives. For example, they may come from the same organization, sector or region. Alternatively, we may have a heterogeneous class composition in which it is difficult to discern any similarities at all among the executives.

With homogeneous classes, we can focus on the learning needs that result from the similarities among the executives. We can tailor our content, activities and commentary to the organization, sector or region that the executives come from. The challenge with this type of class composition is that we may encounter very few differing perspectives on issues, thus providing limited scope for debate and discussion.

With heterogeneous classes, when there are no or few commonalities to draw upon, we have to manage a wide variety of learner needs. We also need to include a range of sectors and regions in our examples. On the other hand, we have a variety of perspectives from the executives, which provides us with rich opportunities for debate and discussion.

13.4 EXECUTIVE EDUCATION COURSE DESIGN

If we are assigned a customized strategic management executive education course, the expectation is that we design the course as well as deliver it. We may also be called upon to design a standardized course for others. Additionally, if we are delivering a standardized course, we need to analyze the course from a design perspective to identify areas in which we can adjust it to meet learner needs. Regardless of the scenario, we need to be familiar with course design and able to implement it to varying degrees with our courses.

We use a course design framework to create an effective and internally aligned course, or to analyze an existing course to identify areas for improvement. There are many frameworks available, developed by academics and practitioners from different realms of education. Here, we use a course design framework that draws upon multiple sources (Nunan, 1998; Grunert O'Brien, 2008; Archer, 2017; Glatthorn, 2018). The framework presents an iterative rather than a linear process. Throughout the process we revisit earlier stages to make adjustments as needed and ensure the alignment of all of the elements. We briefly discuss the course design elements in the framework as they relate to strategic management courses for executives (see Figure 13.1).

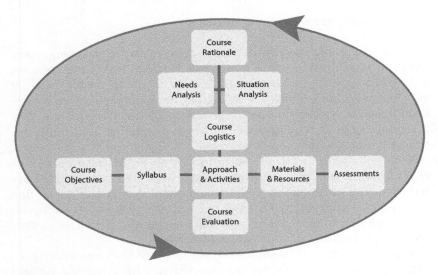

Figure 13.1   Course design elements

The *course rationale* is a brief statement that captures why a course is important. It is useful when marketing a course to executives and their employers. It is very difficult to persuade executives to pay substantial course fees if the course rationale is not clear, comprehensible and convincing. A strong course rationale should answer the following questions:

- Who is the course for? What is the profile of the typical executive the course is designed for?
- Why is it important for these executives to take the course? How will they benefit? How will their organizations benefit?
- Why should executives choose to take this course and not one from another institution?

Once we have a clear rationale for our course, we conduct a needs analysis and situation analysis, either sequentially or in parallel.

A *needs analysis* examines information from various course stakeholders (possibly including some executives, representatives from their employers, and course administrators) about what the course should help executives learn. In addition to helping design the course, it can help communicate that the course will be relevant and beneficial to the executives who take it.

A *situation analysis* identifies contextual issues that may constrain how the course is designed and delivered, impacting the overall success of the course. It allows us to be proactive about potential barriers to the success of the course through questioning and analysis in a number of categories:

- *Institutional factors:* Does our institution have the resources to develop and deliver the course? Is our financial plan for the course sound? Does our institution have the credibility to deliver the course?
- *Instructor factors*: Do we have instructors who will be credible in the eyes of executives? Do we have instructors who are confident enough to manage the strong comments and opinions of executives? Do we have instructors who can engage interactively with the executives?
- *Learner factors*: Do the executives want to be in the course? How will the executives' lives outside of the classroom constrain their performance in class? What kind of payoff will the executives have for being successful in the course? What expectations do the executives have of themselves, the course and the outcome of the course? Do the executives buy into the value of the course?
- *Change factors*: Are the executives' organizations, at all levels, ready for change that the executives may want to implement as a result of what they learn in the course? We are doing our executives a disservice if we teach them strategic management and then send them back to organizations that are not ready for change.

We also have to be practical about how our course will be implemented by answering *course logistics* questions. Executives need their courses to be accessible and to fit into their schedules. They also expect courses to be well-organized and smoothly run. They immediately notice and criticize any hint of disorganization. Some logistical questions to address in the course design stage include:

- How long will the course be?
- Will the course be online, classroom-based or blended?
- How many classes will there be? How long will each class be? What days of the week will the classes occur on? When will the classes start and finish?
- Where will the course be held? Are the facilities accessible from the executives' workplaces? Are the facilities suitable for executives? Do the facilities have visual support space (whiteboards, SmartBoards) and presentation technology (projectors, screens)?

- Will snacks, coffee and meals be provided? If not, are there food options close to the facilities?
- What are the attendance expectations? What are the consequences for non-attendance?
- Who will manage the day-to-day logistics of the course? Who will manage executive complaints?

Only once we have completed these initial course design steps and successfully addressed any questions, are we ready to work on the course content.

We start with the *course objectives*, which state what we want executives to learn in the course. Clear objectives allow our course to stay on track. We align everything to our objectives – our syllabus, methodology, activities, materials and resources. There are two sides to our course objectives – what we want executives to know at the end of the course and what we want them to be able to do. This distinction between knowledge and performance or application is extremely important. Executives don't just need to know strategic management. They also need to be able to utilize the learning in their organizations. We therefore need to address both knowledge and application in our courses.

Building from here, we use the needs analysis output to build the syllabus. The *syllabus* lists the content executives will learn in the course. Specifically, it details the topics, the content within those topics, and the order of the topics. In the next section we will explore the strategic management syllabus in more depth.

With our course content determined in our syllabus, we next need to decide how we are going to deliver the content. Given the characteristics of executives discussed above, making good choices about how we enable them to learn is imperative. We cannot teach with a "business as usual" strategy. We determine how we will facilitate learning at three different levels – approach, methodology and activities – all of which must align with our course objectives and content. An *approach* describes in broad brush strokes what we keep in mind as we engage with the learners. Think of this as the strategies we use in our teaching decision-making. A *methodology* describes in more detail the characteristics of the types of activities we use in our course. An *activity* describes the exact steps or tasks we use to deliver one piece of content. These three terms are often used interchangeably. Moving forward we will use "approach" to refer to both an "approach" and a "methodology," and "activity" to refer to specific tasks we use in our courses. In a subsequent section below, we discuss approaches and activities that we have found effective with executive education strategic management courses.

Closely aligned with our approach, methodologies and activities are our *resources* and *materials* choices. Are we going to use a course textbook? Research articles? Practitioner articles? For our materials, are we going to use business learning games? Case studies? Simulations? Also, included in our resource considerations is software we will use, from learning management systems, to online polling, video-streamed communication, and real-time technology-enabled games and simulations. We also need to decide if we want executives to work directly on laptops or tablets, with all of the materials in digital format, or whether we will provide hard copies of resources. We need to be aware that our resources and materials choices are closely tied to our approach, methodology and activity decisions as well as our budget constraints. Certain approaches, methodologies and activities require specific resources and materials, which we will discuss in more detail below.

Our next course design decisions center around *assessment*, whether to assess or not and, if so, how. Unlike other students, executives tend not to focus on grades. While they certainly want to be successful on a course, they do not define this in terms of a grade but in terms of how much they learn that will help them at work. Our assessment decisions need to align with this and so, if we opt to assess, we should focus on application more than on knowledge. Some assessment approaches that do this are strategy development and problem-solving exercises set within authentic complex dynamic contexts.

Our course design process is not complete until we have incorporated a *course evaluation* feedback loop with the executives. Continuous improvement based on feedback is good course design practice and executives, as customers, expect to have the opportunity to critique the course and for us to act upon their feedback. We need both to be open to ongoing informal feedback throughout course delivery and we need to include a formal evaluation at the end of the course. Standard university course evaluations, designed to provide data for professor career advancement, are not appropriate for this. Course evaluation needs to include all elements of the course – the content, instructor, materials and resources, assessments, facilities and customer service. Therefore, a customized course evaluation tool is required.

We will look at several of the curriculum design framework elements in more detail, namely the syllabus and the approaches, methodologies and activities. These are the components in which we have a number of important decisions to make to craft and deliver impactful strategic management courses for executives.

13.5 A SYLLABUS TO LEARN TO BE STRATEGIC

13.5.1 From Strategic Management to Managing Strategically

We only need to go back about a hundred years to find a time when management was almost entirely operational with very little strategy. Back then, strategy was almost the exclusive domain of admirals and generals (although, further back, the politician Machiavelli was an exception).

In practice, strategic management grew out of budgeting and long-range planning, a process in which the future was expected to be predictable. All that was required was extrapolation (Hussey, 2007). The inherent assumption was that the future will automatically be better than the present. As might have been foreseen, this proved to be wrong. Consequently, greater analysis – including competitive analysis and portfolio analysis – was called for to enable better forecasting and this gave rise to strategic planning (Ansoff et al., 2018).

However, strategic planning was labor intensive and slow so, along with hundreds of strategic planning models, strategic planning departments came into existence (Mintzberg et al., 2005). The delegation of strategy formulation to a staff function, introduced a significant bureaucratic overhead, blurred the lines of responsibility, and created a tendency for planning to become an end in itself. In 1977, Ansoff – who is regarded as the father of strategic management (Hussey, 2007) and who was an enthusiastic advocate of strategic planning – acknowledged that almost two decades after the introduction of strategic planning, most organizations were still only conducting long-range planning (Ansoff, 1977). Gradually, strategic planning departments fell out of favor. However, the shadow strategic planning has cast on strategic management remains.

In addition to more attention being given to analysis than to synthesis, traditionally strategic management has been concerned with establishing goals and objectives which deliver on the organization's mission and guide it into the future. Operations management, in contrast, has been focused on the present and on achieving objectives and goals (Ansoff et al., 2018). This divorces thinking from doing, a separation which is compounded by the need for executives to delegate much of the analysis that is required.

The segmentation of management into strategic and operational management, also decouples strategy formulation from strategy implementation. This is problematic as "there is no such thing as an optimal strategy, worked out in advance" (Mintzberg et al., 2005, p. 116). To be truly strategic, executives need to immerse themselves in the day-to-day of strategy implementation and operational management so that strategic learning can occur.

The original concept of strategic management put forward by Ansoff, held that strategic behavior and operational behavior required different organizational architecture (Ansoff et al., 2018). Trying to accommodate both in one organization produces tension and conflict. However, this needs to be harnessed and embraced rather than avoided.

This need for managers to marry thinking with doing and to manage the tensions in an organization so that it can excel at both strategic management and operational management is what gives rise for a need to move from strategic management to managing strategically. Executives need to learn how to manage strategically, balancing long-term and short-term requirements and contributing both to the crafting of sound strategy and its implementation. In the words of Mintzberg et al. (2005, p. 368), while academics can grab hold of a single piece of strategy, managers "must deal with the entire beast."

Managing strategically requires an understanding of strategy and how to craft it, a focus on implementation, and leadership for organizational adaptability. Leadership for organizational adaptability is a concept which evolved from the complexity theory of leadership. It is required "when people with different, knowledge, beliefs, and preferences interact in an attempt to solve problems and resolve conflicts" (Yukl, 2013, p. 292) (see Uhl-Bien and Arena (2018) for more details). Therefore, for executives to learn how to manage strategically, an exploration of leadership for organizational adaptability needs to be included.

13.5.2   Understanding Strategy

There are various views on strategy and an inadequate common understanding of what it is. Consequently, we hold that the starting point should be to explore what strategy is since, as von Clausewitz (1883) notes in his seminal work *On War*, the first task is to clarify terms and concepts that are confused as only after can we hope to consider the issues easily and clearly and expect to share the same point of view.

As a result, the starting point is to help executives learn what strategy means, a task which is not as simple as it may sound since there is little agreement in the literature, as is shown by the following examples of attempts to define it:

- The "determination of the basic long-term goals of an enterprise, and the adoption of courses of action and the allocation of resources necessary" (Chandler, 1962, p. 13).
- A "coordinated and integrated set of five choices: a winning aspiration, where to play, how to win, core capabilities, and management systems" (Lafley and Martin, 2013, p. 5).

- A "coherent set of analyses, concepts, policies, arguments, and actions that respond to a high-stakes challenge" (Rumelt, 2017, p. 6).

Mintzberg (1987b) holds that strategy needs five definitions to be understood, his "5 Ps" of strategy as a plan, a ploy, a pattern, a position, and a perspective. Meanwhile, Porter (1996) in an article entitled "What is Strategy?", which is regarded as a tour de force, just described strategy rather than defined it.

It is also possible for somebody to define strategy in different ways. For example, Lafley in the example given above defined strategy one way with Roger Martin but with Ram Charan as "choices required by clear goals – choices that result in winning with consumers and customers and against competition" (Lafley and Charan, 2010, p. 75). A definition which is of particular interest since, as stated, if something does not result in "a win" it was not a strategy (the definition also makes the existence of competitors a precondition to having a strategy).

Given the difficulty of understanding strategy, the difference between being strategic and tactical, the difference between being strategic and opportunistic, it is important to allow executives to discuss strategy so that they can construct their own understanding of what it is.

13.5.3 How to Craft Strategy

As a result of the traditional scope of strategic management, in the majority of strategic management courses, most of what is taught is strategy formulation: what, why and how to analyse various things and, to some degree or other, how to pull the output of various analyses together to arrive at a strategy.

As there is no single agreed upon definition of strategy there is no agreed upon approach to formulate or craft it. In *Strategy Safari*, Mintzberg et al. (2005) explore 10 schools of strategy. Depending on the school of thought one subscribes to, various approaches and tools are appropriate for use when crafting strategy. Irrespective of our own personal views, it is recommended to explore a range of these tools with executives when discussing strategy formulation. Some of the best known tools are the SWOT analysis, the BCG Matrix, PESTEL Analysis, the Value Chain, Porter's 5 Forces, scenario analysis, Pareto analysis and, recently, the business model canvas.

However, as Mintzberg (1987a, p. 70) points out, there "is no one best way to make strategy." Consequently, it is also valuable to discuss Crafting Strategy (Mintzberg, 1987a), where the executive is likened to a potter as tacit knowledge is needed in addition to explicit knowledge derived from analysis. Mintzberg (1987a) points out that not all strategy is deliberate, that some of it emerges, and some "intended strategy" gets left unrealized. The *craft* comes into play in learning once strategy has been formulated and knowing what intended strategy to discard and what emergent strategies to incorporate. Purely deliberate strategy precludes learning once the strategy is formulated; emergent strategy fosters it.

Although crafting strategy can be challenging, in practice, most of the problems organizations encounter arise from strategy implementation not strategy development.

13.5.4 Strategy Implementation

Too many executives "believe their strategy job is largely done when they share their aspirations with employees" (Lafley and Martin, 2013, p. 46). This position is reinforced by traditional strategic management education which assumes strategy formation and strategy implementation are separate, sequential activities while in reality they tend to be intertwined (Mintzberg et al., 2003). However, as von Moltke (1890) noted in his seminal work *On Strategy*, no plan of execution extends with certainty beyond the first moment of its implementation. Consequently, to manage strategically, executives need to do more than merely formulate strategy and communicate it. They need to be open to strategic learning and to modify their plans to accommodate it. In the words of Mintzberg, they need to discard some elements of "intended strategy" and supplement the remaining "deliberate strategy" with emergent strategy to arrive at realized strategy.

However, this brings us back to the traditional separation of *strategic management* and *operations management* (Porter, 1996; Ansoff et al., 2018). As discussed, the former involves setting an organization's objectives and goals appropriately for the environment in which it operates, while the latter is mainly concerned with delivering organizational outputs that contribute to the achievement of these objectives. This clearly limits the scope of strategic management to *strategy formulation*, with *strategy implementation* being the domain of operations management. There are some voices in favor of rethinking the division. Slack et al. (2007), for example, hold that operations managers not only need to implement and deliver on strategy but they also need to enable the organization to refine its strategy. They even go so far, in line with Hayes and Wheelwright (1984), as to state that operations managers help drive strategy.

In addition, Mintzberg et al. (2005) note that in 1984, Walter Kiechel suggested in *Fortune* magazine that only about 10 percent of formulated strategies get implemented and add that Tom Peters (author of *In Search of Excellence*) claims that this figure is widely inflated.

As a result, to manage strategically, rather than focus on strategy formulation, executives need to focus on learning how to draw on strategic learning to craft and implement strategy. We need to prepare them for this by discussing implementation challenges, and helping them develop the communication and change management skills needed to effectively implement strategy.

Tools such as balanced scorecards and strategy maps can form part of the discussion but the critical thing is to get them thinking about what derails so many carefully formulated strategies when it comes to deployment and what they need to do to overcome those challenges.

From a very practical perspective, our executives have responsibilities that encompass both strategy formulation and strategy implementation. As such, they are unlikely to be concerned about whether there is a difference between strategic management and managing operations strategically. For the most part, practitioners are not as exacting about the precise meaning of words as academics.

13.5.5 Leadership for Organizational Adaptability

In order to manage the tension between the operational and the strategic, between what Ansoff et al. (2018) call "incremental behavior" and "entrepreneurial behaviour" (which aligns with "exploitation" and "exploration"), executives need to learn how to manage the tensions created by the conflicting requirements these place on an organization and its people. In addition to discussing, for example, "exploration" versus "exploitation" (March, 1991), "blue ocean" versus "red ocean" (Kim and Mauborgne, 2005), and enabling leadership in an adaptive space (Uhl-Bien and Arena, 2018), executives could be put in situations where they need to manage tensions to help them develop this skill.

13.6 APPROACHES AND ACTIVITIES

The objective of strategic management executive education courses is to facilitate learning including, as appropriate, knowledge transfer both from us to the executives and between the executives and their peers. We discuss how we do this from an approach level and then link in examples of activities that fall under those approaches.

13.6.1 Selecting Teaching Approaches and Activities

There are many different approaches for teaching adults, emanating from different fields, and based on different theories of teaching and learning.

The default approach in higher education for teaching any subject matter is *lecturing*. In lecturing, we, as the *knower*, stand at the front of the class and verbally share predetermined content with the class, sometimes supported visually with presentation slides. Learners listen to the lecture and take notes of the key points. This is a highly controlled, teacher-centered, one-way transfer of knowledge.

Lecturing can have a place in the strategic management executive education classroom but it is a limited one. We consciously and intentionally use lecturing in short, bite-sized chunks as a way to efficiently, clearly and directly transfer complex knowledge. However, while there is a time to lecture as a "sage on the stage," there is a much more significant time to be the "guide on the side" with other approaches in which executives interactively explore, process, apply, share and construct knowledge. Because executives are adult learners there is a strong argument for instructional approaches that are less "talking at" them and more "talking with" them. In other words, while there are times at which we deliberately choose to lecture, executives respond more to active and interactive approaches.

We also need to consider the lens through which we are viewing strategic management when determining our teaching approaches. When we teach strategic management, we explore it through an external lens, commenting on what we see as we look at it from the outside. Executives view it through the same lens in their learning process. However, those who run organizations see things from the inside. Strategic management is no longer simply theoretical or abstract when it is seen in a real-world context. Understanding this difference in lenses is key to teaching strategic management in executive education. Consequently, we need learning approaches that provide the best classroom-based approximation of the real-world, viewed from the inside.

Given the variation in our executive learners and the balance we need to strike between knowledge and application, there is no single approach for teaching strategic management in executive education that will work all of the time. Rather, we need to have a range of approaches in our repertoire from which we consciously select the approach that fits the needs of our learners, content and context at a particular point in time. These approaches often take significant time to plan and deliver, more so than lectures. However, they are worth the investment of time and effort as they make the learning experience more relevant, engaging and memorable. In each of the approaches, our role and that of the learners vary. We may shift from facilitator, to guide, to coach, and even to learner. The executives may shift from collaborators, to explorers, to analysts, to problem-solvers. Over a complete course, we integrate our use of these different approaches to deliver an optimal learning experience to executives.

We explore three approaches that are particularly useful in strategic management executive education: constructivism, experiential learning and action learning. For each approach we suggest activities that align with the approach.

13.6.2   Constructivism

Constructivism is technically a theory about learning rather than a teaching approach. However, we start with it because it provides a solid foundation upon which to build our classroom practice for executive education. Constructivism, conceptualized in the field of psychology by thinkers such as Vygotsky (1962) and Piaget (1971), holds that as humans we all construct meaning and build an understanding of our world through our personal experiences. We experience something, reflect on it and then construct knowledge from it.

Constructivism is also the appropriate paradigm for executive education especially as executives bring such a wealth of experience to class, of both breadth and depth. That experience should be the starting point in their exploration of strategic management. In every class, we should provide opportunities for executives to share their personal experiences and build meaning from those experiences around concepts we introduce. Activities that enable this to happen include pair, small group and whole class discussions in which experiences are shared and analyzed, and written reflective personal reports. We cannot emphasize enough the importance of tapping into the experiences of executives in their investigation of strategic management.

Constructivism is important in executive education for a second reason. It clearly places responsibility for learning on the executives. We need to make this responsibility explicit at the beginning of our courses. Our role is to expose the executives to knowledge and ideas. It is up to them to build their understanding of that knowledge and personalize it to their experiences.

13.6.3   Experiential Learning

Experiential learning, in which learning is facilitated through experience, activity, and action, rather than through lectures and textbooks, has been used for many years in various forms. Its most recent iteration is largely based on the work of Kolb (1984). As with constructivism, experiential learning places responsibility for learning on the learner. Learning is an inductive discovery process rather than a passive process. Finally, experiential learning acknowledges that individuals learn differently, based upon how they process their experiences. In order to learn experientially, learners need to be risk-takers, decision-makers, and problem-solvers. They need to be analytical, active, reflective and self-aware. Kolb further elaborated on experiential learning as a circular process, with four stages: concrete experience, reflective observation, abstract conceptualization, and active experimentation.

Experiential learning is a good fit for strategic management executive education. Recall from our discussion on executives as learners, that adult learners appreciate being acknowledged as experts (Kolb et al., 1986). Further, executives like to immediately apply what they have learned to their organizations in order to make their learning relevant, real and memorable. Application facilitates retention, mitigating the forgetting curve uncovered many years ago by Ebbinghaus (1885), which sees people forgetting things almost at once unless they are applied. Experiential learning addresses all of these needs.

An example of experiential learning in a strategic management executive education class, built around the executives' professional experiences, is as follows:

Concrete Experience: Executives work in small groups to share a personal experience they have had in their organization with respect to the topic introduced in a lecture. Alternative activities that can be used in this concrete experience stage include business learning games, scenarios, simulations and case studies, in both regular and digital formats.

Reflective Observation: Executives work in small groups to reflect on the experiences they share. They discuss what they think worked or didn't work in the experience and why. Alternative activities that we can use in the reflective observation stage include individual written journaling and creating a video response to the experience.

Abstract Conceptualization: Executives work in small groups to discuss what they learned from the experience and what they might have done differently. They apply concepts presented in the lecture in their conceptualization discussions.

Active Experimentation: Executives work in small groups to role play scenarios similar to the experiences they shared. They try different ways to manage the scenarios and discuss what worked or didn't work. Other activities that can be used in the active experimentation stage include replaying parts of a business learning game or simulation to experiment with different outcomes.

13.6.4 Action Learning

Action learning is an approach which focuses on solving problems by identifying our existing programmed knowledge and then questioning that knowledge to identify areas for learning (Revans, 1982, 1998). Central to action learning is the belief that learning results from questioning what we already know to find unique and original answers to problems. The questioning in action learning is targeted, using different types of questions (closed and open) to uncover different ways to view the existing knowledge, identify gaps and formulate new knowledge.

Action learning is an effective approach for us to use for a number of reasons. First, it acknowledges the existing "current" knowledge of executives and uses this as the starting point. Second, it uses a targeted and systematic way to enable executives to construct new knowledge. Third, it has a practical and action-oriented outcome. And finally, it is a team-based teaching and learning process which mimics how executives need to operate in their organizations on a daily basis.

An example of how we might implement action learning in our strategic management executive education courses, built around the existing knowledge of the executives is:

Problem: Present a real-life strategic management problem, either a problem of strategy formulation or implementation.

Programmed Knowledge: In small teams, executives share what they already know about the problem and the background to the problem.

Questioning: In small teams, executives ask each other targeted questions to explore their existing knowledge, find gaps and identify new knowledge or perspectives.

Learning: In small teams, executives identify what they have learned and how they will formulate this into action to solve the problem.

To wrap up the activity, the teams present their problem-solving action to the class and support it with their learning.

13.6.5   Additional Learning Design Considerations

In addition to the three approaches above, we should also incorporate additional approaches to help us emphasize different aspects of the learning experience.

Contextualized learning is an approach that, as the name implies, emphasizes the context of the learning activities within a detailed environment, either real or fictional, simulated or virtual (Johnson, 2002). Examples of contextualized learning for strategic management are simulations, case studies and business learning games set in either real or fictionalized settings (the past, the future, a different planet). Contextualized learning is an effective approach to highlight the dynamic complexity of the contexts in which executives function.

Cooperative and social learning involves learners working with each other to accomplish a specified task (Gillies, 2016). For executive education, cooperative and social learning is essential, given that both strategy formulation and implementation involve teamwork. Examples of cooperative and social learning include a team approach to simulations, business learning games or case studies. We can also run team competitions or projects.

As a brief aside, cooperative and social learning is very important in executive education if multiple learners come from the same organization. Those learners can take a team approach to addressing the strategic management issues in their organizations and so benefit significantly from cooperative and social learning. An unfortunate reality for organizations hoping to see change in their organizations is that it is very difficult for a single person who has been changed on an executive development course, to make a difference back in an unchanged organization. Better results can be achieved if an entire team participates in executive education and then together works to bring change to their organization.

Discovery learning involves learners working with hints, clues and otherwise incomplete information, through which they can complete a journey to discover the learning (Bruner, 1961). Discovery learning mimics the reality in which executives function on a daily basis, that of not having all of the information required in order to make decisions. Example discovery learning activities include formulating strategy using different tools but with incomplete information and completing simulations or business learning games designed around incomplete information.

Task-based learning requires learners to complete discrete, real-world tasks. It provides learners with opportunities for application, as opposed to just knowledge learning. The tasks can be complex and lengthy, such as using a tool to formulate or analyze strategy, or simpler and shorter, such as selecting from among two possible tools to use. Simpler and shorter tasks can be used to scaffold learning, providing step-by-step support through a complex task by building on multiple smaller tasks.

13.6.6 Our Repertoire of Approaches and Activities

Pulling all of our approaches together, we have a significant repertoire of educational approaches and corresponding activities to draw from for our strategic management executive education. Remember, it is best not to use one approach all the time but to consciously select the approach that best matches our executive needs and course content at a particular point in time (see Figure 13.2).

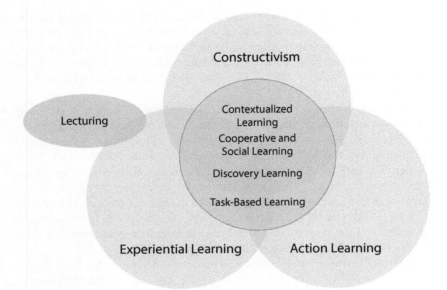

Figure 13.2   Our teaching approach repertoire

13.7   CLASSROOM MANAGEMENT

In addition to selecting and implementing appropriate and impactful teaching approaches and activities, our success in executive education hinges on our ability to manage the real-time complex dynamics of classroom interactions, called classroom management. Successful classroom management includes multiple elements:

1. **Interaction patterns** are how instructors and students work together in the classroom. There are five main interaction patterns we can choose from: whole class led by us; whole class led by an executive; small groups; pairs; and individual. We strategically select our interaction pattern based on our content, time management and learning objectives. For example, whole class led by us is very time efficient and also ensures that all executives receive the same information. Small groups allow for maximum executive participation and experience sharing. Individual work allows executives to move at their own pace and demonstrate their individual ability.
2. **Grouping decisions** are how we select the teams for activities or tasks. We can group executives, for example, according to level of expertise,

ability, sector, organizational role, age or personality. We can group by similarity or difference. Grouping according to any similarity allows executives to tailor their learning to their specific needs. Grouping according to any difference allows executives to share varying perspectives and opinions.

3. **Communication management** ensures that all communication in the class is respectful and professional. We set the ground rules for classroom communication in the first class so that executives know our expectations. These ground rules include one person speaking at a time, no use of derogatory terms and no harassment.

4. **Personality management** is one of the most challenging elements of classroom management in executive education. Most of our executives have strong personalities and opinions. We need to ensure that no single executive dominates the class and that everyone gets heard. We need to ensure that negative or competitive personalities do not bring down the tone of the whole class.

5. **Opinion management** allows for different positions and viewpoints to be expressed in class and for respectful disagreement among those with different positions and viewpoints. If there are two opposing viewpoints, don't ignore the contrary position. We model that seemingly opposing views can both be valid at the same time. Opinion management is important in executive education, not just because executives have strong opinions but because they view strategic management differently depending on their experiences and values. We need to validate and explore these differing opinions as part of our classroom management.

13.8   FINAL THOUGHTS

The successful delivery of strategic management executive education is about balance. The first balance we need to strike in our courses is between knowledge and application. Knowledge is the information about strategic management that is transferred to executives. Application is executives being able to use that knowledge effectively and successfully in real situations to achieve their desired outcomes. The unfortunate default in many higher education courses is an excess of course time and effort spent on knowledge at the expense of application. With strategic management executive education, the course content, while based on theory, has an intended endpoint of application in real organizations. Further, executives need to see immediate, relevant application in order to be motivated to learn and retain their learning. Therefore, we need to consciously avoid the default approach and ensure that we balance knowledge and application in our courses.

A second tension that we need to balance in classes is complexity versus simplicity. Determining "how much complexity is enough for an effective response to the environmental challenges of today" (Ansoff et al., 2018, p. 5) is a vital task to get right both when crafting strategy for an organization and when designing and delivering a strategic management executive education course. As the Nobel prize winning poet Octavio Paz wrote, *too much light, like too much darkness, stops us from seeing*. In an organization, over-complexity in strategy results in the big picture being lost, increased costs of management, employees getting bogged down in the detail, and ultimately in the organization becoming unmanageable. Over-simplistic strategy is equally problematic. The same two scenarios – too much complexity or too much simplicity – lead to the same negative outcomes when teaching strategic management in executive education. Our task, then, is to balance the strategy we present between developing an understanding of its complexity (so that executives can meet the challenges of today's complex business environment) and providing the simplicity through tools and frameworks that help them to cut through the complexity with practical, effective action.

REFERENCES

Ansoff, H.I. (1977), 'The state of practice in planning systems', *Sloan Management Review (pre-1986)*, 18.

Ansoff, H.L., Kipley, D., Lewis, A., Helm-Stevens, R. and Ansoff, R. (2018), *Implanting Strategic Management*, London, UK: Palgrave Macmillan.

Archer, E. (2017), *Curriculum Development: Principles and Practices*, New York, NY, USA: Clanrye International.

Argyris, C. (1980), 'Some limitations of the case method: Experiences in a management development program', *Academy of Management Review*, **5**, 291–298.

Arias-Aranda, D. (2007), 'Simulating reality for teaching strategic management', *Innovations in Education and Teaching International*, **44** (3), 273–286.

Belanger, P. (2011), *Theories in Adult Learning and Education*, Opladen and Farmington Hills, MI, USA: Barbara Budrich Publishers.

Bruner, J.S. (1961), 'The act of discovery', *Harvard Educational Review*, **31**, 21–32.

Chandler, A.D. (1962), *Strategy and Structure: Chapters in the history of the industrial Enterprise*, Cambridge, MA, USA: MIT Press.

Collins, M. (1998), 'Critical returns: From andragogy to lifelong education', in Scott, S. (Ed.), *Learning for Life. Canadian Readings in Adult Education*: 46–58, Toronto, ON, Canada: Thompson Educational Publishing.

Ebbinghaus H. (1885), *Memory: A Contribution to Experimental Psychology*, translated by Ruger, H.A. and Bussenius, C.E. (1913). New York, NY, USA: Teachers College Press, Teachers College, Columbia University.

Fenwick, T., Nesbit, T. and Spencer, B. (Eds.) (2006), *Contexts of Adult Education: Canadian Perspectives*, Toronto, ON, Canada: Thompson Educational Publishing.

Gillies, R. (2016), 'Cooperative learning: Review of research and practice', *Australian Journal of Teacher Education*, **41** (3), 39–51.

Glatthorn, A. (2018), *Curriculum Leadership: Strategies for Development and Implementation,* 5th edition. Newbury Park, CA, USA: Sage Publications.

Grunert O'Brien, J., Millis, B.J. and Cohen, M.W. (2008), *The Course Syllabus: A Learner-Centred Approach*, 2nd edition, San Francisco, CA, USA: Jossey-Bass.

Hayes, R.H. and Wheelwright, S.C. (1984), *Restoring Our Competitive Edge: Competing Through Manufacturing*, Hoboken, NJ, USA: Wiley.

Hussey, D.E. (2007), *Strategic Management from Theory to Implementation*, Milton Park, Oxfordshire, UK: Routledge.

Jennings, D. (2002), 'Strategic management: An evaluation of the use of three learning methods', *Journal of Management Development*, **21**, 655–665.

Johnson, E.B. (2002), *Contextual Teaching and Learning: What It Is and Why It's Here to Stay*, Thousand Oaks, CA, USA: Corwin Press.

Kim, W.C. and Mauborgne, R. (2005), *Blue Ocean Strategy: How to Create Uncontested Market Space and Make the Competition Irrelevant*, Boston, MA, USA: Harvard Business Review Press.

Knowles, M.S. (1981), *The Modern Practice of Adult Education: From Pedagogy to Andragogy, Revised Edition*, Englewood Cliffs, NJ, USA: Prentice Hall Regents.

Kolb, D. (1984), *Experiential Learning: Experience as the Source of Learning and Development*, Upper Saddle River, NJ, USA: Prentice Hall.

Kolb, D., Lublin, S., Spoth, J. and Baker, R. (1986), 'Strategic management development: Using experiential learning theory to assess and develop managerial competencies', *Journal of Management Development*, **5**, 13–24.

Lafley, A.G. and Charan, R. (2010), *The Game Changer: How Every Leader Can Drive Everyday Innovation*, London, UK: Profile Books.

Lafley, A.G. and Martin, R.L. (2013), *Playing to Win: How Strategy Really Works*, Boston, MA, USA: Harvard Business Press.

March, J.G. (1991), 'Exploration and exploitation in organizational learning', *Organization Science*, **2**, 71–87.

McDade, S.A. (1995), 'Case study pedagogy to advance critical thinking', *Teaching of Psychology*, **22**, 9.

Mintzberg, H. (1987a), 'Crafting strategy', *Harvard Business Review*, **65**, 66–75.

Mintzberg, H. (1987b), 'The strategy concept I: Five Ps for strategy', *California Management Review*, **30**, 11–24.

Mintzberg, H., Ahlstrand, B. and Lampel, J. (2005), *Strategy Safari: The Complete Guide Through the Wilds of Strategic Management*, London, UK: Pearson Education.

Mintzberg, H., Ghoshal, S., Lambel, J. and Quinn, J.B. (2003), *The Strategy Process: Concepts, Contexts, Cases*, Upper Saddle River, NJ, USA: Pearson Education.

Nunan, D. (1998), *Syllabus Design*, Oxford, UK: Oxford University Press.

Piaget, J. (1971), *Psychology and Epistemology: Towards a Theory of Knowledge*, New York, NY, USA: Grossman Publishers.

Porter, M. (1996), 'What is Strategy?', *Harvard Business Review*, **74**, 61–78.

Revans, R.W. (1982), *The Origin and Growth of Action Learning*, Brickley, UK: Chartwell-Bratt.

Revans, R.W. (1998), *ABC of Action Learning*, London, UK: Lemos and Crane.

Rumelt, R. (2017), *Good Strategy/Bad Strategy: The Difference and Why It Matters*, London, UK: Profile Books.

Shulman, L.S. (1992), 'Toward a pedagogy of cases', in Shulman, J.H. (Ed.), *Case Methods in Teacher Education*: 1–30, New York, NY, USA: Teachers College Press, Teachers College, Columbia University.

Slack, N., Chambers, S. and Johnston, R. (2007), *Operations Management*, Harlow, UK: Pearson Education.

Uhl-Bien, M. and Arena, M. (2018), 'Leadership for organizational adaptability: A theoretical synthesis and integrative framework', *The Leadership Quarterly*, **29**, 89–104.

von Clausewitz, C. (1883), *Vom Kriege*, Berlin, Germany: Ferdinand Dümmler.

von Moltke, H.K.B. (1890) *Über Strategie*, Berlin, Germany: E.S. Mittler & Sohn.

Vygotsky, L. (1962), *Thought and Language*, Cambridge, MA, USA: MIT Press.

Yukl, G.A. (2013), *Leadership in Organizations*, Harlow, UK: Pearson Education.

Epilogue: personal teaching experiences – personal stories

Sabine Baumann

Teaching is personal. Teaching is challenging. Teaching is diverse. Teaching can be messy. Teaching – even the same module – is always different. Teaching is about people.

The idea for this volume has its beginnings in Berlin in 2016. A group of experienced educators had come together on a Strategic Management Society (SMS) Teaching Community Panel to share very personal stories of teaching failures that ultimately became the roots of future teaching success. The panel "Learning from Teaching Failures, Achieving Teaching Successes" centered on typical classroom failures that all educators experience at some point in their career. The description mentioned examples such as the dreadful sensation that comes when the "innovative" case study or exercise that seemed such a good idea during preparation suddenly crumbles to pieces in class, or the similarly devastating mid-semester recognition that the way a course was conceptualized just isn't working for students. Likewise, assessments sometimes expose weaknesses in the teaching concept or the teaching itself, rather than showing ill-preparation on the part of students. In addition, unfavorable student evaluations may reveal that students are right regarding issues with the course or the assignments.

The idea came from a curiosity about why failure in the classroom is so little discussed, although it is such a common occurrence for educators. Best practices are celebrated, but failures are hidden like skeletons in a closet. However, experienced faculty know that it is often the biggest failures that become the sources of their greatest teaching successes. Thus, hiding failures means missing out on sharing what it takes to turn failures in the classroom into those marvelous moments when our students finally grasp a difficult concept and we know that all of the hard work and planning has paid off.

The topic had obviously struck a chord and the room was teeming with a much larger than anticipated crowd. Surprisingly, the experienced educators shared deeply personal stories of teaching failure, and it became clear that even they had had their share of unpleasant classroom situations. They also offered a lot of personal insight and hands-on advice about how they found successful ways to deal with this challenge. The ensuing discussion was very intense, with the audience joining in and sharing their stories and insights. Equally amazing was the range of topics raised in the discussion, ranging from dealing with heterogeneous student groups to teaching particular methods such as Design Thinking, grading, teaching strategic management to particular student groups such as non-business students or executives, tips for junior faculty on how to grow as a teacher, how to bring practice into the classroom, teaching online, and so on. Time ran out far too quickly for all topics to be covered in adequate depth.

Consequently, following the event in Berlin a new idea was born: we should have a teaching panel series in order to dedicate enough room and depth to all these topics. And it should not be the traditional format with little involvement of the audience, but a setting where attendees receive advice that they can really apply in their own teaching. The panel series idea was put straight into practice: in 2017, the teaching panel addressed "Bringing Practice into the Classroom"; the 2018 panel covered "Integrating Design Thinking into the Strategic Management Curriculum"; while in 2019, the panel centered around "I Wish I Had Known That When I Started Teaching! Teaching Advice for Junior Faculty." What makes these panels different is that the panelists set the scene by briefly introducing the topic (no slides!) and offering genuinely hands-on advice. The bulk of the time is left for the always intense and insightful discussion with the audience. It's all about applicability: What works and what doesn't work, and why?; How to . . .?; and lessons learned and feasible practices.

Soon it became obvious that a panel is only a fleeting event, but that a more permanent teaching strategic management resource was needed with the same personal approach and the same degree of applicability for the classroom. Thus, the idea for this volume was born. The editor and contributors wanted to not only make this volume an exciting read, but to also make it truly relevant for teachers of strategic management.

Many of the contributors have been on the SMS teaching panel series on "Turning Teaching Failures into Teaching Successes," some starting out as audience members and then being on the panel the next year. Special thanks go to Brad Shrader (Iowa State University) and Alan Hoffman (Bentley University), who were both instrumental in the panel series, for their continuous support and for sparking the idea for this volume.

The editor and the contributors of *Teaching Strategic Management: A Hands-on Guide to Teaching Success* hope that this volume benefits faculty and instructors of strategic management regardless of whether they are experienced teachers looking for inspiration or beginners in search of this all-important advice on "how to get started?", "what to avoid?" and "how to deal with?". Just like with the SMS panel series, we hope this guide sparks an ongoing sharing of teaching experiences and advice and paves the way to many "marvelous teaching moments."

Sabine Baumann

Index